Texas Log Buildings

TEXAS LOG

Terry G. Jordan

BUILDINGS
A Folk Architecture

University of Texas Press, Austin & London

Library of Congress Cataloging in Publication Data

Jordan, Terry G
   Texas log buildings: a folk architecture

   Bibliography: p.
   Includes index.
   1. Log cabins—Texas. 2. Architecture, Anonymous—
Texas. I. Title.
NA8470.J67 720'.9764 77-24559
ISBN 0-292-78023-0

Printed in the United States of America

To my Texan ancestors, Anglo and German alike,

who perpetuated for a brief time the ancient craft

of log construction.

Contents

Acknowledgments

Much of the research for this book was funded by grants from the Faculty Research Committee of North Texas State University, grants number 34363 (1972–3) and 34354 (1973–4). Most of the information concerning log structures in Texas was derived from the Texas Log Cabin Register (TLCR), a manuscript collection housed in the Archives of the North Texas State University Historical Collection. The Register, an assemblage of notes, photographs, sketches, and other documents pertaining to log buildings in Texas, is based on field observations by a great many persons, myself included. The Register contains a separate manila file for each of the more than eight hundred structures included. A property of the state of Texas, the Register is open to the public.

The Register was compiled under my direction. Most of those who assisted me were North Texas State University geography students or local county members of the Texas Historical Commission. I am indebted to Truett Latimer, Executive Director of the Commission, for calling upon these volunteer members to assist in the task of compiling the Register. Collectively, the volunteer field workers traveled many thousands of miles and contributed tens of thousands of hours of work, not to mention the expenses they bore for film and developing. The Commission volunteers are too numerous to mention, but I am especially grateful to Otis F. Beaty of Mineral Wells, Mrs. Edward A. (Viola) Block of Grandview, Ms. B. R. Reed of Gainesville, Mrs. Howard W. Johnson of Valley Mills, Max S. Lale of Marshall, Opal Lynch of Valley Mills, Rebecca Radde of rural Meridian, Uel L. Davis, Jr., of Freestone County, Sylvia B. Childs of Freestone County, Col. Egon R. Tausch of rural Wetmore, Lt. Col. Thurman G. Smith of Jasper, Charles K. Phillips of Nacogdoches, Mrs. Earl Hines of Burkeville, Clara Scarbrough of Georgetown, Mrs. Robert L. Vance of Lexington, Mrs. Bess H. Habekotte of Brenham, and Mrs. Bill Bryant of rural Bertram. Mr. Beaty, for example, in his capacity as Chairman of the Palo Pinto County Historical Commission, submitted illustrated reports on more than twenty-five log houses in his county.

My own graduate students in cultural geography at North Texas State University were also most helpful in data gathering, in particular Benny R. West of Valley View, Daniel C. Curtis of Fort Worth, John Swenson of Denton, Carlos Cox of Aubrey, and S. Hollingsworth.

Others who have been especially helpful are Dr. Theodore Albrecht of Cleveland, Ohio; Pamela Puryear of Navasota; Lonn and Diane Taylor of Winedale; John Henry Kothmann of Dallas; Dr. and Mrs. Gilbert J. Jordan of Dallas; Clyde McWilliams of Little Elm; Mrs. Barbara Ledbetter of Murray in Young County; various members of the Dallas County Heritage Society; and Mr. B. Carroll Tharp of Houston.

Occupants and owners of log structures due my special gratitude are Mae Mason of Indian Creek Community in Cooke County, Mr. and Mrs. T. E. Mason of Indian Creek, Mr. R. W. Eddleman of Pilot Point, the late Pat Ware of rural Woodbine, Mr. and Mrs. Fred Haynie of Mountain Springs Community, Mr. and Mrs. George S. Klein of rural Argyle, and Mr. and Mrs. Jim Steel of Mountain Springs.

The Texas Historical Commission kindly contributed a large number of photographs to the Register, some of which are used in this book. A few sketches were done by Fred and Barbara Whitehead of Austin and used with the permission of the University of Texas Winedale Inn Properties.

Texas Log Buildings

ONE

A Regional Folk Architecture

Texas is the product of numerous cultural confluences. Over a period of three centuries, diverse ethnic groups founded colonies in the Texas countryside, fashioning a human mosaic with individual hues that remain discernible today, despite the blurring that has accompanied the process of assimilation. The southern Anglo-American, the black, and the Hispano share cultural dominion of the state with Germans, Slavs, Scandinavians, Amerindians, and a host of smaller groups. No less diverse than the people were the physical environments within the state, environments ranging from arid to humid, from dense forests to open prairies, from rugged hills to table-flat plains.

Over the years, the various Texan peoples interacted with the local conditions of terrain, climate, vegetation, and soil to create a myriad of landscapes, Texan "places." As a cultural geographer, I am by training and inclination sensitive to these landscapes, to the material legacy of a diverse peopling. I have been taught to detect and appreciate even subtle differences between places, and each journey through Texas, often on roads I have traveled previously, reveals new dimensions of the cultural mosaic. As a sixth-generation Texan, I not only observe these varied landscapes but also have a genuine and deep fondness for them.

The multiple cultures of Texas find expression in features as varied as architecture, dialect, livelihood, religion, foods, and town plans.[1] This book deals with architecture, one of the most obvious and visible aspects of culture. More exactly, the book is about *folk* architecture.[2] The products of folk architecture are not derived from the drafting tables of professional architects, but instead from the collective memory of a people. These buildings, whether dwellings, barns, churches, or stores, are based not on blueprints but on mental images that change little from one generation to the next. In this sense, we can speak of an "architecture without architects." Folk buildings are extensions of the people and the region. They help provide the unique character or essence of each district and province.

Do not look to folk architecture for refined artistic genius or spectacular, revolutionary design. Seek in it instead the traditional, the conservative, the functional. Expect from it a simple beauty, a harmony with the physical environment, a visible expression of traditional culture. Folk-built structures tell us about the people and how they live. Folk architecture reveals as much about the culture it represents as do the professionally designed glass-and-steel skyscrapers and other delights of the latter-day architectural millennium in our own modern, technological civilization. More than that, folk architecture describes, for those who will observe closely, the physical environment occupied by a particular people. Weather, climate, native vegetation, and terrain leave their mark on the style and material composition of the folk house and other traditional structures. Even a people so far removed from Nature and ancestral folkways as we of late-twentieth-century urban Texas can learn much about our forefathers and the land they settled simply by investigating their buildings. And, conversely, a knowledge of the lifestyle of nineteenth-century Texans can help us understand many individual elements of the folk architecture. In sum, folk architecture cannot profitably be studied in and of itself, for it is integrally bound to both culture and environment.

Texas offers different styles of folk architecture. Many of the immigrant ethnic groups, both large and small, implanted their own distinctive architectural style, based in their cultural heritage and modified, if necessary, to fit the physical and cultural setting of the new homeland. Throughout Texas, folk architecture is a relict form. Most such structures are decaying products of bygone days and vanishing rural folkways. The folk house long ago became a badge of economic failure, to be occupied with shame by those who did not succeed in our competitive economic system. In our headlong rush to what we perceive as the "good life," to the city and suburb, to the industrial society, we have thoughtlessly discarded the folk architecture of our ancestors. But our forefathers built for permanence, and, in spite of neglect, abandonment, and vandalism, many architectural specimens of their handiwork survive. To some, these relics are unsightly nuisances. To a few of us, cultural geographers and sundry other eccentrics, they are interesting and worthy of study and preservation. Subversive though it may be, our minority finds the relict Texan folk architecture more appealing than the great majority of professionally designed structures we see risen and rising around us today.

Log Culture Complex and Social Stigma

I have chosen log folk architecture as the subject of this book. The term *log construction* will be understood to mean walls built of horizontally laid timbers notched to one another at each corner. Occasionally, some Texans have used the term in a broader definition, to include buildings of picket (*palisado*) construction, consisting of timbers or poles driven vertically into the ground. No attention will be devoted to palisade structures in this study, though they are certainly deserving of research.

My interest in Texas log construction began some ten years ago. I was attracted for several reasons, but perhaps mainly because the simple beauty of these pioneer buildings appealed to me and because they are among the most endangered of traditional Texas structures. Soon log construction will vanish altogether from districts where it was formerly common. Once too numerous to attract much attention, log buildings will soon be too few to permit meaningful research. My investigation of Texas log structures came at the eleventh hour and had an urgency about it.

There was a time when log structures were so plentiful and so universally accepted that they literally dominated the cultural landscape of most of the eastern half of Texas. Houses, stores, inns, churches, schools, jails, barns, and other buildings were of log, as were the ubiquitous split-rail fences. One writer has called this overwhelming presence in the landscape the "log culture complex."[3] In the accounts of some nineteenth-century Texas travelers, we can sense an awareness of the log culture complex. Their remarks were normally matter-of-fact, occasionally denigrating. Noah Smithwick, describing the Austin Colony capital of

San Felipe in 1827, spoke of "twenty-five or perhaps thirty log cabins strung out along the west bank of the Brazos River"; while the town of Brazoria in 1831, according to a northern visitor, "contained about thirty houses, all of logs except three of brick and two or three framed."[4] Mary Eubank, whose first visual impression of Texas in 1853 was the hamlet of DeKalb in Bowie County, noted "a small place called Decab . . . but I think Decabin the most appropriate name."[5] The Englishman William Bollaert provided us with one of the most striking visual portrayals of the Texas log culture complex in a sketch he made of a farmstead in Montgomery County, north of Houston.[6] In Bollaert's 1843 drawing are thirteen structures, all of logs, including a house, six slave cabins, a smithy, a corncrib, a well, a water trough, and various others.

So greatly has the landscape changed in the past hundred years that today the student of folk architecture must search diligently to find surviving specimens of the log technology. No human endeavors can achieve permanence, least of all wooden craftsmanship. To survive over any significant period of time, wooden architecture must be perpetuated, passing from one generation to the next. In Texas, log construction did not retain the transferral from generation to generation. Most log buildings in the state were erected in the 1800's, and I am aware of none built since 1945.

The precipitous decline of log construction was due in part to a social stigma. Log houses became symbols of the frontier, of backwardness, of deprivation. Status could be gained by discarding the log house and replacing it with one of frame, brick, or stone. At the very least, socially upward-mobile folk were expected to conceal the logs with milled siding. Even as early as 1826, founding father Stephen F. Austin was bearing with resignation his log cross, confessing that "we Still

live in log cabins."[7] Jacksonian democracy made it socially acceptable for a presidential candidate to have been born in a log cabin, but it was most assuredly not fitting for the candidate to continue living in one. Lyndon Baines Johnson wished mightily and in weak moments even claimed that he had been born in his grandfather's log house at Johnson City, a house architecturally more elegant by far than his actual frame birthplace, but I never heard that he expressed a desire to live there. It is no accident that the LBJ State Park is dotted with restored log houses but that the nearby Johnson family ranch house is of stone. Ironically, all of the LBJ Park log dwellings were built by Gillespie County Germans, whose descendants rarely supported Johnson politically.

By the third decade of the twentieth century, even birth in a log cabin was no longer socially acceptable. In 1925, a Texan recalling the 1850's was moved to remark that "it was not a disgrace to be born in a log cabin in those days."[8] Some misguided log house dwellers tacked artificial brick siding onto the exterior walls to conceal their shame (Fig. 1-1). One who did not is a friend of mine—an elderly woman of Indian Creek Community in Cooke County, in the heart of the East Cross Timbers. She was born and raised in her fine dovetailed log house almost eight decades ago, and she has never lived anywhere else (Fig. 1-2).[9] When I first met her in the early 1970's, she was stoically enduring her nonelectric, rough-hewn dwelling as a badge of spinsterhood. "If I had a'married, I'd not have to live in a house like this," she maintained. Her brother, who lives nearby, refers contemptuously to the dwelling, his own birthplace, as a "nigger house," though blacks have never lived there. If this woman's attitude has changed since I first visited her home, it is probably because I have brought five hundred or so of my

1-1. A log house sheathed with artificial brick siding. (TLCR, Freestone Co. No. 6, photo 1969; courtesy Freestone County Historical Survey Committee)

1-2. Inhabited, unadorned log house in North Texas. (TLCR, Cooke Co. No. 3, photo 1974)

1-3. "The old house rough hewn—marked by decay." (TLCR, Johnson Co. No. 16)

students to look at, admire, measure, and photograph the structure in the intervening years. I suspect, instead, that she regards me and my students as slightly demented.

Perhaps the log house stigma and abandonment were best summed up in excerpts from a poem published in 1886 by Martha Whitten, recalling the Texas log dwelling of her childhood. The poem, "The Dear Old Home," reads in part:

The old house rough hewn – marked by
  decay
In time was torn from its site away;
One statelier far the acres graced.
The old with the new had been replaced.
It had spacious rooms, and an airy hall,
And roses climbing o'er the outer wall
· · · · · · · · · · · · · · · · · ·
Thus time and progress have altered all
But still that home with joy we recall.[10]

The decline of residential function is a clear and obvious indication of the threatening disappearance of log houses (Fig. 1-3). Already by the mid-1930's, log farmhouses accounted for only 0.7 percent of all occupied rural dwellings in Texas, according to a government survey.[11] Fifty or sixty years earlier, in the 1870's, the percentage was likely well above fifty. The survey covered a sample of twenty-five Texas counties (Table 1-1). The highest percentages and numbers of occupied log farmhouses in the 1930's were found in Big Thicket counties, such as Polk and Orange; in the piney woods of Deep East Texas counties, such as Bowie; in Cooke and other Cross Timbers counties; and in the wooded Hill Country of Central Texas, including the capital county of Travis. The total number of log houses observed in the twenty-five counties was 316. If we assume that the sample counties were representative ones, we can estimate a total of about 3,300 occupied log farmhouses for the entire state in 1934. If we also assume that many log houses cov-

TABLE 1-1. *Occupied Log Farmhouses in Selected Texas Counties, 1934*

County	Number	% of all farmhouses
Anderson	25	0.8
Bee	0	—
Bexar	5	0.2
Bowie	71	1.9
Brazos	8	0.3
Cooke	30	1.3
Dallas	0	—
Frio	0	—
Hale	0	—
Harrison	9	0.4
Hemphill	0	—
Hidalgo	2	0.1
Hill	2	0.1
Hunt	0	—
Kerr	5	0.7
Nolan	0	—
Orange	16	2.6
Polk	110	5.4
Randall	3	0.5
Stephens	1	0.1
Tom Green	0	—
Travis	22	1.0
Washington	5	0.2
Wharton	2	0.1
Wilbarger	0	—

Source: U.S. Department of Agriculture, *The Farm-Housing Survey*, pp. 5–6.

ered with siding went undetected in the survey, we might raise the total to perhaps 4,000 or 5,000. Today I would estimate that there are no more than 600 or 700 occupied log houses in Texas, if we exclude those used as hunting cabins or weekend cottages. But such an estimate is tentative at best and impossible to verify. Some people are unaware that the homes they occupy have a log core, so skillfully and so early was the siding applied.

Log structures are much more consumable today as cords of well-seasoned firewood or as ready-made fence posts than as functional dwellings. Grass fires annually take an additional toll of these buildings, and others succumb to rot and insects. Back in the 1930's and 1940's, when big lumber companies were buying up huge chunks of East Texas farmland to put in pine plantations, log houses by the hundreds were bulldozed to attain the lower tax rates awarded to properties containing no residences.

A few log houses have been dragged off to zoolike restoration projects, to stand empty and unused, protected from vandalism by unsightly barbed-wire-crowned link fences or drowned in concrete sidewalks (see Appendix 1).[12] An additional handful are restored, with widely varying degrees of accuracy, as conversation pieces or weekend cottages by the wealthy of Houston, Dallas, or some other city.

Bases for Diversity

I suppose I was also attracted to the study of log buildings because my ancestors, Anglo-Americans and Texas Germans alike, constructed and lived in such dwellings. It intrigued me that people as diverse as Deep East Texas Anglos and Hill Country Teutons employed this method of construction. I was also fascinated by the many subtle ways these two groups placed their distinctive cultural imprint on the log buildings they erected. If one error has consistently been made by writers considering Texas log folk architec-

ture, it is an assumption that log construction is a basically uniform phenomenon, that there is only one way to build with logs. As a geographer, I was attracted by the spatial variations I observed in log construction from one part of Texas to another.

This spatial diversity has a number of root causes. One, already implied, involved cultural heritage. Anglo-Americans and Germans were by no means the only ethnic groups in Texas to build log structures. Afro-Americans acquired log building techniques during their slavery years, and many of the finest Texas log houses were built by black slave craftsmen. The typical slave cabin was log (Fig. 1-4). After emancipation, blacks continued to use log construction, and a high percentage of the Depression-vintage log houses were built by blacks (Fig. 1-5). The Cherokees, Choctaws, Alabama-Coushattas, and other immigrant Indian tribes who came from the southeastern United States to East Texas had also adopted log construction from the Anglos, and in fact members of these so-called Civilized Tribes may have erected the first log buildings in Texas, prior to 1815. The Alabama-Coushatta group in the Big Thicket retained log dwellings as their dominant type of housing into the 1930's. The United States governmental officials, who obviously regarded log housing as substandard, in 1928 began replacing the log dwellings of the Alabama-Coushattas with wooden frame homes.

Nor was the log culture complex uniform even within the Anglo-American population. Anglo settlers from the coastal plain of the Deep South or Lower South constructed log buildings different in numerous ways from those built by immigrants from the Upper South, including such interior states as Missouri, Arkansas, Tennessee, and Kentucky. In Texas, the lower southern subculture and its distinctive log architecture were implant-

1-4. Slave quarters, Polley Plantation, Wilson County. (TLCR, Wilson Co. No. 1, photo 1936; courtesy Historic American Buildings Survey, Library of Congress)

1-5. A latter-day dogtrot log house, built in 1937 by an East Texas black man. (TLCR, Walker Co. No. 5, photo 1973)

ed in East Texas, while interior and northern Texas were peopled from the Upper South (Fig. 1-6).

A variety of immigrant groups directly from Europe copied Anglo-American log construction styles after arriving in Texas. Among those were the Germans of south-central Texas, the Norwegians of the Bosque County hills, the Wends or Sorbians of Lee County, the early Czech settlers in Austin and Fayette counties, and some of the Irish Catholics in the border area of Goliad, Refugio, and Victoria counties. The Swiss and Alsatian German colonists in Medina County introduced their own distinctive type of log construction from the hills and mountains of central Europe.[13]

Another basis for the varied development of log architecture in Texas can be found in the physical environment. The pioneers who settled Texas found a diverse land, and their perception of environmental conditions influenced the character of their log structures. The declining size and diminishing frequency of trees to the west through Texas halted the advance of the log culture complex, permitting only scattered and isolated occurrence of log buildings in the western half of the state. Average room size declined in response to the smaller size of trees in west-central Texas (Fig. 1-7). Houses in the tall pine forests of East Texas had rooms measuring 16 to 20 feet or more on a side, while many log dwellings in the West Cross Timbers averaged no more than 12 or 13 feet. In Young County, on the western perimeter of major log construction in Texas, the average log room

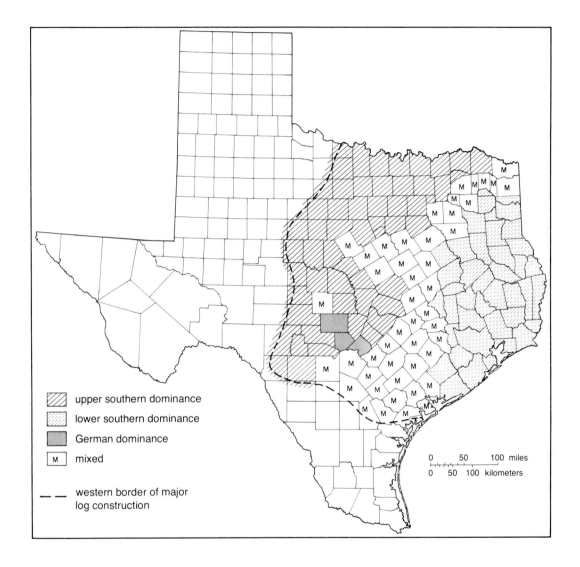

1-6. Generalized population origins in nineteenth-century Texas.

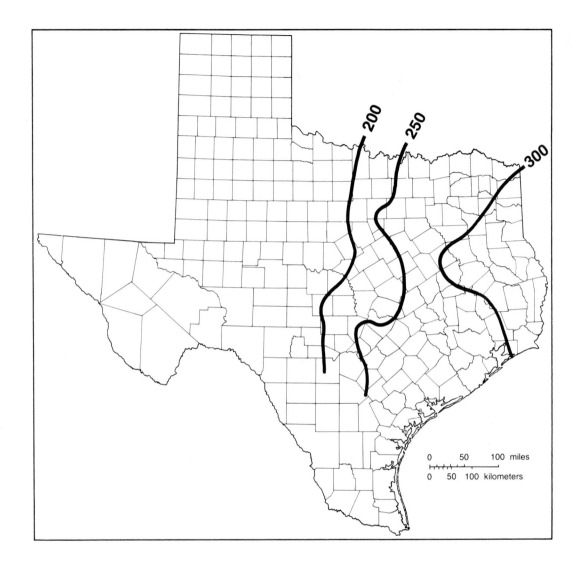

1-7. Isolines for average square footage per log pen (average exterior width × length) in Texas. (TLCR)

measured only 10 1/2 × 12 feet, in Comanche County only 12 1/2 × 13 1/2 feet.[14]

The type of wood locally available was also an important variable. Craftsmen in Texas built log structures out of pine, oak, cedar, cottonwood, pecan, cypress, gum, elm, bois d'arc, and probably several other types (Fig. 1-8). Oak, cedar, and pine account for the great majority of Texas log structures. Post oak seems to have been very popular, and cedar was used in preference to other woods wherever it was available. Each wood presented certain advantages and disadvantages to the builder, causing him to choose among alternate techniques. Notch type, roofing, and other facets of the architectural style could be influenced by the type of wood being used.

Perception of local conditions of climate and weather may have encouraged the popularity of one or another type of floorplan. In hot, humid East Texas an open passageway or "dogtrot" was often left in the center of the log house,[15] a feature less popular in North Texas, where winter "northers" turned dogtrots into frigid wind tunnels. A log kitchen built separate from the house was another warm climate feature most common in East Texas. The environmental influence was apparent in other, diverse ways. For example, availability or absence of native stone or firing clay could help determine the building material used for foundations and chimneys. Insects, also a feature of the natural setting, influenced the choice of wood type and the style of foundation. Termite infestation meant taller foundations for log houses. In all these ways and more, the physical environment helped shape the details of log folk architecture.

Still another variable in log construction was the level of craftsmanship. Some log buildings were erected by amateur laborers at communal "log rollings" and "house raisings."[16] As a rule, such structures display very crude craftsmanship, and in fact relatively few dwellings of this type survive. Others, including the majority of log houses, were constructed by professional or semiprofessional carpenters working for hire. Not many of their names have passed down to us, but we can find mention of such as Sebe Barnes of Callahan County, Thomas J. Shaw of Parker, S. D. Brown and Alexander Boutwell of Cooke, J. H. Chrisman of Coryell, James Wilson of Panola, and William Richey of Hunt.[17] "Such men will be readily procured," wrote Edward Smith in 1849 concerning northeastern Texas, where the price of a log house ranged from $20 to $75. The cheapest was "a plain log hut, eighteen feet square, with a rough wooden floor," built by two men in two days, while the $75 version was a house of hewn pine logs, containing two rooms "separated by an interval of twelve to fifteen feet," requiring three men three days to finish. If wood other than pine was desired, the price of the deluxe version was raised slightly.[18] Not infrequently these craftsmen were black slaves, as were many antebellum southern artisans of all kinds. For example, the previously mentioned James Wilson, log carpenter from Tennessee, owned a black man named Simpson who was his equal as a craftsman. Together they went from place to place in Panola County building log houses.[19] Some slaveowners rented their black artisans to neighbors for the duration of a house or barn raising.

Even though many log structures were built by professional craftsmen, these buildings are none the less a reflection of *folk* architecture. These carpenter-craftsmen belonged to the traditional culture and cannot be separated from it. They were unschooled men perpetuating traditional techniques, migrating with the mainstream of Middle Atlantic people, following the flows and eddies of west-

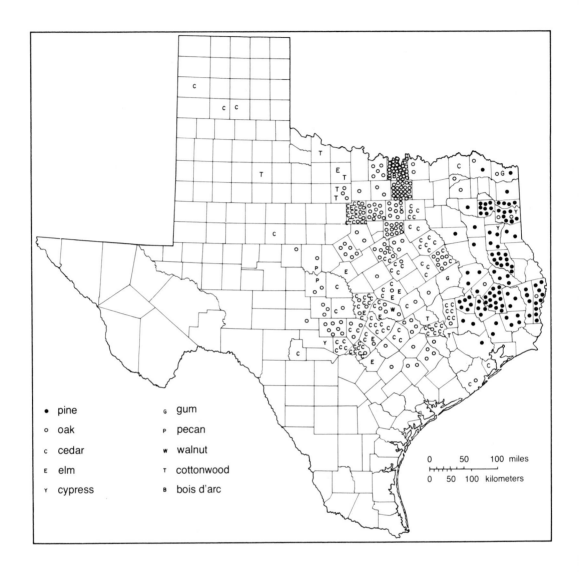

1-8. Type of wood used in log construction in Texas. (TLCR and early travel accounts)

1-9. Expert craftsmanship on log corner timbering in south-central Texas. The Zimmerscheidt-Leyendecker house, built in the 1830's by a German cabinetmaker. (TLCR, Colorado Co. No. 2)

1-10. Sided log house of a well-to-do family, built in the 1850's near Grapevine, today in the Old City Park Restoration, Dallas. (TLCR, Tarrant Co. No. 9)

ward movement. In ancestry and culture, they were like the people for whom they built.

It is the log products of these craftsmen that particularly delight the student of folk architecture, and it is the professionally built log structures that will command most of our attention in this book. As a general rule, technologies and items of material culture in traditional societies decline in quality of craftsmanship with increasing distance from the source region, or hearth. In log construction, Texas is colonial to the Delaware Valley and lies on an outer periphery of log building in the United States. As a consequence, the craftsmanship displayed in Texas log architecture is not nearly so high as in Pennsylvania, Virginia, or even Tennessee. I am as chauvinistically Texan as any, but my field observations in the east-

ern states and in Europe have revealed the Texas structures to be comparatively primitive, on the average. Exceptions can be found—enough to make a study of the Texas log buildings both rewarding and pleasurable. The best Texan ego-builder I have seen is the incredibly well-crafted Zimmerscheidt-Leyendecker log house in the post oak belt north of Columbus in Colorado County, a dwelling attributed to an immigrant German cabinetmaker (Fig. 1-9).[20]

Economic status was another variable to be considered in evaluating folk architecture, particularly the house. Then, as now, a man's wealth or lack of it was reflected in the appearance of his dwelling, even in the early years when virtually everyone lived in log houses. The rich man's log home was larger, taller, and better made than his poorer cultural kinsman's, and more likely to be covered with siding (Fig. 1-10). Because rural wealth and poverty tended to be regionalized within nineteenth-century Texas, an additional regional dimension to log housing resulted.

The architectural variety resulting from differing cultural heritages, physical environments, and levels of prosperity and craftsmanship was pronounced. In a state as culturally, economically, and physically diverse as Texas, considerable regionalization of log architecture was inevitable. Each region boasted its own particular style. This regionalization will be a recurring theme throughout the book.

Perhaps the best way to begin our study is to seek the hearth areas of log construction, to learn how these techniques reached Texas, and to identify the bearers of this architectural tradition. Our quest will take us far into the past, to areas distant from Texas, to alien environments and exotic cultures.

TWO

The Origin & Diffusion of Log Folk Architecture

The log buildings visible in the Texas landscape represent a heritage that originated thousands of miles away across the Atlantic Ocean and far back in prehistory. Though the log cabin became closely identified with frontier occupance in America, it did not originate on our continent. Instead, we must look to Europe and to pre-agricultural times for the antecedent of the Texan log culture complex.

In Europe

Buildings with walls consisting of horizontally laid timbers morticed or fastened at each corner by one or another type of notching seem to have originated in the Mesolithic, or Middle Stone, Age, in northern Europe. Archeological evidence points to the Maglemosian people, seashore dwellers of what is today Denmark, southern Sweden, and northern Germany, as the likely inventors of log construction techniques.[1] In those pre-agricultural times, prior to the decimation of the European woodlands by generations of farmer folk, extensive forests covered most of Europe. Log construction was splendidly suited to such a forest-rich environment, and the technique diffused from its northern hearth area to gain widespread acceptance. By the Bronze Age, log buildings were part of the landscape from southwestern France east into Russia and from Norway to the Balkans.

Areas even farther afield, such as northern Iberia, may have been affected by this diffusion; the evidence is not conclusive.

The great age of forest clearance in Medieval times, lasting from about A.D. 800 until the terrible plagues of the 1300's and 1400's, caused both the retreat of the woodlands and, as a consequence, the contraction of the zone of log construction. Forests and log building alike survived best in the hilly and mountainous districts of central and southeastern Europe and in the colder, less populated plains of northern and eastern Europe, areas unattractive to the farmer (Fig. 2-1). In Scandinavia, Finland, most of European Russia, Poland, Czechoslovakia, the Alpine lands, the Black Forest of Germany, the mountainous spine of Yugoslavia, and the Carpathians, the visitor still today can see houses, barns, mills, churches, and various other structures built of logs.[2] I have examined log buildings in European provinces as diverse as Bosnia, the Salzburg hinterland, and the Four Forest Cantons of Switzerland. It is among the remnant zones of log construction in continental Europe that we must search for the antecedents of the American and Texan structures.

Diffusion to North America

Several different ethnic groups seem to have introduced log building techniques

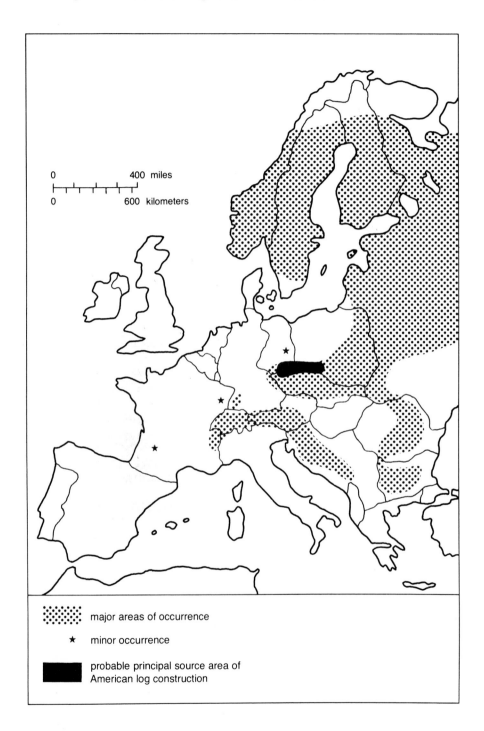

2-1. Distribution of notched log construction in modern Europe.

into North America. Though the British Isles provided the greatest number of settlers to the American colonies, we cannot attribute the introduction to the English, Welsh, Scotch, or Irish immigrants. Many of our American institutions and traditional folkways were derived from Britain—our language is English, our laws English, our prevailing theologies British Protestant and Irish Catholic—and for these reasons and more our part of the world is appropriately known as *Anglo-America*. Yet we look in vain if we seek a British precedent for log construction, because this technique is not found anywhere in the British Isles and apparently never has been.[3] Instead we must look to groups derived from the mainland of Europe.

Swedes, some of whom migrated from Swedish-language areas of present Finland, together with smaller numbers of ethnic Finns, probably made the earliest introduction of log construction into what is now the United States. In the 1630's and 1640's, a small group of these Northmen established the colony of New Sweden along the banks of the Delaware River, in portions of present Delaware, New Jersey, and Pennsylvania.[4] Log construction prevailed through nearly all of the Swedish Empire at that time, so we are not surprised to find log buildings also dominant in New Sweden. Students of folk architecture disagree concerning the importance of the Swedish introduction, but the prevailing opinion among most experts is that it was of relatively little consequence.[5] For one thing, the Scandinavian techniques of log construction are distinctive, as will be described in later chapters, and subsequent American log building displayed traits fundamentally different from those of the Swedish and Finnish structures.[6] Moreover, the New Sweden colony remained very small and isolated. Though annexed by the more powerful Dutch based in New Amsterdam, and soon thereafter by the even

stronger English, the Swedish settlements did not have many outside contacts. Neither the Dutch along the Hudson nor the English in nearby Maryland and Virginia adopted the Swedish building techniques. Instead, the Dutch relied on brick construction, while the English preferred half-timbered and frame construction.

Records do indicate, however, that some persons with British surnames lived in log houses in southeastern Pennsylvania by 1696, or even earlier.[7] These homes may have been purchased from Swedes. In addition, scattered reports of log structures in other early English colonies have been discovered.[8] Captain John Smith, the colonizer of Jamestown in Virginia, had traveled widely in Europe prior to coming to America and had seen log structures in the Balkans and Russia. Other British seafarers had encountered such structures in the port towns of Norway and Sweden. It is conceivable, though unlikely, that early Jamestown had log buildings derived from the continental contacts of Smith and others.[9] In New England, several seventeenth-century garrison houses, or small forts, were of log construction, though apparently few dwellings were.[10] In sum, some log buildings may have been present in various English colonies during the 1600's, but, if so, the log construction techniques failed to spread to the English colonial population at large. The few scattered examples could not have served as the antecedent for the American log culture complex.

Several other minor introductions seem to have occurred in the 1600's. The French in early Québec made some use of log construction with notched corners.[11] Such a diffusion would not have been wholly unexpected, since log buildings were typical of certain parts of France, though not those regions, such as Normandy, that provided the majority of colonists for the St. Lawrence Valley.[12] In any case, stone and half-timbered construction became dominant in New France. The first log structures to appear in the French colony of Natchitoches, Louisiana, in the 1780's or 1790's, were apparently introduced by Anglo-Americans.[13] Such a sequence suggests that log construction techniques did not spread to the interior of North America with the French. Clearly, we should not look to the French for the origin of the typical Anglo-American log building.

The pivotal introduction of log construction seems to have been made by certain German-speaking immigrants who came to the colony of Pennsylvania in the first half of the eighteenth century. Collectively, this group is often misleadingly called the Pennsylvania "Dutch," a corruption of the word *Deutsch*, or "German." By no means were all the Pennsylvania Germans familiar with log construction in their European homeland. In fact, the largest contingent came from Rhenish Germany, particularly the Palatinate, where log buildings were unknown. But some others came from Canton Bern in Switzerland, from the Black Forest of Württemberg, from the German-inhabited western and northern hill fringe of present Czechoslovakia, and from adjacent portions of Silesia and Saxony—in every case, districts where log construction was known.[14] A careful study of the details of log building techniques in each of these German source regions has revealed that only in the Czech hills, including parts of the provinces of Bohemia and Moravia as well as nearby parts of Silesia and Slovakia, can log wall construction exactly like that of the American frontier be found (Fig. 2-1).[15] It seems, then, that the log buildings we observe in the Texas countryside are derived, insofar as the construction techniques are concerned, from a small zone in central Europe, a zone perhaps better known to those who remember the Hitler years as the Sudetenland. The Pennsylvania Germans gave us the log

cabin, along with other vital pioneer paraphernalia, such as the long rifle and Conestoga wagon. In this sense, the districts of Texas where log buildings are found are culturally colonial to Pennsylvania and to Germany.

Once implanted in the Middle Atlantic colonial core area, the German-inspired style of log construction was adopted by other ethnic groups. Even the Swedes, who had their own log tradition, were influenced by the German methods. The English, Welsh, and Scotch-Irish, who shared dominion of Pennsylvania with the Germans and had little or no previous experience with log construction, quickly adopted the German style. The introduction of German log construction occurred between about 1710 and 1740; the spread to neighboring ethnic groups probably took place mainly in the 1730–1750 period, prior to the major era of westward migration.

The various British groups readily accepted this alien technology because it was so splendidly suited to pioneer life in a forested environment. To have built frontier houses of stone, brick, or frame would have been more difficult, requiring masons, sawmills, quarrymen, and kilns. Even so, the use of log construction techniques remained confined largely to the peoples of the Middle Atlantic colonies and their westward-migrating descendants. The English in the Tidewater South and New England never acquired the log technology. One will look largely in vain for log houses in Puritan Massachusetts or among the planters along the southern coast. Boston, Williamsburg, Charleston, and their rural environs contained houses of brick or frame construction. Perhaps the key to British acceptance of log construction in the Middle Atlantic colonies was their close proximity to the Germans. Pennsylvania was America's first "melting pot," where settlers of varied ethnic identities met, mingled, and participated in cultural exchange. New England and the Tidewater South, by contrast, were much less ethnically diverse.

As settlers from the Middle Atlantic colonies began to spread westward and southwestward, beyond the borders of Pennsylvania, they carried log construction techniques with them (Fig. 2-2). Intermarriage became more common with increasing distance from the Pennsylvania hearth area, producing an amalgamated people of mixed British and German ancestry, with lesser admixture of Swedes, French Huguenots, and Dutch. An additional English input into the lineage of this folk occurred when yeomen migrating westward from the Virginia Tidewater met and mixed with the southwestward-moving Pennsylvanians. By the time the vanguard of these Middle Atlantic–Tidewater people had surged through the Appalachians and across the Gulf Coastal Plain and Upper South to reach the borders of Texas, one could no longer distinguish German, English, Welsh, Scotch-Irish, Dutch, French, or Swedish individuality among them. They were one people by then, of mixed ancestry, carrying a diverse cultural baggage that included log construction techniques. It was they who brought the log building to Texas.

Walk among the modest gravestones in the cedar-studded cemeteries where these Anglo-American colonists of Texas are buried and you can read surnames reflecting the mixture of peoples who long before and far to the east had blended to form the old-stock folk of the American heartland and interior South, such surnames as the English Bradford, Gentry, and Wakefield; the Pennsylvania German Eddleman, Foutch, and Baugh; the Scotch-Irish McKitrick, McQuinn, and McElhannon; the Welsh Jones, Davis, and Williams; the Swedish and Dutch Anderson, Thomason, and Van Zandt. Read these names and hundreds of others of like origin and you will perceive the diverse ethnic character of the colonial seaboard from the Hudson Valley to the Chesapeake Tidewater. And you will appreciate how many ethnic lines were crossed by the German log technology.

Meanwhile, other groups possessing knowledge of log construction approached Texas from quite different directions. Notched log buildings were known as early as the 1700's in Mexico and spread with Hispano settlers into northern New Mexico.[16] The techniques employed in Mexican log construction were different in several respects from those of the Anglo. These Hispanic log buildings abound today in five major areas of Old Mexico, including one district just south of Monterrey, not too far from the Texas border. In New Mexico, they are seen frequently in the highlands and wooded valleys from south of Albuquerque to beyond Taos. I have no evidence that this Hispanic log tradition ever penetrated Texas, though there are inconclusive hints that such structures may have existed in the 1700's at Los Adaes and in Gil Ybarbo's colony around Nacogdoches.[17] How the log construction techniques entered Mexico in the first place is a mystery, though German-born priests or miners may have been the bearers.

The only documented non-Anglo introduction of log construction into Texas occurred in the Castro Colony in Medina County, just west of San Antonio. There, a few individual builders derived from Switzerland and possibly also from the Alsace constructed a number of log dwellings and barns that reveal a distinctly non-Anglo influence (Figs. 3-10 and 4-20). Curiously, none of the numerous Texas settlers directly from Norway and Sweden seem to have introduced their respective log traditions, adopting instead the Anglo methods. The same is true of the Texas Germans, excluding those in Medina County, possibly because very few of these immigrants came from log construction areas within Germany.

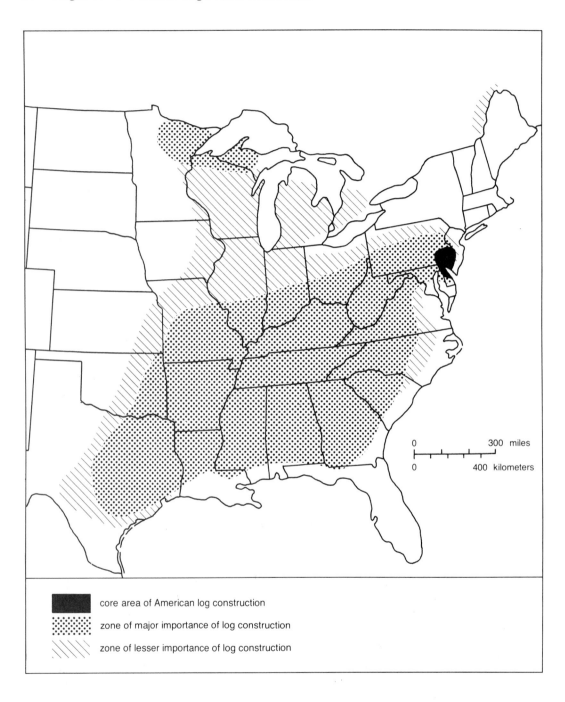

2-2. Distribution of log construction in the eastern half of Anglo-America.

Elsewhere in the United States, a number of nineteenth-century introductions of log construction occurred. Finns who settled the North Woods of Minnesota, Wisconsin, and Michigan erected many distinctive log structures, quite different from those of the Anglos, as did some German colonists in Wisconsin.[18] These later northern introductions had no impact on Texas.

Distribution in Texas

The earliest documented log buildings in Texas date from the 1812–1825 period and were erected by Anglo-Americans. Earlier ones may have existed, either among Indian immigrants from the southeastern states or the Anglo adventurers who penetrated Spanish Texas in the 1790's. Anglo-inspired log structures were built in Natchitoches, Louisiana, at least by 1795 and probably as much as a decade earlier, located only about fifty miles east of the Texas border.[19]

Settlements on the south bank of the Red River in the northeastern corner of Texas were the scene of the first substantial numbers of log buildings in the state, shortly before 1820. A second major implantation occurred soon thereafter in south-central Texas, where Stephen F. Austin settled his "Old Three Hundred" families in 1821–1824. Other nuclei of the log culture complex developed in the years that followed, and soon the various implantations began to coalesce. Within a half-century, log construction spread across the eastern half of Texas as the dominant pioneer building method, a spread halted near the one-hundredth meridian by the diminished size and increased scarcity of timber (Fig. 2-3). But traditions do not die easily. Even to the west, on the Great Plains, Anglo pioneers built log structures whenever possible, often hauling the timber many miles to the construction site. In Swisher County, on the treeless South Plains, some early settlers hauled logs all the way from Palo Duro Canyon for their houses.[20] An enterprising settler in nearby Oldham County, determined to have a log house in spite of the vegetational facts of life, reportedly stole timbers at night from a Rock Island railroad trestle under construction over the Canadian River in 1887. A few nights of such pilferage provided him with materials for a comfortable log dwelling.[21] In the Davis Mountains of Trans-Pecos Texas, highland forests permitted a modest amount of log construction, as was also true in the wooded canyonlands of the Palo Duro–Mulberry Creek area, lying below the Cap Rock in the Panhandle counties of Armstrong and Randall. Ten log cabins have been located at isolated sites in the mountains of Jeff Davis County and another in adjacent Presidio County, both in the Trans-Pecos area.[22]

Most early West Texas settlers, however, bowed to environmental pressure and built palisade (picket), sod, stone, or adobe walls. After the coming of the railroads, imported milled lumber allowed box frame construction to prevail in Anglo West Texas.[23] In the Mexican-dominated brushlands of South Texas, log structures never challenged the traditional Hispanic adobe, stone, brush, and palisade construction (Fig. 2-3).

The time depth of log construction was shallow in Texas, particularly in comparison to the Appalachians and certain other regions of the eastern United States. In parts of West and west-central Texas, log construction was confined to a period of a decade or even less. Across most of the eastern half of Texas, the duration was on the order of thirty to fifty years, at least as far as dwellings were concerned. Cribs, barns, and other outbuildings made of logs persisted longer. The last phase of log construction occurred in the 1930's and early 1940's, centered in the pine forests

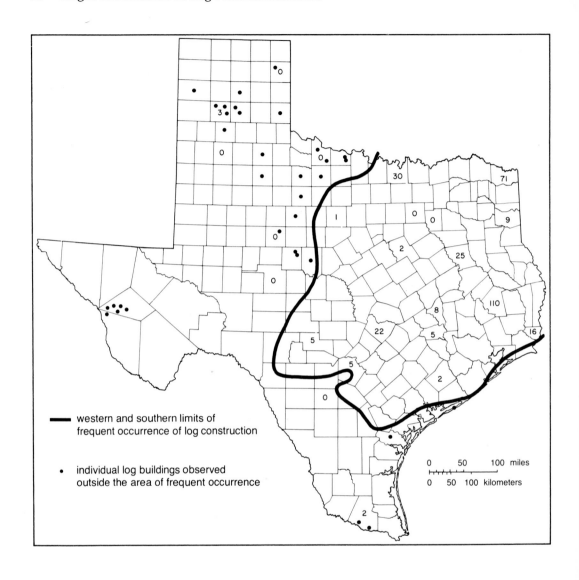

2-3. Distribution of log construction in Texas. Numbers indicate how many inhabited log farmhouses there were in selected counties in 1934. (TLCR and U.S. Department of Agriculture, *Farm-Housing Survey*)

of East Texas and particularly in the Big Thicket of the Southeast, a revival encouraged by the Great Depression. Many unemployed city folk in that era returned to the country homes of their childhood and reverted to the building methods of their fathers to provide new homes. Overall, then, the log construction phase in Texas lasted from about 1815 to 1940. During that century and a quarter, a great variety of log structures were erected in the eastern half of Texas, providing ample subject matter for this book.

The preceding discussion of origins and diffusion will serve as a background for Chapter 3, which is devoted to the raising of a log wall. The practices and techniques of log craftsmen will be our concerns, as will some of the numerous options available to builders.

THREE

Raising a Log Wall

The essence of log folk architecture is found in the construction of the wall. No other features, whether floorplans, roof forms, or chimney types, are unique to log structures. The wall, and the wall alone, makes the log culture complex unique. In this chapter and the one that follows, our concern will be the wall construction.

Preparations for Construction

The first step in log construction, usually accomplished by the prospective owner prior to the arrival of the carpenters or the neighbors who were to erect the structure, was to select, cut, trim, and haul the logs. A Wise County pioneer recalled that his father and a hired hand went "into the woods and selected nothing but straight oak trees and cut down sufficient of these to build the double log house. They hauled the logs to the place where the house was to be built, and then all the neighbors came in."[1] Cutting was best done in winter, when the sap was down, and Anglo-Texan superstition demanded that the trees be felled during the dark phase of the moon. Timber cut at such periods during the winter reportedly seasoned well and remained free of insects. After felling the trees, the axeman removed branches and tops, leaving the trunks a foot or two in excess of the de-

sired length. The logs were then dragged by oxen or rolled to the construction site.

The site was chosen with care. Normally it was well drained, and locations atop low hills or embankments were popular, usually adjacent to a road, path, or track. Texans showed definite preferences in the directional orientation of their log dwellings. A detailed analysis of about one hundred log houses in the East Cross Timbers of Denton and Cooke counties revealed that over half, 53 percent to be exact, face south. Of the remainder, 21 percent face east, 18 percent west, and only 8 percent north.[2] The preference for cardinal directions evident in the East Cross Timbers is in part a reflection of the semirectangular land survey pattern of that region. Roads run north-south and east-west, following the survey and property lines. In parts of Texas where the survey and roads are not oriented to the cardinal points, log houses often face other directions, usually fronting a road. The Old Spanish Road, or Camino Real, between San Antonio and Nacogdoches, trends generally southwest-to-northeast, and many log houses built along it duplicate the directional alignment of the road. Even with these departures from the east-west axis, southern exposure is the rule, allowing the summer breezes to ventilate the dwellings and alleviate somewhat the discomfort of the subtropical climate. No directional preference is evident in the siting of log outbuildings.

3-1. Wooden foundation pier, East Texas. The sill log rests directly on the pier. (TLCR, Sabine Co. No. 1; courtesy Texas Historical Commission)

The Foundation

The foundation of log structures varies from one part of Texas to another. In the east and southeast, one encounters the deep southern tradition of tall piers made of brick or log to elevate the house two or three feet above the ground (Figs. 3-1 and 6-18). An observer in northeast Texas in the late 1840's described the typical log house foundation there as a two-foot pier.[3] The preferred wood for use as piers in East Texas was cypress, though post oak and bois d'arc piers can be found. Such foundations prevail in damp, warm regions because of the termite problem.[4] According to local belief, termites will not infest structures that far above the ground. The practice of raising houses on piers can be traced back to the Chesapeake Tidewater region of Virginia, where it was well established in colonial times. Barns, cribs, and other outbuildings in East Texas are normally equipped with shorter piers and left to the mercy of the termites.

Foundations in the interior central portions of Texas are lower and consist of flat stones, in keeping with upper southern tradition. In parts of the East Cross Timbers, a single block of hand-hewn ferrous sandstone is placed at each corner of the log structure (Fig. 3-2). Equally common in upper southern counties are foundations of two or three layers of limestone placed atop one another, raising the structure a foot to fifteen inches above ground level.[5]

The regional pattern observed in Texas corresponds very well to that within the South as a whole.[6] In Georgia, for example, tall piers prevail on the coastal plain and low stone foundations in the mountains of the north.[7] A close spatial correlation is evident in Texas between the low stone foundation and settlement by upper southerners from Tennessee, Kentucky, Missouri, and Arkansas. Similarly, the settlement zone occupied by

3-2. Hewn sandstone foundation, Cooke County, North Texas.

lower southerners from the coastal plain of Alabama, Mississippi, Louisiana, and Georgia is dominated by taller pier foundations.

Typically, the space beneath the East Texas log house was left open, to be the scene of territorial disputes among chickens, lazy dogs, and playing children. Southern breezes ventilated the space and filtered up through the floorboards. The lower stone foundations and more confined space beneath the upper southern house of interior Texas were often concealed by a skirting, particularly if the house was covered with milled siding. Some upper southern log houses were equipped with cellars.

In many West Texas log homes, a quite different method of construction was employed. These dwellings were dugouts, or semidugouts, formed by excavating several feet of a hillside or stream embank-

ment. The log wall formed a superstructure. Instead of resting on a foundation, the logs lay atop a lower wall of masonry or directly upon the earth at the top edge of the excavation.

Preparing the Logs

Various methods, some crude and some requiring the expertise of craftsmen, were employed to prepare logs for use in a wall (Fig. 3-3). The simplest, and most ancient, technique was to leave the logs round, either peeled or with the bark intact. This technique, which can be traced to the earliest log construction in mesolithic Europe, came to North America with both Swedes and Germans.[8] In Texas, round logs occur in structures throughout the zone of log construction. They were typi-

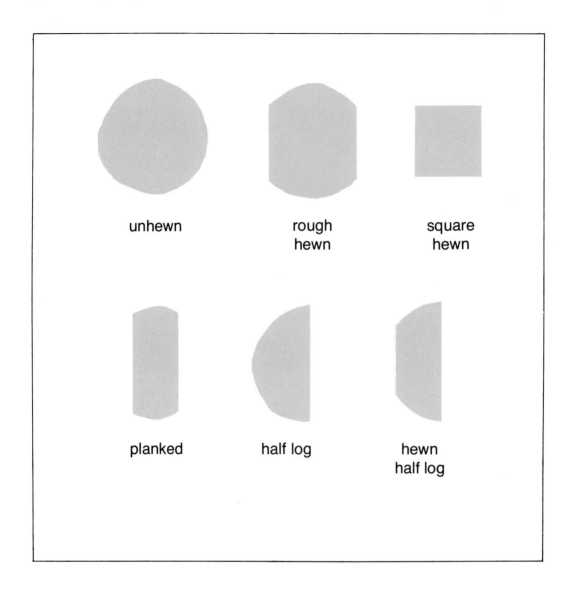

unhewn   rough   square
                hewn   hewn

planked   half log   hewn
                                half log

3-3. Methods of log preparation.

cally used in the first crude pioneer cabins, in barns and other outbuildings, and in the houses of the Great Depression revival of log construction. John B. Billingsley, describing log cabins in the infant community of Dallas in the 1840's, spoke contemptuously of "logs just as nature formed them."[9] Noah Smithwick recalled a similar sight at San Felipe in Austin's colony twenty years earlier.[10]

As a rule, log structures made of round timbers indicate hasty, careless construction performed by minimally skilled workers. That such buildings are so widespread and numerous in Texas is evidence of the low quality of log craftsmanship prevailing in the state. Round-log construction dominated both the very early pioneer phase and the very late Depression-era period of log building in Texas. The last generation of log builders, in the 1930's, retained only this most primitive method, having forgotten the better techniques known to their grandfathers and fathers.

Round logs occur frequently on most types of outbuildings in all parts of Texas, reflecting the minimal concern that farmers had for the appearance and quality of these structures. The large majority of outbuildings were constructed by amateurs. Also, round logs are more common on structures built of softwood, particularly pine.[11] Only in the piney woods of East Texas are substantial numbers of houses built of round logs to be found. But even in East Texas, most of the older houses are hewn. An aged native of Nacogdoches County who is familiar with many log dwellings in that region reports that "all of the log houses for family residence in the western part of the county that I have known were constructed of hewn pine logs," adding that the same is true of Rusk, Cherokee, San Augustine, and eastern Nacogdoches counties.[12] Most of the round-log houses in East Texas date from the 1900–1940 period. In the interior sections of Texas, round-log

dwellings are hardly ever encountered, in keeping with upper southern practice.[13]

The more skilled preparation of logs involves "hewing," or squaring, accomplished by cutting off two or more rounded sides to produce flattened surfaces. A hewn wall displays a more finished appearance, can more easily be made tight against the weather, and presents flat surfaces that are more usable. By hewing the interior side of the wall, the builder increases slightly the amount of living space inside the house. An added advantage of hewing is the removal of the outer "sapwood," leaving only the more resistant, durable "heartwood" of the log.

The first step in hewing a log is to score it with a broadaxe, at frequent and regular intervals, on the sides that are to be flattened. With a chalked string, a straight line is placed lengthwise on the log, and the carpenter "hews to the line."[14] Most craftsmen use a foot adze, a hoelike cutting instrument with a curved blade and long handle. Grasping the handle of the foot adze with his right hand about one-third of the way up from the blade, the carpenter rests the bottom of his right forearm on his right thigh. His left hand holds the handle near the butt end. Straddling the log, he makes short chopping strokes parallel to the surface of the log, chipping off the rounded bark surface in small chunks between each score. The craftsman moves backward as his work progresses. An alternative method is to use a broadaxe to hew the log, a practice normally confined to amateurs.[15] Some houses are built of squared timbers produced by whipsawing or sawmills (Fig. 6-18). Most hewn logs retain the deeper part of the score marks on their flattened surface. The absence of such marks is a certain indicator of sawn or milled logs.

Only rarely are all four sides of the log hewn, producing a squared beam. More commonly, only two sides are hewn, the inner and outer surfaces of the wall. Such two-sided hewing is called "planking" and results in a timber about five to seven inches thick.[16] The remaining two sides of a planked log, the top and bottom, are left rounded, usually with the bark intact. A typical planked pine log observed in a house in Nacogdoches County measured about six inches in thickness by thirteen inches in height. An early-day resident of Wise County, in the oak woods of the West Cross Timbers, referred to planking when he described how workers "hewed down two sides of the logs with sharp broadaxes in order to make both walls of the house smooth."[17] Planking is the normal method of hewing, in both Texas and the Upper South.[18] Four-sided hewing is usually limited to the larger top and bottom logs in the wall, the sill and the plate. All milled logs have four flat sides, as do most that are whipsawn.

Squared or planked logs occur most frequently in houses and other buildings intended for human occupance, such as schools, churches, jails, and kitchens. Among the outbuildings, only smokehouses are typically built of hewn logs.

Hewing or planking, as described above, is normally accomplished before the log is placed in the wall. A cruder method of planking, typical of pioneer cabins, is "rough hewing." The structure is erected with logs left round, after which an axeman shaves off some of the rounded surface. A pioneer of Cooke County, describing the construction in 1846 of his first log cabin, recalled that "I put the logs up round when I built my house in the spring; then in the fall I took a chopping ax and hewed the logs down smooth."[19]

A third basic method of preparing logs occurs mainly in the pine forests of East Texas (Fig. 3-4). The round log is split in half lengthwise, producing two timbers with a half-round, or semilunate, end shape. The half-round logs are then placed in the wall with their flat side toward the interior of the structure (Fig. 3-5). Half-log construction of this type is characteristic of many buildings in the

Deep South, and its presence in Texas should be regarded as an indicator of lower southern cultural influence.[20] In East Texas and the Deep South alike, half-log construction appears on both houses and outbuildings. Most often it is employed on pine wood. Upper southern folk only rarely used half-log construction, and, when they did, the outer curved surface was normally hewn.[21] A description of the half-log technique survives in the narrative of a Texas black woman, who recalled that, when slave cabins were built in Gonzales County, "they split the trees in two, and that made the sides of the house, and the round side was outside."[22]

Significantly, none of the three methods of preparing logs described above was prevalent in Scandinavian house construction at the time of Swedish and Finnish migration to the Delaware Valley. In Scandinavia, house logs were shaped with a drawknife rather than an axe or adze, and the finished log was gently rounded on the inside and outside of the wall. The bottom of the log was shaped to form a concave groove that fit snugly against the log below it.[23] This basic difference strongly suggests that the American log culture complex is not primarily of Scandinavian origin.

Sills, Joists, Wall Logs, and Plates

Having prepared the logs, the carpenters next selected two of the largest to use as "sills" (Fig. 6-13). Normally hewn on all four sides, the sills are thicker than the logs above them, ranging from eight to as much as eighteen inches square.[24] Sills are very substantial beams of wood. One oaken sill found in an Alabama log house measured twelve by twelve inches by twenty feet and still weighed 870 pounds after hewing and a century or so of weathering.[25]

The sills rest directly on the foundation

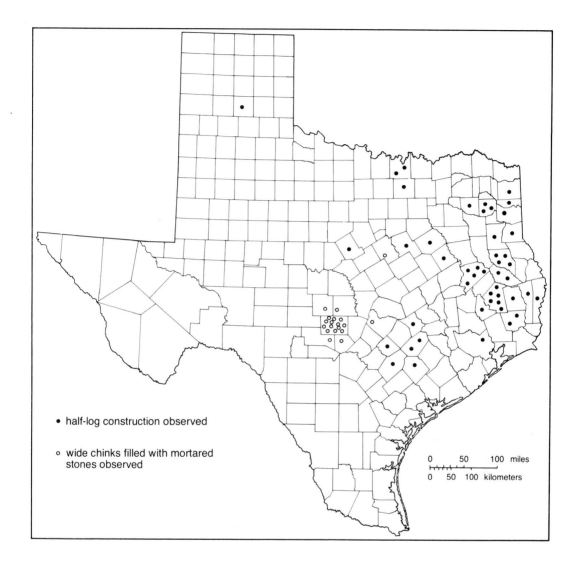

• half-log construction observed

○ wide chinks filled with mortared
  stones observed

3-4. Distribution of half-log construction and wide chinks filled with mortared stones in Texas. (TLCR)

3-5. Half-log construction, North Texas. (TLCR, Denton Co. No. 1)

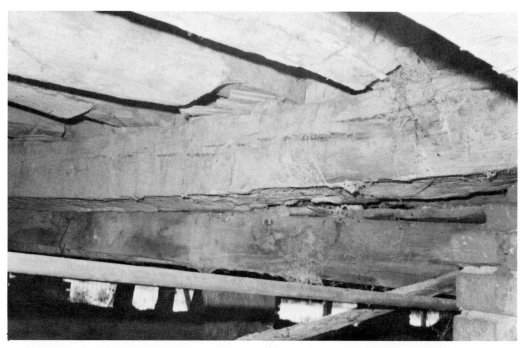

3-6. Floor joists, or sleepers, beneath the Cartwright-McCreary log house, one of the oldest surviving log structures in Texas. (TLCR, Fort Bend Co. No. 1; courtesy Mrs. R. L. Wallace)

piers or stones on the eave sides of the structure and bear the entire weight of the building. Normally, log houses of the eastern half of the United States have side-facing gables, so that the sills lie in the front and back walls.[26] Occasionally a third sill is present, situated halfway between and parallel to the others, adding more stability to the floor. If the structure is to have a wooden floor, the sills are morticed and floor joists lap-jointed into them. The joists, usually called "sleepers," reach from one sill to the other and support the floor boards (Figs. 3-6 and 6-13). Sleepers are spaced at intervals of about two feet. In most cases, they are hewn only on the top side and are made from tree trunks smaller in diameter than those used for wall logs.[27] Square hewn sleepers occur mainly in houses with cellars, as are found occasionally in upper

southern counties in Texas. The cellars cause the sleepers to be exposed to view, prompting the carpenter to give them a more finished appearance.

Two additional logs are then placed as the lowest members of the other two walls of the structure, notched into the sills at either end. Various notch styles are possible, as will be described in Chapter 4. Walls are raised to the desired height by adding more logs on all four sides, each notched into the one immediately below. A carpenter's level is helpful in making certain that each log, beginning with the sills, rests evenly, but some craftsmen relied on eye measurements alone. The logs immediately below the eaves are called "plates," and they support the rafters. Plates, like sills, are larger than ordinary wall logs. They are often placed so as to project beyond the

3-7. Spliced, lap-jointed lower log, Coles house, Washington County. (TLCR, Washington Co. No. 3)

logs below and cantilevered to permit the roof gables to extend beyond the end walls of the structure.[28] If the building is two rooms or more wide, the plates usually span the entire width of thirty to forty feet.[29] Because timbers of this length were unavailable in most of Texas, not to mention the difficulty of lifting such beams into place atop the wall, elongated plates usually consist of two timbers lap-jointed and pinned together lengthwise. The same is often true of sills (Fig. 3-7).[30]

Normally, the plates are the topmost logs, resting on the highest logs in the gable end walls. Occasionally, though, the gables are also built of horizontal logs, in which case the plates forfeit their topmost position. Rafters rest on the plates (Fig. 6-25). In rare instances, the gable walls extend one log higher than the plates.[31] More detail on gable and roof construction is contained in Chapter 5.

If the building has an upper story or loft, and most do, joists must be inserted at the desired height. In simple one-story cabins, houses, and barns, joists for the upper floor rest atop the plates, perpetuating the dominant construction method in Scotland and Ireland, where this technique is applied to stone houses. Joists for the upper floor in story-and-a-half structures rest two or more logs below the plate, a practice of German origin. In better crafted log buildings, the upper story or loft joists are morticed into the wall logs, with the butt ends visible from outside (Fig. 3-8).[32] The alternatives are to wedge them between two log walls or rest them loosely atop the plate, a solution typical of outbuildings and crudely

3-8. Upper-story floor joists, hewn and morticed, Blaine house, near Dew in Freestone County. (TLCR, Freestone Co. No. 3, photo 1969; courtesy Freestone County Historical Survey Committee)

3-9. The completed log pen. (TLCR, Montague Co. No. 5)

built cabins. Usually, if the structure is built of hewn or planked logs, the upper-story joists are hewn on all four sides and morticed into the walls. The joists are left exposed on the underside, the ceiling of the lower story. Joists, like sleepers, are placed on two-foot centers.

Lifting logs into place atop the wall during construction is a logistic problem. The traditional solution was to roll them up an inclined plane consisting of two or more poles reaching from the ground to the top of the wall, at a slope of about twenty or thirty degrees. This inclined plane is called a "skid."[33]

As the wall is raised, preparations are made for the desired apertures, usually one or two doors, a small window, and a fireplace gap. These openings are cut after the wall is fully raised, but the top logs to be cut for each opening are sawn part-way through when placed in the wall, to facilitate insertion of the saw later. To prevent severe slippage or sagging during the cutting of the apertures, wooden wedges are placed between the logs near the cutting line. After the sawing is completed, the openings are framed with rived boards to stabilize the severed logs, and then the wedges are removed. The framing boards are pegged or nailed into the ends of the cut logs. Under no circumstances are the sill or plate logs severed, since the structural strength of the building would be too greatly weakened (Fig. 3-9).

Chinks and Chinking

Care is taken in erecting the wall so that the individual logs do not rest flush against one another but instead remain separated by a crack or "chink" of an inch or more width. An early traveler in northeastern Texas described chinks of four to six inches width, and in some Texas log structures chinks are as wide as eight to ten inches.[34] The chink provides an important clue to the specific European origin of most Texan and eastern American log construction. In Europe, chinks occur only in the log buildings of Czechoslovakia and adjacent portions of central Germany, mainly the provinces of Bohemia, Moravia, and Silesia, suggesting that Pennsylvania Germans derived from those areas exerted a primary shaping influence on American log construction techniques.[35] The purpose of chinks may have been to allow for subsequent warping of the logs, since many log structures were built of improperly seasoned wood. Chinks also allow builders to accommodate the natural taper of logs.[36] Less skill and time are required to build a chinked wall, important considerations on the frontier.

Elsewhere in Europe, including Scandinavia and the Alps, logs are carefully shaped to eliminate tapering and permit a snug fit against one another, leaving no chinks. In Texas, the chinkless log wall is extremely rare, occurring mainly in Medina County, where it was seemingly introduced by German-speaking settlers of Swiss or Alsatian origin in the 1840's (Fig. 3-10). A few sawn pine log buildings in Deep East Texas also display the chinkless method.[37]

The next step is to cover or fill the chinks, so that cold air and rain cannot blow in through these cracks. In the Deep South, the most common solution was to nail rived "sealing boards" horizontally over the chinks on the inside wall, and occasionally also on the exterior.[38] In East Texas, where settlers from the Deep South were prevalent, such rived-board covering is the dominant type, particularly in the Big Thicket area.[39]

Chinking in central and northern Texas, in counties settled by upper southerners from such states as Tennessee, Kentucky, and Missouri, is quite different from that of East Texas, consisting of one or another kind of filler daubed over with plaster. Several distinct types of filler occur. One very common upper southern method involves the use of thin slats of split wood, tightly wedged at a slant into the chink (Fig. 6-13).[40] According to a pioneer of Wise County, these slats were "made out of green wood and were the shape of a thin brick."[41] An early resident of northeastern Texas wrote of "pieces of timber split for the purpose and driven in with an axe."[42] An alternative solution is to use small, flat fragments of rock to fill the chinks, a practice found widely through interior Texas wherever stone is abundant.[43] Both split wood and flat stone chinking are found widely in the upper southern source regions of the settlers of interior Texas.[44]

The filler is daubed both inside and out to form a tight wall. Daubing material differs from one district to another, depending upon what substances are available locally. In limestone areas, a mortar composed of lime and sand is prepared.[45] Sifted wood ashes are often added in the preparation of lime mortar, and perhaps also granulated salt.[46] If no limestone is available, clay is a satisfactory substitute. The clay, mixed with animal hair, moss, straw, grass, broomweed, or the like and worked with water, produces a long-lasting plaster.[47] In the absence of both clay and limestone, ordinary mud can be used.[48] A slave cabin in Gonzales County was described by a former resident as being chinked "just with mud."[49] If the wall logs are planked instead of fully hewn, the plaster or mud gains extra stability by adhering to the rough bark surfaces on

3-10. Chinkless log wall construction, with half notch and false corner·timbering, in the Medina County German area. This is the Joe Bendele house at Castroville. (TLCR,

Medina Co. No. 1, photo 1936; courtesy Historic American Buildings Survey, Library of Congress)

the top and bottom of the logs. The use of lime, clay, or mud has ample precedence in the eastern states contributing settlers to Texas.[50]

German log house builders in the Texas Hill Country developed a unique method of chinking. Unusually wide chinks were left as the wall was being raised, to be filled in with sizable hewn blocks of limestone or sandstone, firmly mortared into place (Figs. 3-4 and 3-11). The end result is a wall consisting as much of masonry as of logs, as much the product of a stonemason as of a carpenter. So distinctive is this method that it provides an almost unfailing mark of identification for German-built houses in the Hill Country. I know of no European or American precedent for mortared hewn-stone chinking, and I am inclined to believe that the technique originated in the Fredericksburg area.

Not all log structures are chinked. Writing of early cabins in the Austin Colony, George Erath recalled that "the Texas wind found the cracks between the logs," while Noah Smithwick described an early San Felipe house as unchinked.[51] Frederick Marryat made a similar accusation concerning a log structure in Bowie County in the early 1840's.[52] Perhaps the majority of log outbuildings were never chinked.

One of the most lamentable mistakes typically made in log house restorations is the use of modern commercial cement for chinking. The cement is both inaccurate and potentially very damaging to the logs. Its use is an error of the same magnitude as using concrete blocks for foundation stones or ordinary machine-cut commercial shingles for roofing.

Covering the Wall

Many log houses are sided over or otherwise covered, concealing the exterior and interior walls and completely hiding the logs. Occasionally, covering is applied even to barns and other log outbuildings.

Most commonly, horizontal or vertical siding forms the exterior covering (Fig. 6-19). Vertical siding, of the board-and-batten type, is confined to log houses of the lower socioeconomic groups, though an even greater stigma was attached to unadorned exterior walls with exposed logs. Horizontal siding is more expensive than board-and-batten, and it early became a symbol of economic success. Some log houses received a sheath of siding at the time of their construction, while others had to await this distinction for a generation or more.[53] Francis Bingham, a pioneer plantation owner of Brazoria County, covered his new hewn log house with boards from his own sawmill as early as 1831, making it perhaps the first log dwelling in Texas to be so distinguished.[54] Sam Houston's "Wigwam" house in Huntsville is a fine surviving example of horizontal siding over logs.

Status seeking was certainly a powerful stimulus for applying milled siding, but another consideration was protection for the log wall. Exposed to weathering, even the best seasoned oak logs will decay. The protective motive for siding is suggested by those Texas houses with siding on all exposed walls but unadorned logs under the shelter of porches. In later years, simulated brick siding and sheet metal covered many log structures. Another traditional solution, very rare in Texas, was to plaster the exterior walls, completely covering the log surfaces.[55] Also rare is the painting of exposed logs, though I have occasionally seen Texas barns and cribs bearing coats of whitewash or red paint.

Interior walls are often left uncovered, but even the lower socioeconomic groups frequently affixed a wallpaper consisting of pages torn from mail-order catalogues or newspapers. Wainscoting or wall boards grace the finer log houses, and a

3-11. Log wall with unusually wide chinks, filled with hewn, mortared stones. This type of construction is confined mainly to the German Hill Country around Fredericksburg. (TLCR, Gillespie Co. No. 10, photo 1973)

light blue paint was often applied to the ceiling.

In the construction and adornment of a log wall, perhaps no single feature or technique was as crucially important as the corner notching. Chapter 4 is devoted to the various methods of fastening logs together at the corner.

FOUR
Corner Notching

If any single element can properly be called the key to log construction, it is the corner notch, the joint where logs from adjacent walls are attached to one another. The entire weight of the building exclusive of the sills and floor rests on the four corners and therefore on the notches. Not only is the notching weight bearing, but it also holds the walls laterally in place by preventing horizontal slippage. If the notching is faulty, the entire structure is faulty.

To fashion the notch, the carpenter or "corner man" normally uses a small axe or, for less complicated notches, a hand saw. A carpenter's square, chisel, and ruler are useful, and patterns showing the proper slope angles are sometimes employed. A skilled workman can fashion even the more complicated notches with only an axe, using it in the manner of a chisel for the fine fitting. Most of the work on the notch is performed on the ground, but final exact fitting is accomplished atop the wall.

Eight distinct notch types are found in Texas, only four of which account for the great majority of log structures in the state.[1] These four dominant styles are the *half-dovetail, saddle, "V,"* and *square* notches (Fig. 4-1). Much less common are the types called *full-dovetail, semilunate, half,* and *double* (Table 4-1; Fig. 4-2). Several other styles which occur in the eastern United States, such as the diamond notch, are not present in Texas.[2]

The Full-Dovetail Notch

Though uncommon in Texas, the full-dovetail is a parent type from which several local notch styles were derived. It is formed by cutting slants or "splays" in different directions on the end of the log, one on the top and the other on the bottom, in the manner of a common cabinetmaker's joint (Fig. 4-3).[3] The result is a locking joint of superior strength, possessing the added advantage of draining rainwater to the exterior.

Full-dovetail notching occurs widely throughout Europe, including the source areas of both Swedish and German immigrants to the Middle Atlantic colonies.[4] I have personally seen the full-dovetail notch on houses in the mountains of Bosnia and the old Swedish-settled area of southwestern New Jersey. In Europe, full-dovetailing is found in both chinked and chinkless construction. The chinked Czechoslovakian type seems to be the principal prototype of the American dovetailed log buildings, since the Swedish-built houses along the Delaware are typically chinkless. Full-dovetailing in the United States is confined, as an important notch type, to the Delaware Valley, eastern Pennsylvania, and portions of the Great Valley of the Appalachians as far south as northwestern Virginia.[5] Elsewhere, in areas influenced by Middle Atlantic log construction, full-dovetailing is rare, even in Ohio and other states

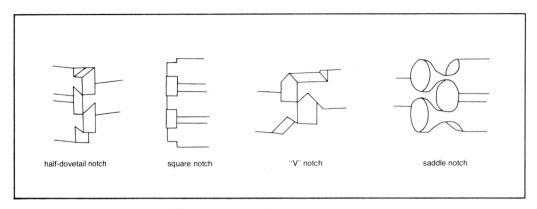

4-1. Most common types of log corner notching in Texas.

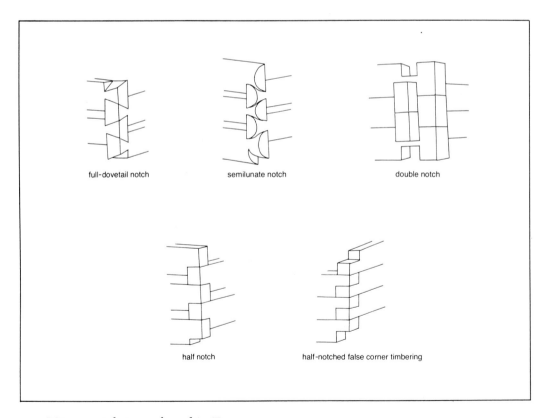

4-2. Minor notch types found in Texas.

TABLE 4-1. *Types of Log Corner Notching in Texas*

| Type of notch | Log houses* | | Log outbuildings | |
	Number	%	Number	%
Half-dovetail	187	35	17	10.5
Square	136	25	16	10
"V"	112	21	36	22
Saddle	78	14.5	82	51
Semilunate	10	2	6	4
Full-dovetail	7	1	0	0
Double	4	0.75	1	0.5
Half	3	0.5	3	2
Diamond	0	0	0	0
Other types	0	0	0	0
Total	537		161	

Source: TLCR; also includes a few outbuildings observed in the field but not listed in the Register.
*Includes dwellings, courthouses, churches, schools, jails, offices, and stores.

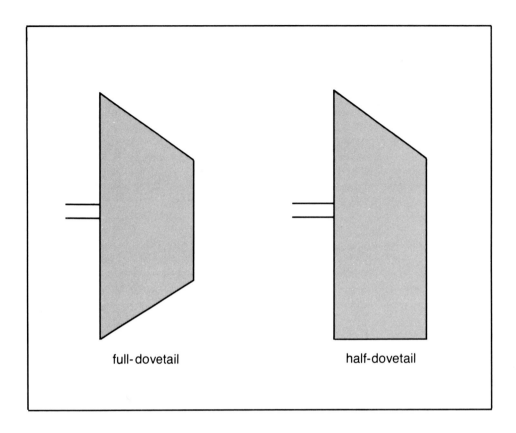

full-dovetail   half-dovetail

4-3. Dovetail notches.

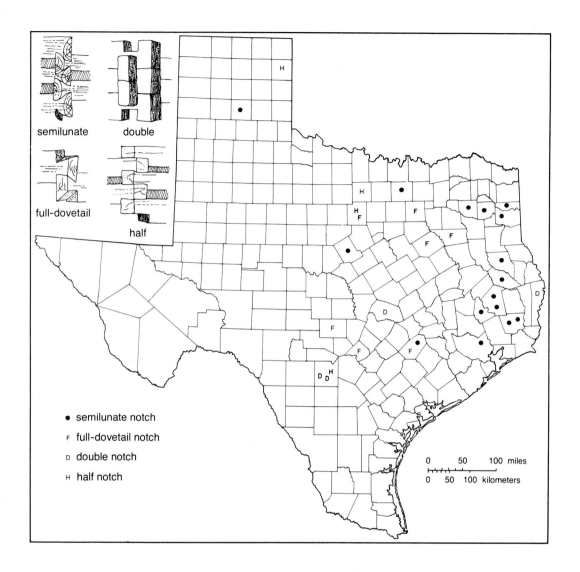

semilunate   double

full-dovetail

half

● semilunate notch
F full-dovetail notch
D double notch
H half notch

0   50   100 miles
0   50   100 kilometers

4-4. Distribution of minor types of log corner notching in Texas. (TLCR)

close to the American hearth of log construction.[6] In Wisconsin and possibly other upper Midwest states, full-dovetail notching was reintroduced by nineteenth-century European immigrants and is locally important.[7] Only about 1 percent of all Texas log houses are full-dovetailed (Fig. 4-4).

The Half-Dovetail Notch

By contrast, the half-dovetail notch, also called the "mitre dovetail," is very common throughout most of the eastern United States and is the dominant type in Texas log houses (Fig. 4-5).[8] The difference between the half- and full-dovetail is that the former type has a splay or slant only on the top side of the tongue of the log (Figs. 4-3 and 4-6). Obviously, the full-dovetail is parent to the half-dovetail. Evidence suggests that half-dovetailing evolved in central Europe, possibly Czechoslovakia, but it is uncommon there.[9] The transition from full to half may have occurred again in America, in the region peripheral to southeastern Pennsylvania. Half-dovetailing, though somewhat easier to fashion than its parent type, still produces a firmly locked joint and retains the water-draining advantage. It is a superior type identified with fine craftsmanship.

The half-dovetail notch was first used extensively in the border region of Virginia and West Virginia rather than in Pennsylvania. It became dominant through most of the Upper South and Ohio Valley, in areas as far-flung as the hills of Arkansas, the North Carolina Piedmont, and the southern half of Ohio.[10] Some residents of North Texas call the half-dovetail a "Missouri notch," suggesting its importance in that state. Some confusion exists concerning the chronology of the half-dovetail, for it is said to have dominated the latter period

of log construction in Ohio and the early period in Alabama.[11] Because Texas drew so heavily on the Upper South as a source of settlers, it is not surprising that the half-dovetail notch is the most common type in the state. It was no doubt a half-dovetail that H. H. Halsell, a pioneer of Wise County, was describing when he recalled that "the logs were put up, the ends being trimmed to dovetail together."[12]

The half-dovetail is particularly prevalent when hardwoods, mainly various species of oak, are used for construction.[13] It occurs less frequently in cedar, pine, and other softwoods. Half-dovetailing is generally used on planked timbers, though it occurs occasionally on half-round logs (Figs. 4-7 and 4-8). Upon completion of the structure, the ends of the dovetailed logs were normally sawn off flush to form a "boxed" corner.[14] Sometimes, though, the ends were left slightly projecting, producing an "overhanging dovetail" corner.[15]

All knowledge of how to fashion this once-prevalent notch type seems to have died out in Texas. Indeed, the procedure for cutting a half-dovetail corner is almost forgotten everywhere in America. Fortunately, a present-day craftsman of the southern Appalachians who remembers the technique was interviewed recently by the authors of *The Foxfire Book*, and he demonstrated for the camera how to fashion the half-dovetail.[16] First, the craftsman used an axe to cut a 30° to 45° slope on the top side of the end of a hewn or planked log, sloping down from what was to be the inside of the wall toward the outside. The sloped surface was smoothed with short, careful strokes of the axe. Then another log was placed atop the first and at right angles to it, with care taken that it lay exactly horizontal. A ruler about one inch wide was rested on the cut slope and a line drawn along the top edge of the ruler on the side of the second log. The ruler was then placed vertically, resting on the hewn interior wall surface

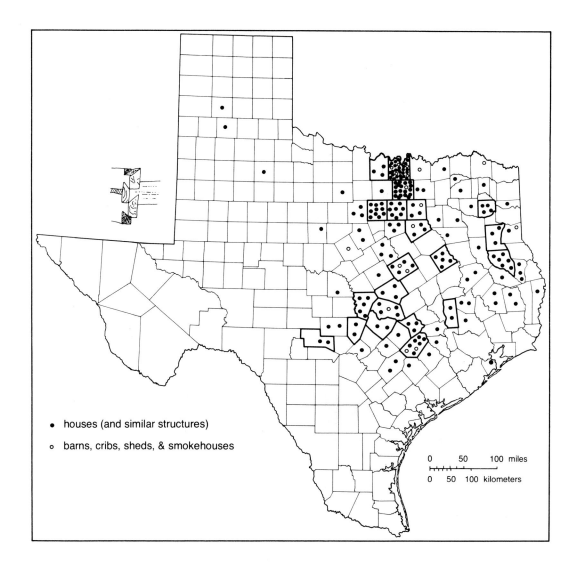

4-5. Field observations of half-dovetail–notch log corner timbering in Texas. In counties with dark outline, half-dovetail notching accounts for 33 percent or more of all houses observed (only counties with at least four observations are included). (TLCR)

4-6. Inspecting half-dovetail notching on an oaken log house in North Texas. (TLCR, Denton Co. No. 29, photo 1973; courtesy Roy Bray and the *Texas Magazine*, published by the *Houston Chronicle*)

4-7. Half-dovetail notch on massive planked logs, Central Texas. (TLCR, Freestone Co. No. 1; courtesy Freestone County Historical Survey Committee)

4-8. Half-dovetail notch on half-round pine logs, Big Thicket area, dating from about 1885. (TLCR, Polk Co. No. 16, photo 1973; courtesy Mrs. John Winter)

of the first log and a vertical line was drawn to intersect the sloping line on the second log. This line-drawing process was repeated on the opposite side of the second log. These lines could also be drawn by using a pattern cut to the desired slope angle, making the ruler unnecessary.

Following the guidelines, the carpenter cut a sloped surface on the bottom side of the second log, matching the slope already cut on the lower log. The two were fitted together, and, if not sufficiently snug, high places were shaved off with chisellike strokes of the axe. If wide chinks were desired, a minimum of wood was removed in cutting the sloped surfaces. To narrow the chink, deeper notch cuts were made, maintaining the same angle of slope.

The Saddle Notch

The saddle notch is probably the most ancient of all types (Figs. 4-1 and 4-9). It is almost always used on logs that are left round rather than hewn, and it is fashioned by hollowing out a saddle-shaped depression near the end of the log, shaped to fit the rounded contour of the adjacent log or another saddle.[17] Two subtypes of the saddle notch can be distinguished, the "single" and the "double" (Fig. 4-10). The double saddle is formed by cutting depressions into both the top and bottom of the log, while the single saddle notch, the simpler of the subtypes, has a depression cut only on one side of the log (Fig. 4-11). Both subtypes of the saddle notch form a locked joint, and the ends of the logs are left projecting beyond the corner, rather than being cut off flush as in the dovetailed types.[18] The single saddle notch with the depression cut on the bottom of the log drained rainwater better than did the double type or the top-notched single type, since it lacked a depression on the top side of the log which could catch and hold moisture. Pennsylvania Germans seem to have introduced the subtype notched only on the bottom, since this style is very common on log barns in the German-settled counties of that state.[19]

The saddle notch was likely developed as early as mesolithic times in Europe. After being introduced to America by both Germans and Swedes, it became very common throughout the zone of log construction in the United States. Saddle notching was the dominant type used in the early pioneer cabins, since it could be fashioned by relatively unskilled workers.[20] The professionally built log houses which replaced pioneer cabins display saddle notching much less frequently. Saddle notching also dominated the twentieth-century phase of log house construction in East Texas and the Deep South as a whole, reflecting the lower level of craftsmanship typical of this late period. To find any substantial number of saddle-notched dwellings, one must visit the woodlands of the Lower South, including East Texas (Fig. 4-12).[21] As a rule, saddle notching is most common in softwoods, particularly pine and cedar (Fig. 4-13).[22]

Saddle notching is the prevalent type on most kinds of outbuildings throughout Texas and the eastern United States (Table 4-1).[23] Barns, cribs, well houses, cotton sheds, and similar structures were usually built by amateurs rather than professional carpenters, and saddle notching was often the only type known to them. Overall, then, the saddle notch is found mainly on early pioneer cabins, twentieth-century log houses, and various kinds of farm outbuildings. It is most common in unhewn softwoods, particularly in the lower southern pine region.

4-9. Saddle notch on pine logs, a typical East Texas construction. (TLCR, Walker Co. No. 5, photo 1973)

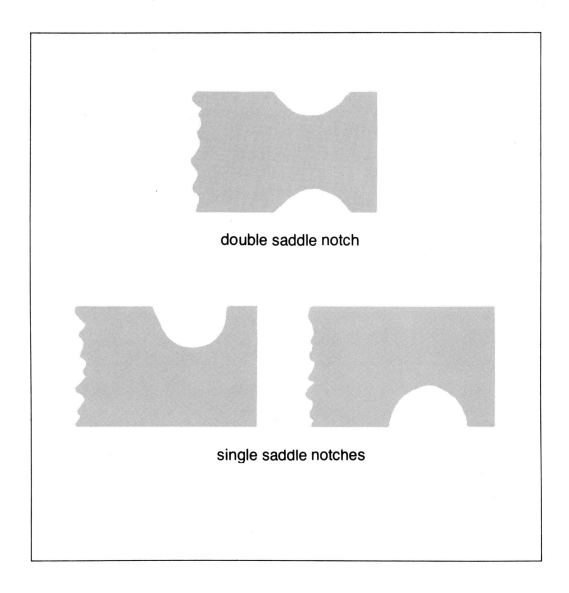

double saddle notch

single saddle notches

4-10. Saddle notches.

4-11. Single saddle notch on an East Texas log barn. (TLCR, Sabine Co. No. 2B; courtesy Texas Historical Commission)

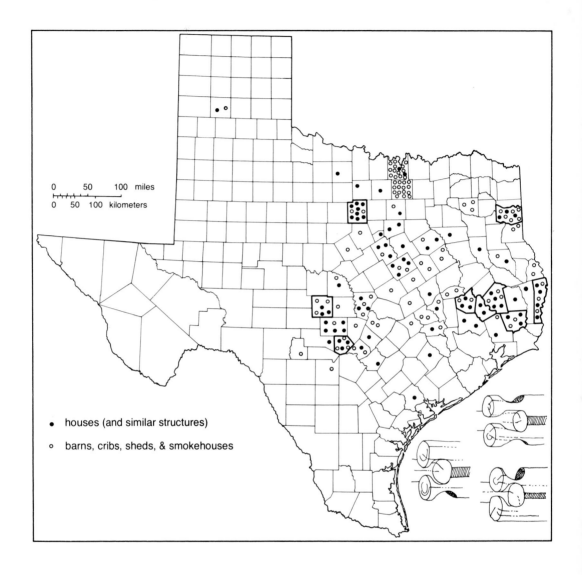

4-12. Field observations of saddle-notch log corner timbering in Texas. In counties with dark outline, saddle notching accounts for 33 percent or more of all houses observed (only counties with at least four observations are included). (TLCR)

4-13. Saddle-notched cedar logs, on a Hill Country barn. (TLCR, Comal Co. No. 4; courtesy Theodore Albrecht)

4-14. "V" notch on an oaken log house in North Texas. The "V" notch is confined mainly to the northern and central parts of Texas, settled from the Upper South. (TLCR, Cooke Co. No. 16, photo 1972)

The "V" Notch

"V" notching, so-named because of its inverted V-shaped joint, was developed in Europe, apparently as a variant of the saddle notch (Figs. 4-1 and 4-14). The Schwenkfelders, a German religious sect from the province of Silesia, seem to have introduced the "V" notch into Pennsylvania in the 1730's, and it became the most common type on Pennsylvania German log houses.[24] "V" notching does occur on some Swedish houses along the Delaware, but apparently this represents a borrowing from the nearby Germans.[25]

"V" notching is found throughout most of Pennsylvania, particularly in the German counties, and its spread west was mainly by way of the central Appalachians and Ohio Valley.[26] It is the dominant type in the mountains of western Maryland and Virginia and occurs widely through Kentucky, Ohio, Indiana, Illinois, and Missouri. Generally, the further south one goes in the eastern part of the United States, the less frequent the occurrence of "V" notching. In the Blue Ridge and Great Valley of the Appalachians, the "V" notch prevails as the dominant type about as far south as the Virginia-Tennessee border, beyond which it is less common.[27]

In Texas, "V" notching is very closely associated with settlers of upper southern and German heritage. It occurs almost exclusively in the interior central and northern parts of the state and is extremely rare in East Texas (Fig. 4-15). Clearly, "V" notching reached Texas by way of the Ohio Valley and Missouri. The Hill Country Germans of Central Texas presumably learned how to fashion the "V" notch from upper southerners in their vicinity, since the large majority of Texas German immigrants were not derived from provinces where this type of corner notch was known.

The "V" notch forms a solid, locked corner and is used both on hewn logs and on those left in the round. Perhaps more often than not, "V" notching occurs on square-hewn logs rather than planked ones. If the logs are hewn, the corner is boxed, but round logs are left projecting beyond the corner, as with the saddle notch. Rainwater is drained out of the joint fairly well, though the "V" notch is inferior to the dovetail types in this respect. "V" notching occurs frequently on both oak and cedar logs. It is not uncommon to find saddle and "V" notching intermixed on walls, an additional suggestion that the "V" is derived from the saddle type. On both houses and outbuildings, the "V" notch accounts for about one-fifth of the log structures in Texas (Table 4-1).

The Square Notch

The square notch, often called a "quarter" notch in Texas, is apparently derived from the dovetail types and possibly also from "V" notching (Figs. 4-1 and 4-16). It was developed in Europe and is common in northern Bohemia, the principal source area of American log construction.[28] Curiously, all previous scholars who dealt with this type declared it to be an Americanism with no European precedent. Henry Glassie, for example, argued that square notching first appeared among English settlers in central Virginia.[29] Possibly, but, if so, the American development was a secondary, independent invention. The widespread distribution of square notching in America, from Wisconsin to Alabama and Idaho to Ohio, suggests instead an early introduction from Europe.[30]

We might best regard square notching as a degenerate type because it requires much less skill to fashion than most other styles and does not produce a locked joint (Fig. 4-17). It probably evolved as less skilled craftsmen de-

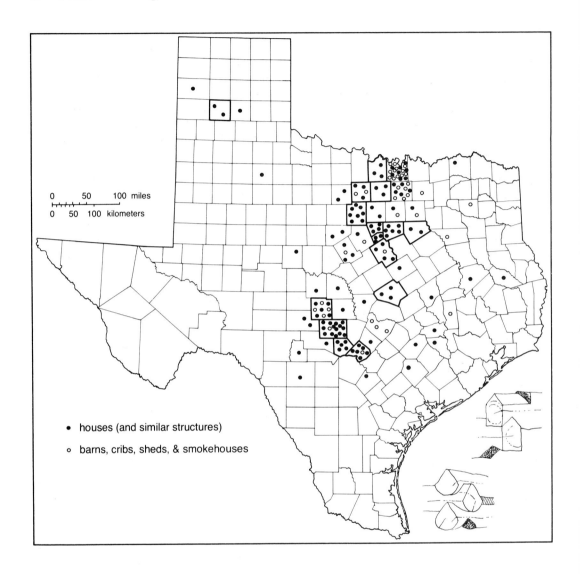

4-15. Field observations of "V"-notch log corner timbering in Texas. In counties with dark outline, "V" notching accounts for 33 percent or more of all houses observed (only counties with at least four observations are included). (TLCR)

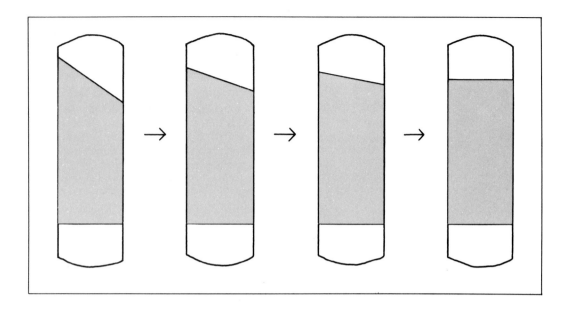

4-16. Evolution of the square notch from the half-dovetail notch.

4-17. Square notch on a log house in Central Texas. Square notching occurs widely through eastern and central parts of the state. (TLCR, Hays Co. No. 1; courtesy Theodore Albrecht)

creased the angle of dovetailing, or both angles of the "V" notch, until the angle reached 90°, forming a notch consisting only of right angles (Figs. 4-16 and 6-13). Because this notch is not locking and cannot hold together simply by gravity, each joint must be pegged or nailed to assure the survival of the structure. Pegging the logs provides sufficient shear strength, at least until the pegs rot out from the rainwater that tends to collect on the flat surface of the square notch.

Degenerate forms of material culture, such as the square notch, often appear when uninitiated culture groups accept a technology from another group, usually on a periphery or outer zone of usage. The farther from the source region and parent population of a technique or technology, the more primitive the level of skill normally is. In the case of the square notch, an American independent invention perhaps occurred among the English in central Virginia, in the zone where Anglo-Saxons migrating westward from the Chesapeake Tidewater first encountered the log technology of the Middle Atlantic folk.[31] The square notch may have been their fumbling effort to copy an alien technology. More likely the Virginia English were simply attracted to the least complex notch style they found in the Middle Atlantic technology. The square notch could easily be fashioned with a saw, a tool the Tidewater English were familiar with, minimizing reliance on the axe and adze.

Square notching is most widely encountered across the inner coastal plain of the South, from the Virginia Piedmont to East Texas, areas settled largely by persons of English stock derived from eastern Virginia.[32] It is relatively rare in the Upper South, though numerous examples can be found in eastern Kentucky, Ohio, and southern Illinois.[33] A few examples are even found in southwestern New Jersey, the old zone of seventeenth-century Swedish settlement. The widespread occurrence of square notching in the coastal plain of the Gulf southern states is perhaps a reflection of the remoteness of the Deep South from the American source area of log technology, the Delaware Valley.

In Texas the square notch is the second most common type on dwellings and similar structures (Table 4-1). It appears most frequently in eastern and east-central Texas and seems to have been fashioned mainly by migrants from Alabama, Mississippi, and Louisiana (Fig. 4-18).[34] Upper southern settlers rarely employed the

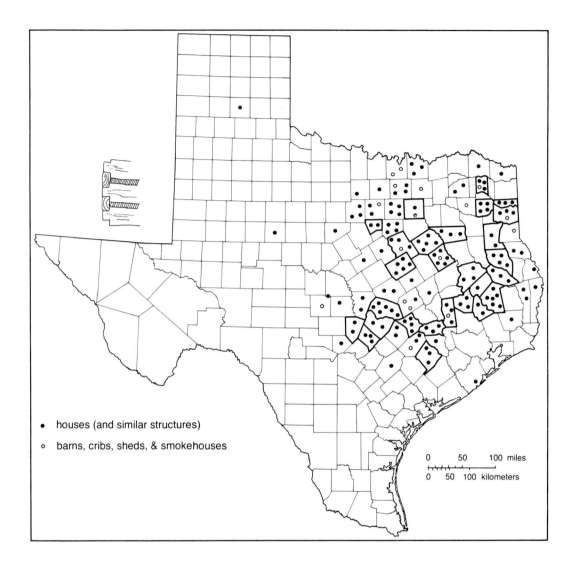

4-18. Field observations of square (quarter)-notch log corner timbering in Texas. In counties with dark outline, square notching accounts for 33 percent or more of all houses observed (only counties with at least four observations are included). (TLCR)

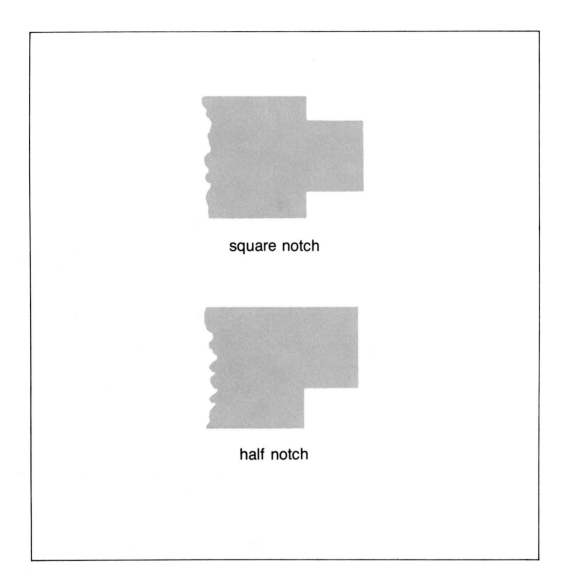

square notch

half notch

4-19. Comparison of square and half notches.

square notch. In Cooke County, an upper southern stronghold in North Texas settled mainly from Missouri, no examples of square notching were found on the thirty-six log houses observed in field research.

A still further degeneration from the square notch seemingly produced the *half* notch, the simplest of all forms (Fig. 4-19).[35] To fashion this notch, the builder had to remove only one square of wood from the bottom corners of each log. Pegging is required to hold the half-notched corner in place, since it shares the unlocked character of the parent square notch. Throughout Texas the half notch is rare. However, on many square-notched structures, occasional half-notched joints appear, usually to rectify minor misfits in the wall.

Both the square and half notches are normally applied on hewn logs, but they can be found also on round and half-round timbers. As with dovetailed notching, the projecting ends of square-notched logs are typically boxed at the corners, but less careful builders sometimes left the ends projecting.

Closely related to half notching is the technique called *false corner timbering*, in which the tiers of logs on adjacent walls are even instead of alternated and no chinks are present (Fig. 4-2).[36] This inferior method, typically achieved by use of the half notch, is extremely rare in Texas, though it does occur with some frequency in Old Mexico. The Medina County region of Alsatian and German-Swiss settlement contains the only significant number of false-corner-timbered buildings in Texas, though very few survive even there (Fig. 3-10).

The Double Notch

The double notch is very similar to the square notch, differing only by virtue of a projection at the corner which causes it to form a locked joint (Fig. 4-2). Looked at another way, the double notch is simply a saddle notch with a square-shaped saddle. Those readers familiar with the popular toy known as Lincoln Logs will at once recognize the double notch.[37] A variant type known as the single notch is occasionally found, typified by notching only on one side of the log, similar to the single saddle notch.[38]

In Europe, double notching is very common, dominating the zones of log construction in Scandinavia, the Alps, and much of the East European plain.[39] It seems to have originated in central or eastern Europe and spread from there to much of the remainder of the continent.[40] Normally, this notch produces a chinkless wall quite different from the typical American construction. Double notching rarely occurs in the United States, though Finnish immigrants introduced it into the North Woods of the upper Midwest in the late nineteenth century.[41] Much earlier, Spanish settlers carried it from Mexico, where it is very common, to the mountain country of northern New Mexico.[42] Double notching dominates the Hispanic Rio Arriba still today, producing buildings clearly different from those built by Anglo-Americans in adjacent districts.

The Mexican and New Mexican zones of double notching apparently never influenced Texas. Chinkless double-notched walls occur infrequently in the state and appear to have been common only among the Medina County ethnic Germans (Fig. 4-20). A few examples can be found in pine log buildings of twentieth-century vintage in East Texas (Fig. 4-4).[43]

4-20. Chinkless, double-notched house on the southwestern periphery of the log construction zone in Texas. This structure was built by Joseph Rudinger, an immigrant from Alsace, in the colony of D'Hanis, Medina County, about 1850. The double-notch and the chinkless construction are very rare in Texas, suggesting that Rudinger learned

these techniques in Alsace. It is also possible that Swiss settlers in the same colony are responsible for this introduction. (TLCR, Medina Co. No. 2, photo 1972 by Ted Powers; courtesy Marcia Jackson and Texas Historical Commission)

4-21. Semilunate notching on a house in the pine forests of East Texas. This type of notch is found almost exclusively on pine logs and is relatively rare in Texas. In most cases, half-log construction employs half-dovetail notching instead of semilunate. (TLCR, San Jacinto Co. No. 3, photo 1973)

The Semilunate Notch

Somewhat more common in Texas is the semilunate notch. Apparently an American invention, the semilunate is found almost exclusively in the Deep South, where it is applied to half-round pine logs. The natural round shape of the log surface is preserved in the configuration of the notch, producing something akin to a full-dovetail joint (Figs. 4-2 and 4-21).[44] Or, perhaps better, the semilunate is simply half of a saddle notch. Not all half-round logs are notched in the semilunate manner, but all semilunate notches occur on half-round timbers.

In Texas, the Deep South association of semilunate notching is at once evident from its spatial distribution (Fig. 4-4). The large majority of examples observed in the field are found in East Texas, the main settlement area of lower southerners.

Several other types of corner notching occur in America, besides those mentioned in the preceding sections.[45] Notable is the diamond notch.[46] However, none of these is known to exist in Texas (Table 4-1).

Choosing a Notch Type

A number of causal factors influenced the craftsman's choice among notch types. The area of origin of the builder, reflecting his cultural background, was one such factor. Another, of equal importance, was the type of wood available to the craftsman.

The cultural geographer is by inclination attracted to an analysis of the cultural heritage of builders as a key to the decision-making process. In their study of Wisconsin log structures, for example, L. R. Brandt and N. E. Braatz began with the hypothesis that the ethnic background of the builder was the most im-

TABLE 4-2. *Five Major Notch Types in Texas as Related to Place of Origin of Settlers*

	In counties dominated by upper southerners[1]	In counties dominated by lower southerners[2]	In counties dominated by Germans[3]	In counties with a mixed population
Total number observed of five major types[4]	242	126	41	115
	(%)	(%)	(%)	(%)
Full- or half-dovetail	44	30	10	30.5
"V"	26.5	2	61	15
Saddle	10	21.5	22	16.5
Square or half	19	41	7	37
Semilunate	0	5.5	0	1

Source: TLCR.
[1] Upper South = Arkansas, Missouri, Kentucky, Tennessee, North Carolina.
[2] Lower South = Louisiana, Mississippi, Alabama, Georgia, South Carolina.
[3] Germans = settlers directly from Germany.
[4] Houses, churches, jails, etc.—no cribs included.

portant cultural factor influencing corner notch type.[47] The regional pattern of corner timbering in the eastern United States, described earlier in this chapter, reveals that dovetailing and "V" notching are more common in the Upper South, the Midwest, and the Pennsylvania source region, while square, saddle, and semilunate types occur more frequently in the Lower South, particularly in the Gulf and Atlantic inner coastal plain.

Builders of log structures in Texas should reveal their sectional origins by retaining the prevalent notch types of their former home districts, if the factor of cultural heritage is an important one. East Texas, settled by lower southerners, should display different frequencies of notch types than Central Texas, where upper southerners were numerically dominant (Fig. 1-6). Both of these settlement areas, moreover, should differ from the German counties of south-central Texas, and a transitional zone of mixed ethnic origin also ought to reveal a unique combination of notch types.

The relationship of notch type and place of origin in Texas is shown in Table 4-2. It is noteworthy that half-dovetailing and "V" notching are more common in the upper southern counties, while the square, saddle, and semilunate notch types are found more frequently in the lower southern area. Notice, too, how the notch percentiles for the counties with mixed population fall in between the extremes of the upper and lower southern areas in every case. By far the most striking correlation is that between Germans and use of the "V" notch, and the associated avoidance of dovetailing in the Hill Country German counties. The Germans in question came largely from half-timbering areas in Hesse, Nassau, and Lower Saxony and thus had no log construction heritage in Europe. Most likely, preference for the "V" notch was related to their practice of placing sizable stones mortared together as chinking, requiring a wide gap between logs (Fig. 3-10). Additional evidence for the importance of ethnic background is found in the concentration of double notching in the Alsatian and Swiss-German settlements of Medina County.

The choice among notch styles was also strongly influenced by the type of wood available to the builders (Table 4-3).[48] Almost half of all oaken log houses observed in Texas are dovetailed, while those built of pine are most often saddle or square notched. Cedar timbers usually display saddle or "V" notching, and all semilunate notching occurs in pine. In general, we can say that dovetailing predominates for hardwoods, while saddle, "V," square, and semilunate notchings are prevalent in softwoods. The findings in Texas strongly suggest that log "corner men" usually knew how to fashion two or more different notch styles and that

TABLE 4-3. *Five Major Notch Types in Texas as Related to Type of Wood*

	Oak	Pine	Cedar	Elm
Number observed*	167	85	72	8
	(%)	(%)	(%)	(%)
Full- or half-dovetail	44.5	28	21	25
"V"	22	2	28	37.5
Saddle	8.5	31.5	30.5	25
Square or half	25	29	21	12.5
Semilunate	0	9	0	0

Source: TLCR.
*Houses, churches, jails, etc.—no cribs included.

they allowed the available type of timber to influence their choice among those types. This view is supported by the fact that many log houses were built by professional carpenters. As experts in log construction, these builders were surely aware of at least several of the cornering techniques.

I selected one small area, consisting of two adjacent counties in north-central Texas, to test the relative importance of place of origin versus wood type in the choice of notch style (Table 4-4). Both of these counties, Palo Pinto and Parker, were settled largely by upper southerners

TABLE 4-4. *Population Origin, Wood Type, and Corner Notching on Log Houses in Palo Pinto and Parker Counties, Texas*

Parker County		Palo Pinto County	
Population origins			
Leading states of birth (as % of non-Texas native-born, 1880)[1]	Leading states of residence prior to removal to Texas (as % of all immigrants, 1865–1880)[2]	Leading states of birth (as % of non-Texas native-born, 1880)[1]	Leading states of residence prior to removal to Texas (as % of all immigrants, 1865–1880)[2]
Tennessee 22	Arkansas 20	Missouri 17	Arkansas 23.5
Missouri 12	Tennessee 15.5	Tennessee 13	Missouri 21
Arkansas 9	Missouri 14	Alabama 12	Mississippi 12.5
Kentucky 8	Mississippi 11	Arkansas 10	Tennessee 8.5
Georgia 8	Kentucky 6.5	Mississippi 9	Alabama 8
Upper South[3] 51	Upper South[3] 56	Upper South[3] 48	Upper South 56
Lower South[4] 24	Lower South[4] 25	Lower South[4] 31	Lower South[4] 29

Type of notch		(%)	(%)
	Half- or full-dovetail	77	17
	"V"	15	33
	Saddle	0	33
	Square	8	17

Type of wood		(%)	(%)
	Cedar	0	70
	Oak	100	26
	Elm	0	4

Source: TLCR.

[1] U.S. Census, 1880, 1:530.
[2] H. L. Kerr, "Migration into Texas, 1865–1880," Ph.D. dissertation, pp. 87, 88 (based on census schedules).
[3] Upper South = Arkansas, Missouri, Tennessee, Kentucky.
[4] Lower South = Louisiana, Mississippi, Alabama, Georgia.

in the period 1850–1890, with Arkansans, Tennesseans, and Missourians dominating. A detailed study of population origins reveals no significant difference between the two counties. But even though Palo Pinto and Parker lie adjacent to one another in the hills of north-central Texas, their respective forest covers are quite different. Parker is traversed by a belt of post oak forest, while Palo Pinto contains extensive cedar brakes. This difference greatly influenced the type of wood used for log construction (Table 4-4). Significantly, the notch types also differed, reflecting the dissimilarity of the forests rather than the similarity of population origin. Dovetailing predominated in the oak woods of Parker, while saddle and "V" notching prevailed in cedar-studded Palo Pinto. In the two counties, all dovetailed notches observed were oaken.

Additional evidence that most builders knew how to fashion more than one type of notch is revealed by detailed examination of individual structures. For one thing, the sill log is often or even generally notched differently from those above it. Half-dovetailing frequently appears only on the sill or the log just above the sill, with square or "V" notching on the rest of the wall (Fig. 4-22).[49] I have observed this same sill-wall contrast in East Tennessee. Saddle and "V" notching are often seen to alternate within a log wall, and in some other cases the type of notching changes about three or four feet above ground level (Fig. 4-23). These observations reveal that notch style varied even with position in the wall. When houses were enlarged, the added second pen or upper story often was notched differently from the original part of the dwelling. In extreme cases, as many as three notch styles appear on the same house.[50]

An analysis of structure types provides even more evidence that a variety of notch styles was known locally (Tables 4-1 and 4-5). Dovetailing and square notching account for the large majority of

4-22. On this East Tennessee house, the sill log is half-dovetailed, while the logs above are "V" notched. Similar sill-wall contrasts are seen widely in Texas. (Photo 1974)

4-23. Different notches used on the same log wall. The style changes from "V" notch to half-dovetail about four feet above ground level on this North Texas house. (TLCR, Denton Co. No. 26, photo 1973)

TABLE 4-5. *Notch Types of Texas Log Outbuildings*

Type of notch	All farm outbuildings	Barns and corncribs	Smokehouses	Miscellaneous small cribs
	(%)	(%)	(%)	(%)
Full- or half-dovetail	10.5	10.5	23.5	5
"V"	21	24	23.5	13
Saddle	51	48	35	66.5
Square or half	12	11.5	12	13
Semilunate	5	6	6	2.5

Source: TLCR; includes also some structures observed in the field but not listed in the Register.

houses and similar structures, such as stores, jails, inns, and offices, but outbuildings are normally saddle or "V" notched. Indeed, over half of all outbuildings in Texas display the saddle notch. Smokehouses reveal a rather different frequency of notch types from other outbuildings. On many farmsteads where multiple log structures are present, more than one notch type is employed even among the outbuildings.

Date of construction can also be causally related to notch type, since knowledge of how to fashion the more difficult notches, such as the half-dovetail, gradually died out in Texas as the decades passed (Table 4-6). Dovetailing accounted for the majority of all log dwellings built in Texas during the 1840's, but for only a small minority built after 1890. Conversely, the easier-to-fashion saddle notch was quite rare on houses prior to the Civil War but occurred on well over half of those erected in the last fifty-year period of log construction. Use of square notching remained fairly constant throughout the era of the log culture complex in Texas, while "V" notching experienced a peak of usage in the postbellum period. In effect, the less complex notches, saddle and square, survived longest, documenting a rapid deterioration of log technology after about 1890. I have interviewed, in the 1970's, a number of Texans who personally built log structures. The only notch they know is the saddle.

Conclusion

Four major notch types—the half-dovetail, "V," saddle, and square—account for the

TABLE 4-6. *Date of Construction for Five Major Notch Types on Texas Log Houses and Cabins*

Date of construction	Number observed*	Full- or half-dovetail	"V"	Saddle	Square or half	Semilunate
		(%)	(%)	(%)	(%)	(%)
Pre-1840	22	41	18	9	32	0
1840–1849	47	53	6	4	37	0
1850–1859	104	36.5	27	10	25	2
1860–1869	68	37	22	13	26.5	1.5
1870–1879	38	23.5	31.5	21	23.5	0
1880–1889	21	19	57	9.5	14	0
1890–1940	29	7	3.5	58.5	27.5	3.5

Source: TLCR.
* Includes also churches, jails, offices, and the like.

large majority of Texas log structures. Usage of these types varied spatially, temporally, and according to the cultural heritage of the builder, the wood, and the type of structure. Texas log carpenters typically knew how to fashion more than one of the notch styles. The quality of log construction in Texas, as evidenced by corner notching, peaked in the antebellum period and experienced a sharp decline after about 1890.

The log structure entailed much more than its walls, though the use of horizontally laid, notched timbers did provide distinctiveness. Builders had many other decisions to make in erecting a log house or outbuilding. Floorplans, roof styles, provisions for heating and ventilating, and various other features were necessary considerations for the prospective owner. In the following chapters, we will look at the more important of these features. We will find that, while the log wall may be attributed to the Pennsylvania Germans, other characteristics of the log folk architecture come from the English, Scotch-Irish, and other ethnic groups of the Middle Atlantic and Chesapeake Tidewater cultural hearths.

FIVE

Construction of Floors, Roofs, & Chimneys

Some quite striking regional and temporal differences can be observed in the flooring and roofing of log buildings and in the construction of fireplaces and chimneys. Different techniques, building materials, and levels of craftsmanship produced a considerable variety of floor, roof, and chimney types, some of which still abound in the landscape, others of which have vanished altogether.

The Floor

In the crudest log dwellings, dating from the earliest years of pioneering, "old mother earth served as floors."[1] Every few weeks the occupants wet down the dirt floor and tamped it to increase hardness and minimize the amount of loose soil particles.[2] A well-maintained dirt floor, regularly tamped and swept, is not as primitive as it might seem.

Even so, persons with wealth or status normally aspired to something better. "Dirt floors were common, but some of those who were considered wealthy made their floors of puncheons."[3] A puncheon is a short, thick board that reaches from the center of one sleeper to the next. For this reason, the exact length of the puncheon is determined by the spacing of the sleepers, usually about two feet apart. The carpenter makes puncheons by riving boards about two inches thick and six to ten inches wide from a log, using a froe

and a mallet. Smoothing is done with a foot adze, working cross-grain, after the floor is installed. A cruder type of puncheon is made by splitting sapling logs in half, leaving the bark intact.[4] In either case, whether boards or split logs, they are lap-jointed onto the sleepers by removing wood from the underside at both ends of the puncheon, done in such a way that they abut end-to-end at the center of each sleeper, leaving no gaps.

Most commonly, the puncheons are not fastened to the sleepers, remaining in place because of gravity and the lap-jointing. In finer houses, though, the puncheons are "pinned down to the sleepers with an auger and wooden pins."[5] The major problem with loose puncheons is warping, a problem solved by pinning. A well-made, pinned puncheon floor, polished and waxed, makes a fine appearance.

A cruder method of installing a floor, common in many poorer quality dwellings, is to rest the puncheons directly on beds of soft dirt or sand rather than on sleepers.[6] Such floors harbor insects and deteriorate quickly. None survive in Texas today, though numerous puncheon-sleeper floors can still be seen.

A step above pinned puncheon floors in quality are those made of sawn boards. Many of the finer log houses, even in the early decades of settlement, had board floors. George Erath, recalling the log folk architecture he had seen in the Austin Colony, mentioned "plank floors," adding that "the planks were sawn by hand."[7]

Still another method of constructing floors is to use stone. One log house in Cooke County is equipped with a splendid flagstone floor, far grander than the dwelling itself, and similar floors are occasionally seen in other parts of the state.[8]

Roof Structure

The roof of the eastern American log house normally has two side-facing gables joined by an uninterrupted sweep of roofing. Dormer windows, hipping, gambrel roofs, and similar departures from the unbroken two-slope roof are rarely encountered. Apparently the American pioneer derived the basic side-gable roof from the British Isles, especially northern Ireland and certain parts of England.[9] Gables occur widely in continental Europe, but are less frequently positioned on the sides of the structure. Front and rear gables are found on some types of American log buildings, particularly barns, but most have side-facing gables.

Gabled roofs on Texas log structures differ fundamentally in construction. The older and less common of these is the "ridgepole-and-purlin" type.[10] The ridgepole runs the length of the roof, reaching from one gable peak to the other, and the purlins, also called "rib poles," are paralleled to the ridgepole and spaced at regular intervals (Fig. 5-1). The log walls of the structure extend up into the gable, and the ridgepole and purlins are notched into the gable logs. W. R. Strong recalled that his Cooke County log dwelling "had gables also built of logs, each log being from one to three feet shorter than the one beneath it," and "rib-poles were laid across from one end to the other" to support the roof.[11] The pitch of these roofs ranged from about 25° to 35°.

Few ridgepole-and-purlin roofs survive in Texas, and they seem to have been common only in the early pioneer period of log construction. The origin of the ridgepole-and-purlin type was seemingly Scandinavia, and the introduction to America perhaps should be credited to the early Swedes and Finns on the Delaware.[12] This style is extremely rare or altogether absent in the Sudeten German source regions of American settlers, though it is seen in the Alpine lands.

Also uncommon in Texas is the "ridgepole-and-rafter" roof type. Here the ridgepole is tied to rafters which reach from the ridgepole at an angle of about 45° to the plates. The rafter is either lap-jointed onto the plate or mortised into it, depending upon whether or not a chisel is available to the builders. The ridgepole is hewn and, if necessary, spliced to attain the desired length. Rafters are more commonly left round, in which case the term "pole rafter" is used. Cedar seems to have been a preferred material for pole rafters in Texas.[13] The ridgepole-and-rafter roof is British in origin, probably derived from northern Ireland, or possibly from England.[14]

A third type of ridgepole roof is sometimes called the "Anglo western."[15] Very gently pitched, the Anglo western roof lacks a true gable structure (Fig. 5-1). The unhewn ridgepole rests directly on the top logs of the pen, and rafters extend from it to the plates. The pitch of the roof, sometimes as little as 5°, depends entirely on the thickness of the ridgepole, since no other elevation is provided. The Anglo western roof, the most primitive of all types in America, is found mainly in the Rocky Mountains. In Texas it is a common type only in the west, particularly the Panhandle, where a scattering of log buildings occurs. Elsewhere in Texas it is rare and can be found only on some smaller log outbuildings.

The dominant type of roof construction on log buildings in Texas is character-

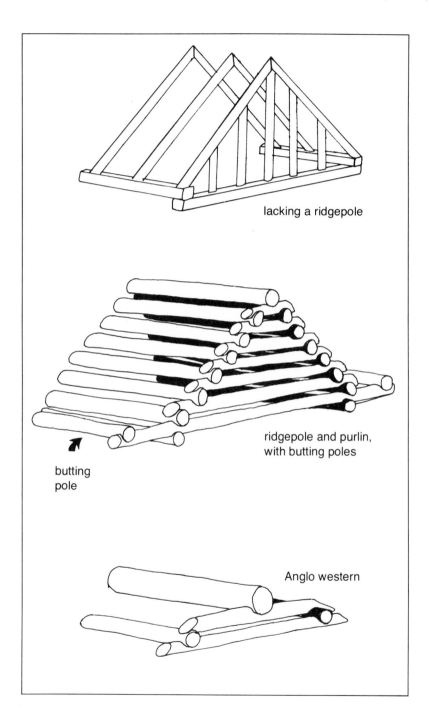

lacking a ridgepole

ridgepole and purlin,
with butting poles

butting
pole

Anglo western

5-1. Roof structure types.

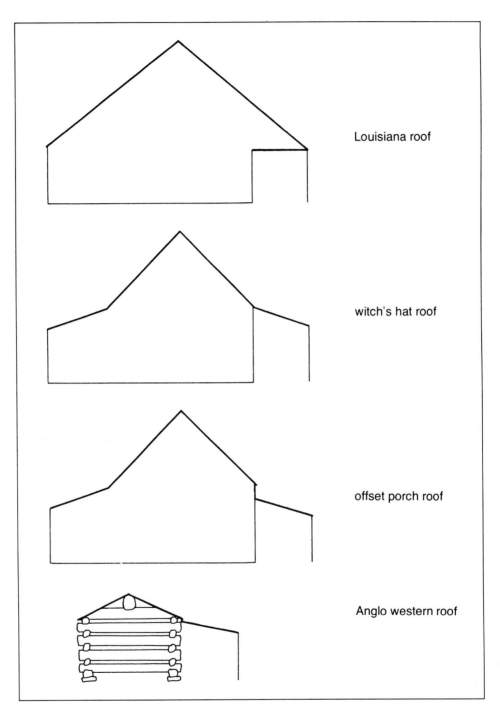

Louisiana roof

witch's hat roof

offset porch roof

Anglo western roof

5-2. Roof profile types.

5-3. Louisiana style roof on a Central Texas log house, the Brock place built in 1850 near Lockhart. (TLCR, Caldwell Co. No. 2; courtesy Texas Historical Commission)

ized by the absence of a ridgepole (Fig. 5-1).[16] Adjacent rafters on opposite slopes of the roof are lap-jointed or mortised together at the roof ridge and secured with a wooden pin. Normally the rafters, either hewn or pole, are spaced at two-foot intervals. Additional stability is provided by lathing, long slats affixed to the rafters, at right angles to them, reaching from gable to gable. Most such roofs have a pitch of about 45°, in common with the ridgepole-and-rafter type. Vertical studs provide additional support for the gable-end rafters, and the gables are enclosed with clapboards, either horizontal or vertical. Logs do not extend into the gable in this roof or in the ridgepole-and-rafter type.

The nonridgepole roof is the dominant type not only in Texas but also in most areas of the eastern United States. It has ample European antecedents, perhaps most notably in Germany. Some roofs of this type are also found in parts of England.

Two principal roof profiles occur in the nonridgepole type. The first, and much more common, is characterized by a break in the pitch at the points where shed rooms and porches begin (Fig. 5-2). The portion of the roof covering the log pen slopes at about 45°, considerably steeper than the roof projections extending over the shed room and porch (Figs. 6-2 and 6-29). Often the porch roof is offset several feet below the main roof. The second type, sometimes called the "Louisiana style" roof, is much rarer and occurs mainly in East Texas.[17] It consists of two unbroken slopes of about 40° extending over the entire structure, with no break for the porch and shed room (Figs.

5-4. Distribution of cantilevered log supports for roof of porch and/or shed room in Texas. (TLCR)

5-5. Hipped roof on a pine log house of twentieth-century construction, East Texas. Ungabled roofs such as this are fairly common on dwellings built after about 1900. (TLCR, San Jacinto Co. No. 5; courtesy G. J. Jordan)

5-2, 6-20, and 6-26). The attic often extends out above the porch in Louisiana style roofs (Fig. 5-3). Occasionally dormer windows are present. Only the finest of East Texas log houses have Louisiana roofs.

Also typically East Texan are cantilevered log supports for the shed room and porch. A log high in each gable-end wall projects six to ten feet to the front and rear, providing most of the support for the roof structure covering the shed room and porch (Figs. 5-4 and 5-7).

In the latter phase of log house construction in Texas, mainly in the pine forests of the east, a new and quite different type of roof construction appeared. This twentieth-century type lacks gables altogether. It results in a four-sided pyramid roof on single-pen structures and a hipped roof if the building is two or more pens

wide (Fig. 5-5).[18] Such roofs are closely identified with log dwellings built and occupied by East Texas blacks, and most date from the 1900 to 1940 period. Structurally they are of greater strength than most of the gabled types. The gableless roof seems to have accompanied a replacement of fireplaces by stoves, a transition which made chimneys unnecessary. A principal function of the gable had been to provide a wind shield for the chimney.

The roof structure usually extends to overhang the log wall on all four sides of the house. On the gable ends, this is accomplished by making the plate two to ten feet longer than the logs below it, so that a cantilevered projection of one to five feet occurs at each gable. In East Texas, this cantilevering is sufficiently long to permit the roof structure to extend flush with or, more typically, *beyond* the outer side of the chimney (Fig. 5-6). If the cantilevered roof surrounds the smoke outlet, the chimney is said to be "hooded" (Figs. 5-7 and 5-8). These overhanging gable roofs are a lower southern type, particularly common in Louisiana, and their presence in East Texas is yet another architectural link between that region and the Deep South.[19] An overhang at the front and back of the structure is accomplished by allowing the rafters to project a foot or so beyond the plate at the eaves.

Roofing Material

The roof structures just described can be covered in various ways. Most primitive is the board or clapboard roof, typical of the early pioneer period and normally applied over the ridgepole-and-purlin structure.[20] As W. R. Strong of Cooke County recalled, "These boards were from three to four feet long and were rove with a froe from oak logs."[21] Oak and pine seem to have been the preferred woods for roofing boards, and specific mention of post oak, white oak, and burr oak was made by early settlers.[22] A Wise County pioneer described roof boards "made out of white oak trees . . . sawed into three-foot lengths . . . ; with a riving tool, the boards were split six to eight inches wide."[23] A house with board roof is said to be "covered," and the boards sometimes reach the entire distance from eaves to ridgepole (Fig. 5-9).

The roofing boards can be affixed to the structure in one of several ways. The simplest method mentioned by pioneer builders is to hold them in place with weight poles. Roofs of this type are equipped with a "butting pole" or "butt log" at each of the eaves. Resting atop cantilevered logs and notched into them, the butting poles lie parallel to and out beyond the plates.[24] Butting by gravity against these poles are

the roof boards and short slats of wood called "knees," which have the double purpose to cover the cracks between the boards and to serve as spacers keeping the weight poles in place. Higher on the roof are additional alternated tiers of knees and weight poles, all supported ultimately by the butting pole (Fig. 6-1). W. R. Strong of Cooke County described such a roof when he wrote of cantilevered logs "a foot or two longer than the others," upon which rested "what was called a butt log."[25] William Banta of northeastern Texas wrote of three-foot boards "split out and placed on the rib poles, and then weighted down with what were called weight poles."[26] Typically, the boards on the prevailing windward slope of the roof project a foot or so beyond the ridge, showing "one foot to the weather," in the nineteenth-century vernacular.[27] Somewhat finer are board roofs fastened by pins or nails to the purlins, in which case the butting pole, knees, and weight poles are unnecessary (Fig. 5-9). I know of no surviving board roofs in Texas, nor am I aware of any obvious European antecedent for this method. The board roof seems to have been an expedient frontier type that developed from the shingle in America.

As soon as the pioneer period had passed, most log structures were "roofed," implying the use of shakes or shingles. This manner of roofing was brought to Pennsylvania by Germans from the hilly areas of central Europe and has little British or Scandinavian precedent. Most British roofs are thatched, and those on log structures in Sweden and Norway are usually of birch bark covered with sod. Some Scandinavian roofs are shingled, but even these differ from American types by virtue of their narrow, three-inch-wide shape.[28]

A "shake," in nineteenth-century usage, is an untapered board split from a log and measuring about 12"–15" wide, 2'–3' long, and 1/2"–1 1/2" thick.[29] Shakes,

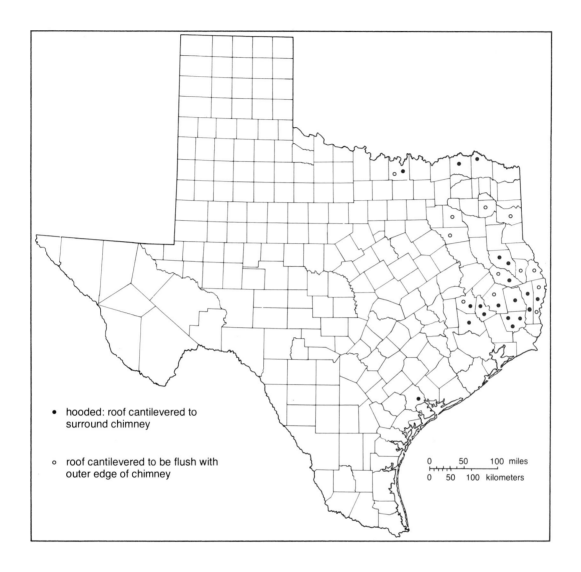

5-6. Distribution of cantilevered roof overhang on chimney gable of log house in Texas. (TLCR)

5-7. Hooded cat chimney, East Texas. The roof was cantilevered to surround the chimney in order to protect the stick-and-mud chimney from the weather. Note also the cantilevered log porch-roof supports. This single-pen pine log house was built about 1844 and has recently been restored and moved to Montgomery County. (TLCR, Walker Co. No. 2; courtesy B. C. Tharp)

5-8. Roof built flush with the outer side of the chimney, Deep East Texas. Note the cantilevered plates and the change from stone to brick construction on the chimney. (TLCR, Sabine Co. No. 1; courtesy Texas Historical Commission)

5-9. Low-pitched board roof on the Woody log cabin, the first white dwelling built in Wise County, in the West Cross Timbers. A "turkey feather" shake roof covers the porch. The Tennessean builder of this single-pen cabin stands on the front porch. (TLCR, Wise Co. No. 1; from B. B. Paddock, ed., *A Twentieth Century History and Biographical Record of North and West Texas*, 1:310–311)

like roofing boards, are manufactured by craftsmen using a froe and the preferred material is oak. Shakes cut in the dark of the moon supposedly do not curl or warp.[30] Unlike boards, they are fastened to the roof in overlapping tiers, like shingles, and they are more common on rafter-and-lathing roofs. Because shakes are untapered, they often stick out at odd angles, particularly after a few years of warping and weathering, producing what is called a "turkey feather" roof.[31]

Shingles, shorter and thinner than shakes, also differ in their tapered thickness. Handmade shingles are tapered with a drawknife.[32] They were manufactured from cedar and cypress at various places

in nineteenth-century Texas, and in time the shingled roof became dominant on log structures throughout the state. Not infrequently, shingles were a third-generation roof, succeeding board and shake predecessors. In shingle and shake roofs, as in the earlier board type, the problem of joining at the ridge is solved by letting the top row on the side facing the prevailing wind project a foot or so beyond the top. Such roofs are said to be "capped" (Fig. 6-4).[33]

Thatched roofs were reported on a few log structures in Texas. These were confined to the settlements of German-speaking people in the Hill Country and in Medina County.[34] Thatching is obviously a technique imported from Europe by the Germans, since the practice was unknown among the Texas Anglos. The low-profile "western" style roof of the Rocky Mountains is often covered with a layer of sod or dirt, a type occurring occasionally on the log semidugouts of West Texas.[35]

Placement of the Chimney and Fireplace

The chimney and fireplace of the Anglo-built log dwelling in Texas are nearly always situated at the center on one of the gable walls, with the chimney extending up to and above the peak of the gable. The chimney structure is exterior to the log wall, necessitating the previously mentioned fireplace gap. Double- and triple-pen houses usually have multiple chimneys, one at each gable.

The exterior chimney centered in a gable wall is of British origin and reached Texas by way of the Chesapeake Bay colonies and the South.[36] Gable-end hearths are confined to western Europe, and the exterior chimney structure is almost exclusively English.[37] By way of contrast, the Swedes and other Scandinavians typically built chimneys interior to the log wall and situated in a corner of the pen, practices duplicated in Swedish log houses of the Delaware Valley.[38] The Pennsylvania Germans, following the tradition of their European homeland, placed the hearth and chimney in the center of the pen, and they relied more on the wood-burning stove than the fireplace as a heating device.[39] The so-called Franklin stove is in fact the typical Pennsylvania German stove, introduced from central Europe. In Texas, one of the hallmarks of the German log house in the Hill Country and Medina County is the absence of exterior, gable-end chimneys. As in Penn-

sylvania, these divergences from the typical Anglo practice are a reflection of the continental European origin of the builders.

British, too, is the relatively shallow firebox of the Anglo-Texan fireplace, designed to maximize heat reflection into the room (Fig. 5-10).[40] Describing the log homes of early northeastern Texas, Andrew Davis recalled that "the fireplace was from 3 to 6 feet wide, and deep enough that large logs could be piled in . . . The hearth was broad, made of well-prepared mortar that would stand fire, or of stone, when it could be obtained. The back and jams were made of the same kind of material."[41] Often a large stone served as the hearth, though many early houses had earthen hearths.[42]

Stick-and-Dirt Chimneys

Construction of the chimney and firebox can be accomplished with various building materials. Most pioneer cabins, as well as many dwellings in flat alluvial plains, where stone and firing clay are not found, were provided with "stick-and-mud," "stick-and-dirt," or "stick-and-daub" chimneys (Fig. 5-11).[43] Early observers in Texas wrote of "wooden" chimneys, made of "sticks laid in mud."[44]

Two rather different methods are used to build stick-and-dirt chimneys in Texas. The more primitive of these, now vanished completely from the state, is the *pen chimney*, built of notched, horizontally laid poles or logs, referred to by one pioneer as "heavy timber."[45] W. R. Strong of Cooke County erected such a chimney for his log cabin in the 1840's, recalling that

we sawed out a place for the fire-place, maybe six feet across, then took short

5-10. A typical fireplace in an East Texas log house. The combination of stone and brick in fireplace construction is typical, as is the curved steel arch support (often a discarded saw blade). (TLCR, Jasper Co. No. 4, photo 1977 by Mike Yancey; courtesy Texas Historical Commission and Mrs. Frank Lindsey)

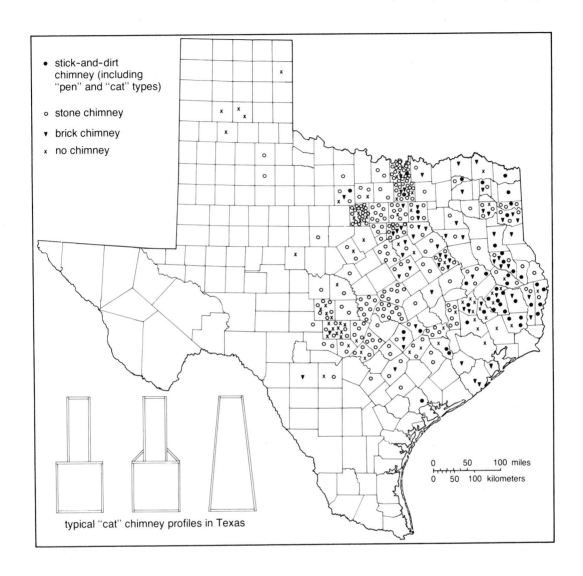

- stick-and-dirt
  chimney (including
  "pen" and "cat" types)
- stone chimney
- brick chimney
- no chimney

typical "cat" chimney profiles in Texas

0   50   100 miles
0   50   100 kilometers

5-11. Chimney types on log dwellings in Texas. (TLCR and early accounts)

logs, notched them down good, and built a [fireplace] pen with three sides around that hole, notching the logs into the house logs like you build a rail pen; this went up about four feet and then narrowed down gradually to the top, using smaller sticks as you went up. Inside this we made a hearth and fire-back of rocks and plastered it inside and out with mud. . . . The eves of the roof were generally extended about six feet on the ends to protect the stick and dirt chimney from the weather, as the rain would melt the mud and cause it to crumble.[46]

This type seems to have been more common in the Upper South and interior Texas. Pen chimneys are seen in the mountains of Kentucky and were still being built there in the early twentieth century.[47]

A more sophisticated type is the *cat chimney* (Fig. 5-7).[48] Four long, peeled poles are erected vertically to serve as the chimney corner posts, reaching two feet or so above the roof ridge. These posts are framed together with short horizontal poles, either attached by nails or inserted into holes bored in the corner posts. Additional stability can be attained by nailing two of the corner posts to the log wall of the house, but normally this is not done. Small slats or sticks, about one inch thick and two inches wide, are laid as cross pieces, stacked over one another and supported by the corner posts. These cross pieces can be nailed or pinned to the posts. Several chimney profiles are possible in pole construction (Fig. 5-11).

Then the pole-and-slat framework is covered with "cats," matlike rolls consisting of clay worked with water and mixed with a binder of moss, grass, hay, straw, or horsehair. The best clays to use are those with some sand content. Mixing is accomplished in a clay pit by barefoot workers who trample the binder into the wet loose earth. The resultant cats are pliable and cohesive, about four inches thick and a foot long. Working from the bottom of the chimney, the builders wrap a cat around each slat, completely covering the wooden framework. A fire is lit to bake and harden the chimney. The well-made cat chimney can last for years, though frequent maintenance work is necessary.

Cat chimneys perpetuate the ancient European construction technique called "wattle and daub," known widely in England, Ireland, Germany, and northern France. Wattle-and-daub chimneys were once common in Northern Ireland, and the American cat chimney was probably introduced by the Scotch-Irish.[49] Stick-and-dirt chimneys were also built by the Swedes, raising the possibility of Scandinavian origin.[50] Very similar chimneys were also built by the French settlers of Natchitoches, Louisiana, employing a construction called *bousillage*.[51] The major zone of occurrence of cat chimneys is the coastal plain of the Lower South and the adjacent Ouachita Mountains of Arkansas.[52] In Texas, cat chimneys were most common in the Big Thicket and in the "Between the Creeks" area of northern Titus County.[53] Few survive today, even in the Thicket, though some accurate reproductions have been built in several restoration projects.[54]

Stick-and-dirt chimneys are dangerous. More than one log house burned down because the chimney caught afire. George B. Erath, recalling life in south-central Texas in the 1830's, told how "the Texas wind found the cracks between the logs and sometimes helped the fire to set the log chimney ablaze. When the log chimney conspired with the fire to roast the occupants on a cold day, nothing remained to do but to climb up on the roof and throw down the chimney, thus placing the small room still more at the mercy of the icy norther."[55] Some log house dwellers, cognizant of the danger, kept a pole beside the house to pry the chimney away if it caught fire.[56] For this reason, most stick-and-dirt chimneys are normally built standing four to eight inches free of the wall above the firebox.[57]

The pole is inserted in this gap, providing leverage for quick dismantling of the blazing chimney.

Stone and Brick Chimneys

In some instances, masonry chimneys replaced earlier stick-and-dirt types after the pioneer years had passed. Most often, however, stone or brick chimneys were built when the houses were constructed. Itinerant masons followed log carpenters from job to job, filling the fireplace gaps with stately, durable chimneys. Sometimes the masons were delayed, and the new homeowner had to improvise a temporary covering for the fireplace gap. George Elam of Bandera County "erected a log house and left the opening for the fireplace, . . . waiting for a chimney builder to come and put up my chimney." He covered the gap with a wagon sheet.[58]

Stone chimneys, usually referred to in the Texas vernacular as "rock" chimneys, were present from the early years of settlement in many areas, particularly the interior, upper southern counties (Fig. 5-11).[59] One observer, writing in 1852, went so far as to say that stone chimneys were built whenever stone was available (Fig. 5-12).[60] The more primitive are built of "rough stone," or fieldstone, but the better ones, the majority, are made of quarried, hewn stone (Fig. 5-13).[61] Early rough stone chimneys are mortared with mud, but often they are so well designed that they remain standing and functional even after the mud weathers away. Hewn stone chimneys are lime mortared and extremely durable. Some truly fine, graceful hewn limestone and sandstone examples can be seen in central and northern Texas. Stone chimneys have ample European precedence, particularly in Britain. They are numerous in Pennsylvania, the Appalachians, the Ozarks, and most other Middle Atlantic–upper southern regions.[62]

Chimneys built of fired brick are more common in the Lower South and were introduced mainly through the Chesapeake Tidewater colonies by English immigrants. In Texas, the greatest numbers are in the eastern portion of the state, the settlement domain of lower southerners (Fig. 5-11). A certain amount of prestige is attached to brick chimneys, and few of the finer log houses lack them.[63] In East Texas, cat chimneys are associated with the lower socioeconomic groups, brick chimneys with the better-to-do people.

Many chimneys in Texas include both stone and brick, with the rock portion forming the lower two-thirds or three-quarters and brick the upper part (Figs. 5-8 and 5-14). Similar chimneys occur throughout much of the South, and the prototype is found in England.[64]

Whether stone or brick, the masonry chimney on Texas log houses is normally built freestanding by six inches or so from the gable wall above the firebox, in the manner of most stick-and-dirt chimneys.[65] One is tempted to label this feature a cultural anachronism, a trait surviving the shift from wooden to masonry chimneys, but closer investigation reveals that such chimneys occur in England. The English freestanding masonry chimney can be seen all across the eastern United States. To construct chimneys in this manner allows for uneven settling of the masonry, reduces the problem of roof seal, keeps unwanted heat out of the house, and lessens the fire danger should pieces of mortar loosen and fall out.[66]

Chimneyless Log Dwellings

By no means do all log houses in Texas have chimneys (Fig. 5-11). Some very early structures had only hooded smokeholes, as at Brazoria, where a traveler in 1831 saw a log house "with a place for a fire in the northern [room] and a hole through the roof for the smoke."[67] As late

5-12. A single-pen, pine log house in Deep East Texas. Note the fine stone chimney, the saddle notching, the hewn cantilevered log supporting the roofs of the porch and

shed room, and the massive sill log. (TLCR, Jasper Co. No. 4, photo 1977 by Mike Yancey; courtesy Texas Historical Commission and Mrs. Frank Lindsey)

5-13. Hewn stone chimney on a log house in the East Cross Timbers. Locally referred to as "ironstone," this ferrous sandstone is easily shaped into blocks for chimney building. (TLCR, Cooke Co. No. 3)

5-14. Brick-topped sandstone chimney, North Texas. Chimneys containing both stone and brick portions are common in Texas and derived from England. (TLCR, Cooke Co. No. 2)

as 1853, a resident of Greenville complained that "there is not a house that can boast a chimney. If a fire is made at all it is in the yard on the south side of the house."[68]

After the Civil War, and particularly after about 1875, most log houses were built without chimneys. Kitchen ranges and wood-burning cast-iron stoves replaced the hearth and fireplace for cooking and heating purposes, and the stovepipe replaced the chimney. In fact, quite a number of existing chimneys were pulled down and the fireplace gaps boarded over in that era. The art and craft of chimney building was in severe decline by 1900 and, if we may judge by the quality of the luxury fireplaces in our modern suburban Texas homes, never revived.

The German log house builders of the Texas Hill Country normally did not build fireplaces. Flues for stovepipe outlets are more typical of the German houses, in keeping with central European tradition.

The chimneys that survive on Texas log houses, and a great many do, are pleasant reminders that craftsmen once passed this way. But in common with all aspects of log folk architecture, these fine chimneys are endangered and inadequately protected for the future.

In the following chapter, we will turn our attention away from the details of construction techniques to consider log dwelling *types*. We will discover, as before, that these types reflect the diverse architectural heritage of the Middle Atlantic and Chesapeake Bay colonists.

SIX

Log Dwelling Types & Floorplans

Log dwellings come in various shapes and sizes. They differ greatly in floorplan, quality of craftsmanship, and the number of "creature comforts" contained. Each region or district displays its own distinctive types of log dwelling, as does each time period during the era of the log culture complex. Even in so restricted an area as Texas, log dwellings are diverse, both from place to place and from decade to decade. In this chapter and several to follow, we will look at some of these spatial and temporal contrasts, both in dwellings and in other types of log structures.

Cabins and Houses

Perhaps the most basic contrast is that between the *cabin* and the *house*. The log cabin, sometimes called a "pole shack," belongs to an early, primitive generation of log dwellings built for temporary occupance in the first, difficult years of pioneering (Fig. 6-1). "With the early settler a cabin comes first," wrote an observer in 1837, "then the hewed log [house], well chinked and daubed . . ."[1] Cabins are small and windowless, built of logs crudely notched and projecting beyond the corners, with the bark remaining intact. The cabin is equipped only with bare-earth floors and stick-and-dirt chimneys. A visitor to the infant town of Dallas in 1844, John B. Billingsley, described such dwellings when he wrote of "two log cabins, the logs just as nature formed them, the walls just high enough for the door heads; the [roof] covering was clapboard held in place by weight poles, chimneys made of sticks and mud, and old mother earth served as floors."[2]

Another observer, commenting on the crude dwellings of Anglo pioneers in the nearby upper Sabine River valley, spoke contemptuously of "miserable twelve-feet-square mud-and-log cabins."[3] The Morris County town of Daingerfield in 1846 could boast only "three or four cabins scarce fit for pigsties," while colonists on the Lavaca River in 1827 lived in "rude log cabins, windowless and floorless . . . absolutely devoid of comfort."[4] Mary Nunley, a pioneer girl of Palo Pinto County, recalled that, upon the arrival of her family, "my father and a hired man made two small cabins in which we lived through the winter . . . on dirt floors" where they "cooked, ate and slept all in the same room." After one year's residence in the cabin, the family moved into a roomy hewn log house.[5]

Log cabins were typically built by communal amateur labor at festive "house raisings." An axe was the only tool needed. W. R. Strong, who came to the East Cross Timbers of Cooke County in 1846, left a fine written account of a log cabin raising:

People were mighty good to help each other in those days . . . If you built a

6-1. A typical log *cabin*, built of round logs and equipped with a board roof and pen chimney. This structure, sketched by a Mr. Tidball in 1791 in a Creek Indian community in the southeastern United States, is typical of the pioneer cabins built later in Texas. It also reflects the extent to which the "Five Civilized Tribes" had adopted Anglo log construction. Note the butting pole, knees, and weight poles on the roof. (From John R. Swanton, *The Indians of the Southeastern United States*, plate 58)

house, everybody for ten miles would come and help you raise it. When I built my first house, the Chadwell's, Dickson's, Eubanks' and old man Billy Brown helped me raise it. My house was a log cabin fourteen feet square with a stick and dirt chimney and covered with boards. . . . I put the logs up round when I built my house in the spring, then in the fall I took a chopping ax and hewed the logs down smooth, then I cut chinkin, out of little poles mostly and chinked the

cracks and plastered them over with mud. I hewed out puncheons for the floor and made a stick and dirt chimney. . . . To make a bed, you took a forked stick and drove it in the dirt floor of the cabin where the outside corner of the bed was to be; a rail laid from a crack in the log house to the fork on the stick, both ways, made the foot and side board; poles were laid across the slats and generally a beef hide laid over that. If you had a one-half inch auger and wanted to be real stylish,

*you bored two holes through four round
poles after scalping the bark off with an
ax, and put poles through both ways for
head and foot board.*[6]

Few log cabins survive in Texas. Most
were occupied only for several years before being replaced by more substantial
dwellings, at which time the cabin was
demoted to the status of barn, chicken
coop, or smokehouse.

The majority of slave quarters in Texas
were log cabins. Indeed, the United States
census in the antebellum period enu-
merated "slave cabins." The typical slave
dwelling consisted of one room, though
some larger ones could be found.[7]

A log *house*, by contrast, is a second-
generation dwelling, built of carefully
hewn timbers, neatly notched at the corners and sawn off flush, tightly chinked,
equipped with a wooden floor and a window or two, and provided with graceful
chimneys of stone or brick. Construction
of a log house "is what might be called
the second step of the pioneer toward a
comfortable habitation," wrote an anonymous Texas traveler in 1837. Commenting on the difference between houses and
cabins in early south-central Texas,
George B. Erath contrasted "double log
houses, with rock chimneys and plank
floors" and "log cabins with the bark on
the logs."[8] The house is larger than the
cabin, in both height and square footage
of living space. Contrary to the popular
image, log houses were not normally
built at communal house raisings by amateurs. Rather, most were constructed by
professional or semiprofessional carpenters, itinerant craftsmen who went from
place to place building houses for hire.
Close on the heels of the carpenters came
masons, who erected the splendid stone
and brick chimneys seen on most second-
generation log dwellings.

Our primary concern in this chapter
will be houses rather than cabins. More

exactly, the focus will be on house floorplans, perhaps the most fundamental trait
of a dwelling. Log construction was applied to a variety of floorplans. The prospective inhabitant chose among many
possibilities, basing the choice on such
considerations as the local climate, family size, and economic status. In making
the choice, the settler was also guided by
cultural heritage, though innovations did
occur. Often, or even generally, the floorplan of log dwellings underwent changes
as the years passed and the family grew.
Simple one-room houses typically became more elaborate forms in this manner.

The Single-Pen House

The simplest and most basic floorplan in
American log houses is the "single-pen"
with side-facing gables. A "pen," in log
house terminology, refers to the unit of
four log walls fastened together with corner notching. All full-sized ground-floor
rooms subsequently added to the house,
whether of log construction or not, are
also called pens. Most commonly, in Texas at least, the log pen forms a single
room, but in some cases the pen is subdivided by light partitions into two or
more rooms.

Single-pen houses are very common in
Texas, the South, and the eastern United
States as a whole (Fig. 6-2).[9] They represent the oldest folk houses virtually
everywhere the log culture complex was
implanted in America. In Texas, single-
pen log houses are more common and
generally dominant in the interior portions, the sections colonized by upper
southerners (Fig. 6-3). They occur
throughout lower southern East Texas as
well but are less common there and nowhere dominant (Fig. 5-7). Single-pen
dwellings suggest a lower socioeconomic

6-2. A story-and-a-half single-pen log house of roughly square floorplan, with rear shed room, in North Texas. The pen measures 15 1/2' × 18'. The half-dovetailed structure was built about 1860 by a Missourian. Note the absence of windows in the log pen and the lack of a front porch. This house, considerably enlarged, is still inhabited. (TLCR, Cooke Co. No. 39, photo ca. 1898; courtesy Mr. and Mrs. Jim Steel, the present inhabitants)

class of people, and there is a correlation between these simple houses and poor agricultural districts. In East Texas, the single-pen dwelling was most commonly a slave quarters (Fig. 1-4).

Two basic types of single-pen log houses occur in the eastern United States, reflecting several different ethnic origins of the American colonists (Fig. 6-3). The older of these types has a *rectangular* shape, with the dimension of the front and rear walls exceeding that of the side gable walls by five feet or more. Typical measurements of these pens are 22' × 16', 24' × 16', 20' × 15', or 30' × 18'. The European groups responsible for introducing this rectangular floorplan were the Scotch-Irish and Germans of the Middle Atlantic colonies. The basic Pennsylva-

nia German log dwelling, also called the "continental" house, consists of a rectangular pen subdivided by partitions into three rooms, one of which serves as a kitchen-parlor and occupies one end.[10] The front door is off-center. A central chimney is located on one of the partition walls. The continental German log house rarely occurs outside Pennsylvania, and none was built in Texas.

Rectangular log houses among Scotch-Irish settlers differ from those of the Germans by having a gable-end chimney and a centered front door directly opposite a rear door.[11] Such floorplans occur widely in Northern Ireland. The Scotch-Irish rectangular pen is often partitioned into two rooms, the larger of which contains the fireplace, but many of these Irish houses

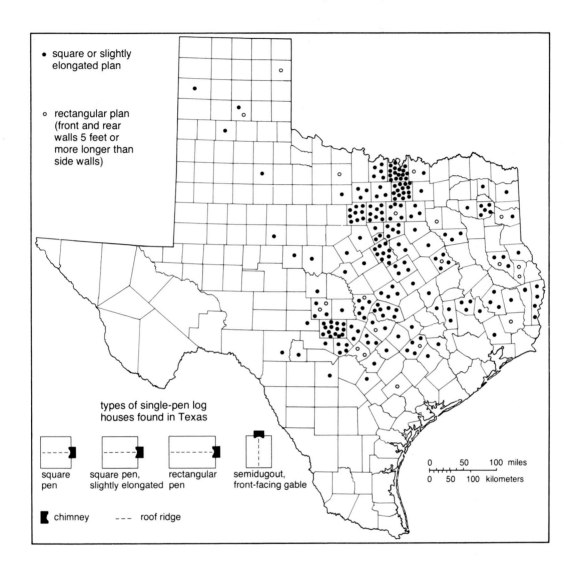

types of single-pen log
houses found in Texas

square
pen

square pen,
slightly elongated

rectangular
pen

semidugout,
front-facing gable

chimney   - - - roof ridge

• square or slightly
  elongated plan

o rectangular plan
  (front and rear
  walls 5 feet or
  more longer than
  side walls)

6-3. Distribution of single-pen log dwellings observed in Texas. (TLCR)

6-4. A Scotch-Irish rectangular single-pen log house, divided by a log partition wall into two rooms of unequal size. The larger room, in keeping with Scotch-Irish tradition, contains the fireplace. Note also the capped roof and the cat chimney. (TLCR, San Augustine Co. No. 1, photo 1936; courtesy Historic American Buildings Survey, Library of Congress)

are unpartitioned (Fig. 6-4). Unlike the German continental house, which is typically of story-and-a-half design, the Scotch-Irish version is single story, though usually equipped with a loft. Both German and Scotch-Irish single pens have side-facing gables. A survey of hundreds of Texas log floorplans revealed only nineteen scattered examples that could be described as Scotch-Irish rectangular single pens (Fig. 6-3). The Louisiana French built rectangular log houses in the Natchitoches area, but examples of their distinctive style are wholly lacking in Texas.[12] Clearly, we must look elsewhere for the antecedent of the typical Texas single-pen log house, for it cannot be attributed to the Germans, Scotch-Irish, or French.

The other basic type of single pen, the type dominant in Texas, has a *square* or roughly square floorplan (Figs. 6-3 and 6-5).[13] Normally, the dimensions of the four walls are equal or within two or three feet of being equal. If the plan is not precisely square, the longer dimensions are on the front and back walls. The majority of such pens measure about 16' × 16' to 18' × 18', though smaller and larger examples can be found. Rarely if ever are square pens subdivided by partitions. In common with the German and Scotch-Irish single pens, the square type has side-facing gables, and it shares the Scotch-Irish characteristic of a chimney centered in one gable end.

Square single-pen dwellings are an English type, descended from the one-bay house of Old England.[14] A *bay* is sixteen feet square in British terminology. The sixteen-foot unit, also called a *rod*, is supposedly wide enough to house four oxen side-by-side, a desirable characteristic in Medieval times in England, before the housing of people and domestic animals under one roof was made illegal.[15] This simple one-room house was introduced into America, as a frame structure, by the English colonists of the Virginia and

Maryland Tidewater.[16] It was copied in log construction in the back country of Virginia, where the Tidewater and Middle Atlantic architectural traditions met and mixed. Wherever square log pens outnumber rectangular ones, the Tidewater floorplan tradition can be said to prevail over the Middle Atlantic.[17] Texas fits this category, for the overwhelming majority of single-pen log dwellings in the state are square or roughly square, and the 16' × 16' pen is very common. So, while Texas is colonial to Pennsylvania in log construction, it is a child of the Virginia Tidewater in the single-pen floorplan. Folk architecture in America generally represents a blending of diverse traditions, and the basic single-pen log house of Texas is no exception.

Another type of single-pen log dwelling found in Texas is the *dugout* or *semidugout* of the western part of the state (Fig. 6-6). Without exception, these crude structures belong to the cabin phase of construction, but they differ in several important respects from cabins and houses in the eastern half of the state. First, the dugout is on a hillside and partially excavated into the slope. The log wall forms only a superstructure, accounting for about half of the total height of the dwelling, the remainder being formed by the excavation. Hillside sites and cellars are very common for German log houses in Pennsylvania, but it is questionable whether the West Texas log dugout perpetuates that tradition. A second difference can be detected in the placement of the door, for the dugout is entered through a gable end. Likely this is a survival of an ancient floorplan, one found in prehistoric Europe and usually present in the American cabin phase as a minority type. The West Texas log dugout, in a broader architectural context, belongs to the "Anglo western" type, found widely through the mountain areas of the western United States.[18] Texas is a meeting ground culturally of East and West, and

6-5. A typical story-and-a-half single-pen log house in the East Cross Timbers. The pen measures 17 1/2′ × 19 1/2′. Note the morticing for the upper-story joists and the half-dovetail notching. (TLCR, Denton Co. No. 11, photo 1973)

6-6. A log semidugout, West Texas. Log construction was applied to such structures in the 1870's and 1880's in areas where sizable trees were rare. (From the Erwin E. Smith Collection of Range-Life Photographs, Library of Congress)

the characteristics of log housing provide additional evidence of these contrasts. The log architecture of West Texas seems in many respects more akin to that of the Rocky Mountains than to that of East Texas and the South.

The Basic Double-Pen House

In many cases, single-pen houses were enlarged some time after their construction to become double-pen types (Fig. 6-7). Other dwellings were built initially with two full-sized rooms. The second room was added to a gable end of the first

pen, producing a house of much greater width than depth, with side-facing gables. Such enlargements are common in several parts of Europe. These houses appear in several distinct log floorplans, the simplest being the *basic double pen*.

The basic double-pen house is formed by placing an abutting second pen on the gable end opposite the chimney (Fig. 6-8). Both pens are square or nearly so, connected to one another by a door at the mid-point of the dividing wall. Each pen has a front door. If the two pens were built simultaneously, both are log, and the front and back walls normally consist of a single span of logs reaching the entire thirty-to-forty-foot width of the dwelling

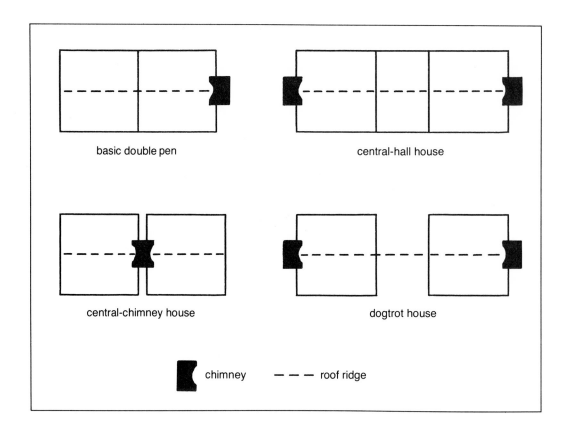

basic double pen

central-hall house

central-chimney house

dogtrot house

■ chimney   — — — roof ridge

6-7. Major types of double-pen log houses in Texas.

6-8. A basic double-pen house in the West Cross Timbers. Only one of the pens is log. (TLCR, Palo Pinto Co. No. 11, photo 1973; courtesy Palo Pinto County Historical Survey Committee)

(Fig. 6-9). A log partition wall, notched into the front and back spans, separates the two pens. Rarer are basic double pens consisting of two separate, abutting log pens, usually a reaction to the absence of timbers of sufficient length.

More commonly, the basic double pen was formed by adding a second pen to an original single-pen house. In these enlargement basic double pens, the second room is normally not of log construction, but of frame or stone (Figs. 6-8 and 6-10).

The basic double-pen house is apparently of English origin and can be traced to the Chesapeake Tidewater districts of Virginia and Maryland.[19] This house, in frame construction, is well represented in the Tidewater. Others suggest a possible

Irish origin and attribute introduction to the Scotch-Irish of Pennsylvania.[20] A multiple origin is certainly possible, for the basic double pen occurs very widely in the eastern United States. Log examples have been observed in Indiana, North Carolina, the southern Appalachians, Georgia, and elsewhere. In Middle Tennessee, a major source of Texas settlers, a basic double pen with two front doors is the prevalent type and has been labeled the "Cumberland House."[21] Nearly all basic double pens in Texas are of the Cumberland variety. In most log construction areas, however, the basic double pen is a minority type, nowhere dominant or absent.

In Texas, the same distributional pat-

6-9. Basic double-pen house in the piney woods of East Texas. A log partition wall creates two rooms of equal size in this single-story dwelling. (TLCR, Walker Co. No. 6, photo 1973)

tern can be observed. The basic double pen occurs in all areas, but not as a prevalent type (Fig. 6-11). The East Texas examples usually contain a single span of pine logs divided into two pens by a log partition wall (Fig. 6-9), while those in upper southern interior Texas almost always consist of a frame pen added to a single-pen log house (Fig. 6-8). This difference is seemingly attributable to the smaller size of timbers available in central Texas. In the Hill Country German counties, the second pen is typically of stone or half-timbered construction (Fig. 6-10.)[22]

The Central-Chimney Double-Pen House

Closely related to the basic double-pen house is the central-chimney type, also a double pen. A second pen is placed at the gable end containing the chimney, so that the fireplace becomes centrally situated between the two pens and the chimney is engulfed by a single span of roof (Fig. 6-7). The fireplace opens into both pens, or two fireplaces share the same chimney. The two pens are usually built three or four feet apart, with the intervening space occupied by the chimney, fireplace, stairs, and storage space. In the eastern American vernacular and in many folk architec-

6-10. A basic double-pen house built by Germans in Fredericksburg. One of the pens is log, the other stone. Note the absence of a chimney and fireplace, a typical feature of Hill Country German log dwellings. The "V" notching and wide, rock-filled chinks are also typically Texas German. (TLCR, Gillespie Co. No. 26, photo 1977)

ture publications, the central-chimney double pen is called a "saddlebag" house.[23] In Texas, however, the vernacular meaning of "saddlebag" house is quite different, so we would best avoid use of this term.[24]

The idea of a central fireplace is an ancient one, found in many parts of Europe, particularly in the British Isles. In the prototypical European example, there was no chimney involved. Instead, smoke rose from the hearth and escaped through a hole in the roof. While this ancient form rarely appeared in America, the idea of an interior fireplace was part of the cultural baggage of both British and German colonists. In the typical Pennsyl-

vania German rectangular single-pen house, as we have seen, the chimney is internal, on a partition wall. The transition from this to a chimney placed between two separate pens would not have been difficult. Other scholars attribute the central-chimney double-pen house to Tidewater Anglo-Virginians and claim a British antecedent.[25]

Central-chimney double-pen houses occur widely through the eastern United States but rarely as a dominant type. They appear most frequently in West Virginia, Indiana, Kentucky, and southern Illinois but are said to be extremely rare in Ohio.[26] Relatively few are seen in the coastal plain South. In climatic terms,

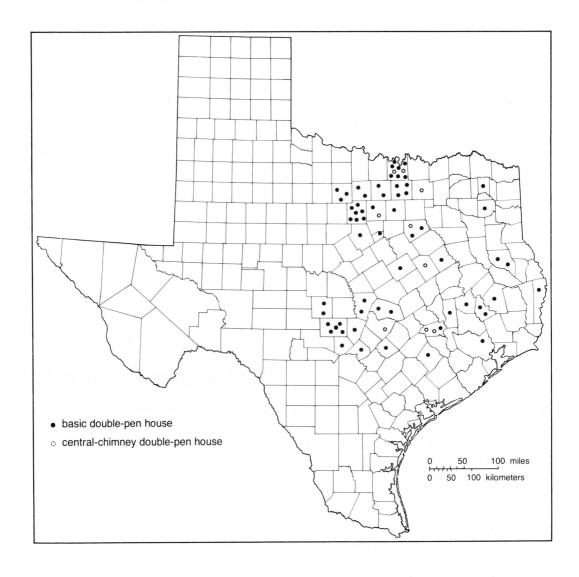

6-11. Distribution of basic double-pen and central-chimney double-pen dwellings observed in Texas. Includes some houses having only one log pen, the second pen being of frame or stone construction. (TLCR and early accounts)

the heat-retaining attribute of the central chimney makes good sense in colder areas, and perhaps for that reason this house is principally a northern type.[27]

Few central-chimney double pens were built in Texas.[28] None at all have been found in East Texas, and the majority of the eight examples recorded in the state is located in upper southern counties (Fig. 6-11). They may have been more common prior to about 1850, when Texas and much of North America remained in the grip of the "Little Ice Age" and winters were colder. Noah Smithwick, recalling life on the prairies near Austin in the 1830's and 1840's, declared that status-seeking men there often built large double-pen houses with "a big double chimney" between the pens.[29] One of the earliest log houses in the Austin Colony, that belonging to Judge John P. Coles at Independence in Washington County, was of the central-chimney type. Normally, both pens of the central-chimney type are log, but in Texas several were formed by adding a frame pen to an existing single-pen log house.

The Dogtrot and Central-Hall Houses

Another, much more common Texas double-pen house type is variously referred to in the vernacular as the "dogtrot," "dogrun," "two P," "two pens and a passage," "central passage," or "saddlebag."[30] Here the second pen is placed on the gable end opposite from the chimney and separated from the other pen by an open space of about seven to fifteen feet (Figs. 6-7 and 6-12). Describing such a house at the Texas river port of Brazoria in 1831, a visitor spoke of "two square houses, about fifteen feet apart, . . . constructed of logs, . . . and the space between them being covered over by a roof,

a broad passage is left, sheltered indeed above, but quite open at both ends."[31] The average width of the open passage or breezeway in Texas dogtrot houses is about 10 1/2 feet, with the narrowest example observed measuring 7 feet and the widest 14 (Fig. 6-13).[32]

The dogtrot house is splendidly suited to a warm climate zone and is particularly common across the inner coastal plain of the Deep South, from Georgia into East Texas.[33] It occurs as far north as Indiana, Illinois, and Iowa and is seen throughout most of the Upper South as a minor type.[34] In Texas, dogtrots are most common in the eastern sections settled from the Lower South (Fig. 6-14). So prevalent is this floorplan east of the Trinity River that one writer has called it the "East Texas House."[35] An early visitor to northeast Texas felt that dogtrots represented "the usual construction of cabins in this country," while another traveler in Brazoria County called it "the plan common to the country dwellings of farmers in Texas."[36] By no means was the log dogtrot exclusively a rural house type, for it could be seen in early towns, such as Austin and San Felipe, as the dominant type.[37] Westward through the upper southern domain in central and northern Texas, the dogtrot is less common, though nowhere absent. By way of comparison, only 16 percent of the thirty-one log houses observed in upper southern Cooke County in North Texas are dogtrots, while in the East Texas county of Polk, fully 50 percent of the twelve houses observed display the dogtrot plan.[38] For some reason, many Texans mistakenly believe that the dogtrot is the most typical traditional folk house throughout the state. Some misguided "restoration" projects have resulted from this misconception. Perhaps the most notorious is at Weatherford, where two excellent single-pen houses were moved in from different parts of Parker County and placed together under one roof as a counterfeit dogtrot.

6-12. Recently abandoned dogtrot log house near the Red River in northeast Texas. The "V"-notched structure has off-center front doors in each pen, a hooded brick chimney, and rear shed rooms. It belongs to the type I, first generation of dogtrots. (TLCR, Lamar Co. No. 1, photo 1966)

Some prestige was clearly attached to the open-passage floorplan. Noah Smithwick described them as the houses of "vain" men, while an English visitor placed dogtrots among "the better sort" of log dwellings.[39] Dogtrots were built throughout the 125-year duration of the log culture complex in Texas. The earliest date from 1815 to 1820, and the most recent one detected was constructed in 1937 (Fig. 1-5).[40]

The function of the open passageway was to funnel cooling breezes and relieve somewhat the discomfort of subtropical summers. John Barrow, in the 1840's, described the breezeway as the place "in which the occupants take their meals, and indulge in rest during the heat of the

day."[41] Farm animals and dogs occasionally disputed the human claim to this space, as did swarms of insects and birds in flight.

Two distinct types of log dogtrot houses can be detected in Texas and the South.[42] First-generation dogtrots evolved from original single-pen houses. They usually contain slightly oblong pens, often of slightly different size, and each pen has a front door and no original front windows (Fig. 6-12). Frequently the second pen is of frame rather than log construction. If both pens are log, the notch type often differs from one to the other. Second-generation dogtrots consist of two square pens of equal size built at the same time, with a uniform notch style, no front

6-13. Open dogtrot of the Tom Ireland log house, at Webbers Prairie in western Bastrop County. Note the square notching, the wood slat chinking, the sill log, and the sleepers. (TLCR, Bastrop Co. No. 1, photo 1937; courtesy Historic American Buildings Survey, Library of Congress)

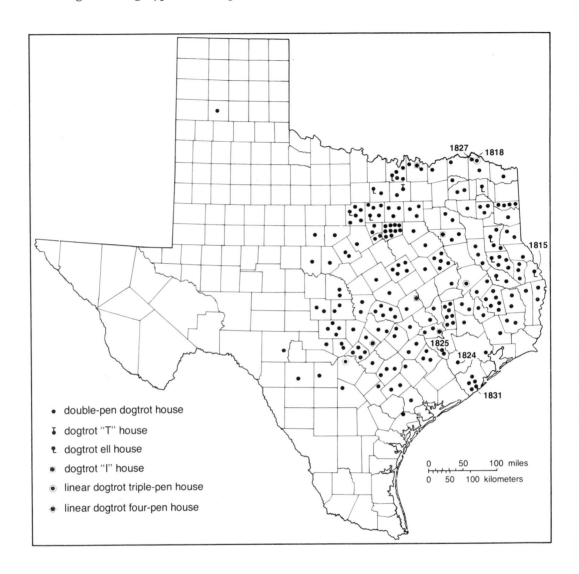

6-14. Distribution of dogtrot and central-hall log dwellings observed in Texas. Includes central-hall floorplans. No effort has been made to distinguish dogtrot houses from central-hall types. Dates are for earliest documented local examples with open breezeway. (TLCR and early accounts)

doors, and one or two front-facing windows in each pen (Fig. 1-10). Texas offers abundant examples of both types.[43]

Much controversy surrounds the origin of the dogtrot house. Some scholars have found similar structures, called "pair cottages," in Sweden, Finland, and the Swedish colonies on the Delaware, suggesting a Scandinavian origin.[44] One of the two pens of the European pair cottage serves as a kitchen, and several other floorplan features differ from those of the American dogtrot. Still, the possibility of Swedish-Finnish origin cannot be discounted. Further evidence for Swedish origin is suggested by the occurrence of the vernacular term *saddlebag* to describe dogtrots both in the old Swedish districts of New Jersey and in East Texas, an obvious linkage between the oldest, easternmost American log construction area with one of the more recent, southwesternmost districts.[45] The widespread distribution of the dogtrot also suggests an introduction from Europe. Some other scholars have called attention to the similarity between the dogtrot house and the *double-crib barn*, a log outbuilding with an identical basic floorplan, derived from the German Alpine lands and very common in the American zone of log construction.[46] The double-crib barn will be discussed in more detail in Chapter 8, but its candidacy as the prototype of the dogtrot house merits mention here. In the double-crib barn, the open passageway is used as a place to park the farm wagon and to hang tools and implements.

Still another possible prototype for the dogtrot is the central-hall house, identical to the dogtrot except that the open passage is walled in front and back to form a hall, with front and rear doors providing access.[47] Central-hall houses are very common in Europe, especially in England and Ireland.[48] They seem to have developed gradually from the ancient, previously described central-fireplace house.

Such structures began in antiquity as oblong single-pen dwellings, with the humans living in one end and the domestic animals in the other, separated only by the open hearth (Fig. 6-15). There were two entrances, centered in the front and rear walls to provide draft for the fire. In time, partitions were developed to separate the human and animal quarters. The fireplace was moved to a gable end and provided with a chimney, leaving the central portion of the house to be a hall. In more recent times, the animals were expelled from the house and it became exclusively a human abode.

This European central-hall house was introduced to the American colonies by various groups, particularly the Scotch-Irish and English. Its main implantment was in the Chesapeake Tidewater.[49] We can easily imagine how builders of the central-hall house, upon experiencing the subtropical discomfort of the American South, might have decided to eliminate the front and rear walls of the hallway in order to improve ventilation. A central-hall prototype of the dogtrot is further suggested by the transition to an enclosed central-hall arrangement that occurred in most dogtrot houses after about 1900. The majority of trots were enclosed to form halls or parlors, and few open passages remain today.

Whatever their origin, many early American dogtrot houses seem linked to eighteenth-century central and southwestern Virginia, as well as Tennessee.[50] Henry Glassie was clearly in error when he placed the origin of the dogtrot in eastern Tennessee as late as 1825.[51] By that date, the dogtrot was already common in Texas (Fig. 6-16). From Virginia and Tennessee, the dogtrot spread to the Gulf Central Plain, where it attained even greater acceptance. In its enclosed central-hall form, this double-pen house diffused over much of the eastern United States.

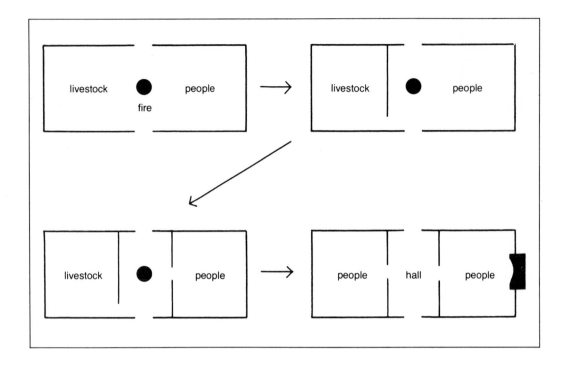

6-15. Evolution of the British central-hall house in Europe.

6-16. One of the earliest illustrations of a dogtrot log house in Texas. This drawing, dating from 1831, depicts a farmhouse on the McNeil Plantation in Brazoria County, near the Gulf of Mexico. It was engraved by J. T. Hammond. (From *A Visit to Texas*, following p. 38)

Triple-Pen Houses

The addition of a third full-sized room is possible in a variety of forms, producing triple-pen houses (Fig. 6-17). Perhaps most common are triple pens resulting from attachment of a third room on the rear, producing "ell" and "T" houses. This third room was often a kitchen.

In the *basic ell*, the third room is added directly behind one of the front rooms of a basic double-pen dwelling, so that the floorplan takes the shape of the letter *L*. Similarly, a *dogtrot ell* or *central-hall ell* occurs when a third pen is attached behind one of the original pens of those floorplan types (Figs. 6-14, 6-18, and 6-19). The third room has a roof ridge running perpendicular to that of the main part of the house. Ell additions are of British origin and occur frequently on Texas log houses.[52] The ell pen is usually of frame construction, though log examples do occur. The third pen is sometimes separated from the main part of the house by a rear dogtrot or passageway, particularly if the room is a kitchen, but most often it abuts one of the front pens.[53]

In "T" triple pens, the third pen is added to the rear center of the house, producing a T-shaped floorplan. Such additions are much rarer than ells and are seen most commonly as enlargements of basic double-pen and central-hall plans, forming *basic "T"* and *central-hall "T"* houses. A "T" addition on a dogtrot house has the disadvantage of blocking the flow of breeze, and perhaps for that reason the dogtrot "T" is rare.

Another type is the *linear basic triple pen*, formed by adding a third pen to the chimneyless gable of a basic double-pen house, producing an extremely wide dwelling. Closely related, and more common, is the *linear dogtrot triple pen*, which results when a third room is added to a gable end of a dogtrot house. Two famous examples of linear dogtrot triple

pens in Texas are the Rice family home at Crockett, long misleadingly called a "stagecoach inn," and the Wright plantation mansion in Red River County (Fig. 6-20).[54] The Rice home, recently relocated and restored at nearby Mission Tejas State Park, was constructed alongside the Old Spanish Road beginning in 1828 and had already attained its triple-pen width by 1834.[55] The Wright house, unlike the Rice place, has the dogtrot enclosed as a hall.

Four-Pen Houses

Rarely does the log folk house in Texas attain four-pen dimensions, and in fact houses of that size are unusual anywhere in the United States. The few Texan examples are truly impressive structures (Fig. 6-21). Regrettably, the finest four-pen log house in Texas was deliberately destroyed several years ago, and the only surviving specimen is endangered.

The Claiborne Kyle house in Hays County is a *linear dogtrot four pen*, possibly unique in Texas and the entire South (Fig. 6-22).[56] The four pens are lined up in a row, two on either side of a typical dogtrot, and all four were built at the same time, in the 1840's. Large double fireplaces are positioned centrally in both two-pen segments of the house. The imposing seventy-five–foot width of the Kyle dwelling is reminiscent of the English longhouse, and the practice of enlarging dwellings by increasing the width is unquestionably of British origin.[57]

The *foursquare*, or *block*, is another four-pen Texas log folk house. Focused on two intersecting, cross-shaped hallways, the foursquare owes an obvious debt to the symmetry of the Georgian style architecture (Fig. 6-21). Perhaps the earliest such house was built in antebellum times near Madisonville in East Texas, "a big log house, four rooms in it, and the great

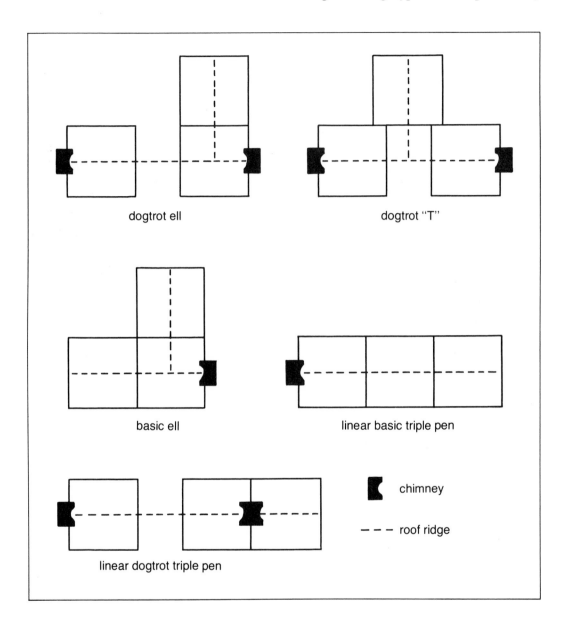

dogtrot ell

dogtrot "T"

basic ell

linear basic triple pen

linear dogtrot triple pen

chimney

– – – roof ridge

6-17. Some triple-pen floorplans.

6-18. Dogtrot ell house in East Texas. The square-notched pine logs were whipsawn or milled, rather than being hewn with axe and adze, permitting almost chinkless construction. Note also the wooden foundation piers. (TLCR, Angelina Co. No. 1, photo 1936; courtesy Historic American Buildings Survey, Library of Congress)

6-19. Sided story-and-a-half dogtrot ell house, Deep East Texas. the rear portion of the ell serves as a kitchen, the front portion probably as a dining room. (TLCR, Sabine Co. No. 1; courtesy Texas Historical Commission)

6-20. A linear triple-pen central-hall log house, the Wright Plantation home in Red River County. The dogtrot was enclosed as a hall and a frame third pen was added to the near end of the original house. Note the Louisiana style roof. (TLCR, Red River Co. No. 2; courtesy Texas Historical Commission)

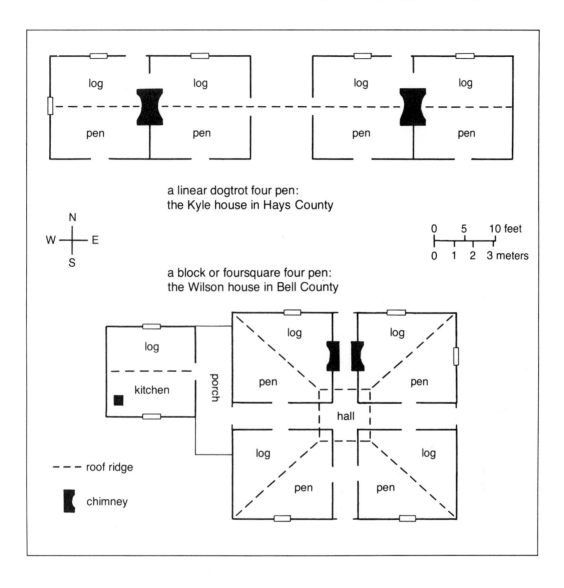

a linear dogtrot four pen:
the Kyle house in Hays County

a block or foursquare four pen:
the Wilson house in Bell County

6-21. Examples of four-pen log houses found in Texas.

6-22. Lap-jointing at juncture of two log pens of a linear dogtrot four-pen house, the Kyle home in Hays County. Built all at one time, the Kyle house originally had a double fireplace centrally positioned in each end. The logs were spliced because timbers of sufficient length could not be found. (TLCR, Hays Co. No. 1; courtesy Theodore Albrecht)

hall both ways through it."[58] A postbellum foursquare, the Wilson house in Bell County, was torn down several years ago. Built in the late 1860's by two brothers from Mississippi, it served initially as their multifamily dwelling.[59] A truncated pyramid roof and two interior chimneys added to the Georgian appearance of the Wilson house. With its destruction, Texas lost one of its most distinguished log houses.

Second Stories

All of the floorplans described, from the humblest single pen to rambling three and four pens, can easily accommodate a second story. Even the smallest single-story cabin usually has at least an open half-attic sleeping loft for children. Such lofts are common in Ireland and Scotland, and their presence in Texas log dwellings is a survival of the British tradition. In both Britain and Texas, the loft is supported by joists resting atop the front and rear walls of the house. Lofts are most often found in cabins rather than houses, and access is by means of a ladder.[60]

More common, particularly in houses, is a one-and-a-half-story development, with the upper level reached by a stairway.[61] In Texas, such houses are widely referred to as "two-story," and the dogtrot version is called a "saddlebag." The amount of headroom in these upper half-stories varies from one house to another, depending on the height of the log wall (Fig. 6-23). Floor joists for the second story usually rest three or four logs below the plate. In contrast to the loft, the upper half-story is of German origin and common in the continental German log houses of Pennsylvania.[62]

The stairway in story-and-a-half single-pen houses is normally tucked away in a corner adjacent to the fireplace or, less commonly, a corner on the opposite end

of the room from the fire. The steep stairs make a ninety-degree turn to accommodate the corner, as in many Pennsylvania German houses. The stairway is often boxed in and provided with a door at the foot (Figs. 6-24 and 6-34).[63] In central-hall and dogtrot houses, the stair leads up from one side of the central passage in a straight sweep and is less commonly boxed (Fig. 6-25).

The real status symbol in Middle Atlantic folk architecture is a full second story. It informs neighbors and visitors that the owner is economically successful and wants to show his wealth. The second story in such houses has a boxed square ceiling, unlike the sloped ceilings of the story-and-a-half. Full second stories were never added to single-pen houses in Texas and only very rarely to the basic double-pen and central-chimney types.[64] Rather, they are confined almost exclusively to dogtrot or central-hall types, resulting in what is known as the "I" house. Simply described, the "I" house is two rooms (or two rooms and a hall or passage) wide, one room deep, and two full stories in height.[65] The "I" house is so-named because it occurs frequently in Indiana, Illinois, and Iowa, states beginning with the letter *I*. Better names for it might be "two-story dogtrot," "two-story central hall," or "two-story basic double pen."

The traditional antebellum plantation "mansion" of the old Cotton Belt is often simply a log "I" house with a grand porch attached in front and siding affixed to conceal the logs. As such, the log "I" house appears here and there in the riverine plantation districts of Texas, but it is not a common type (Figs. 6-14, 6-26, and 6-27). The finest surviving example is the Foster house, built about 1852 near the banks of the Brazos River in Milam County and today restored at Log Cabin Village in Fort Worth (Fig. 6-28).[66] Most of the others, such as Holland Coffee's "Glen Eden" on the Red River, have perished.

6-23. Upper half-story of a North Texas log house. The two small windows flank the exterior chimney, and the top of the stairwell is seen at the left. (TLCR, Cooke Co. No. 2, photo by Lynn Harris)

6-24. Boxed-in staircase in a North Texas log house. The steep stairs make a right angle at the corner of the pen, adjacent to the fireplace, and can be closed off by the door. (TLCR, Cooke Co. No. 2, photo by Lynn Harris)

6-25. Top of a steep, straight staircase in the upper-story hall of an East Texas central-hall log house, originally a dogtrot. Note also the rafter attachment to the plate. (TLCR, Sabine Co. No. 1; courtesy Texas Historical Commission)

The "I" house is of English origin, at least in its central-hall form. Over much of England, as well as Wales and Scotland, the central hall "I" house can be seen in brick or stone construction, consisting of rooms approximately sixteen feet square separated by halls on both stories that are about ten feet wide. Two-story dogtrot houses apparently do not occur in Europe.

Shed Rooms

Another common, almost universal, means of enlarging a log house is the *shed room*, also called a "side" room. These are typically about one-half to two-thirds the width of a pen and are added on the back side of a house, directly behind a pen. In Texas, as in the eastern United States, shed rooms range from seven to twelve feet in width.[67] The name *shed room* is derived from the single-slope shed roofs covering these additions. Attached to the main roof at the eaves, the shed roof projects at a lesser pitch, forming a break in the profile (Fig. 6-2). In rare instances, the shed room is built of logs, but the difficulty of attaching a new log wall to an existing one usually dictated that the shed room be of frame construction or, in the Hill Country German counties, of stone (Fig. 6-29).[68] The large majority of Texas log houses have rear shed rooms, and they occur on every type of floorplan. Much more rarely, shed rooms are placed on a gable end of the house (Fig. 3-10).

Shed rooms are of British origin. They are seen most commonly in western England and may have been introduced from that region initially to the Chesapeake Tidewater.[69]

The Porch

Most, but by no means all, Texas log houses are equipped with a roofed porch, usually running the entire length of the front side of the house (Fig. 6-18). Some porches are smaller, covering only an area adjacent to the front door. The full-sized porch is about half the width of a pen, similar to the shed room. In many houses, the porch roof is attached a foot or two below the eaves, forming an offset. Back porches are less common and occur primarily in the lower southern domain in East Texas.

Porches are common throughout the Middle Atlantic and Tidewater zones, most frequently and almost universally in the Deep South.[70] A substantial number of log dwellings in the Upper South and the upper southern districts of Texas lack porches (Fig. 6-2).

The origin of the porch is not clearly understood. Some European houses have porchlike structures, but the log house porch may be derived from the West Indies or even Africa. Porches are certainly much more common on American houses than in any British, German, Swedish, or Dutch areas in Europe, suggesting an alien influence or an American invention.

The Room on the Porch

An occasional feature of the Texas log house is the "room on the porch." This small enclosure amounts to half of a shed room, or one-quarter of a pen. It is formed by enclosing a portion of the front porch with walls, resulting in a room approximately eight feet square. The room on the porch often serves as a sleeping place for a widowed grandparent.

Since the full-sized porch is more common in the Deep South, the room on the porch is also of greater importance there.

6-26. Full two-story dogtrot "I" log house, the McAdoo Plantation mansion in Washington County. Note the Louisiana style roof. This house was torn down in 1950. (TLCR, Washington Co. No. 4, photo ca. 1940; courtesy Pamela Puryear)

Such rooms have the disadvantage of blocking off some of the breezes needed to cool the porch, and for this reason they never became very popular. Like the shed room, the room on the porch is typically of frame construction but occasionally is seen in log.

The Kitchen

Perhaps most commonly, the kitchen is part of the log house. In the early years of pioneering, cooking was done at the fireplace in the main room of the house, or even out-of-doors. As the house was enlarged, a shed room or ell addition often became the kitchen.

In a great many houses, however, a freestanding log pen was built to serve as a kitchen, or "cook house." Such kitchens are either completely separate from the dwelling or are attached only by a roofed walkway or porch (Fig. 6-30). The main reason for building freestanding kitchens was to remove unwanted heat from the house. The amount of heat that built up in a well-chinked log house from a cook stove or fireplace, winter or summer, could be well-nigh unbearable, particularly in the subtropical climate of Texas. The old saying "If you can't stand the heat, don't stay in the kitchen" has

6-27. Dogtrot "I" house covered with siding, the George Crist house in Limestone County. Built in the early 1860's, the house also has a single-pen frame addition on the right side. (TLCR, Limestone Co. No. 4, photo 1908; from the Joseph E. Taulman collection, University of Texas Archives, Austin)

largely lost its meaning, for our modern kitchens cannot rival those of the Texas folk house in heat production and retention. A separate kitchen also lessened the danger that fire might destroy the house.

The freestanding log kitchen displays a fairly standard floorplan (Fig. 6-30). A single-pen structure, the kitchen is entered by way of a door in a gable end. At the opposite gable end is either a fireplace and hearth or a cook stove. Many kitchens are windowless, but most are provided with a small window on each side for cross ventilation. The gable-entrance single pen is an ancient type of log building, traceable to prehistoric Europe, and there is little question that the log kitch-

en of Texas and the South is a latter-day representative of that ancient floorplan. Other kitchens, a minority, have side-facing gables and are identical in floorplan to single-pen houses. As a rule, kitchen pens are somewhat smaller than those of the house. Dimensions of 12' × 12' or 14' × 14' are common, though many kitchen pens are slightly elongated.

The tradition of freestanding kitchens is found all through the South, particularly on the coastal plain in the Lower South. The practice of connecting the kitchen to the house with a roofed passageway may have a Scandinavian antecedent. In the previously mentioned log pair cottage of northern Europe, a possible

6-28. Gable-end view of a dogtrot "I" house, a Brazos River plantation mansion now restored and reconstructed at Forest Park in Fort Worth. (TLCR, Milam Co. No. 1, photo 1976)

6-29. German cedar log house with stone shed room, built by the Becker family in the Texas Hill Country. The opening in the pen may once have been a fireplace gap, but most German houses lacked fireplaces. (TLCR, Kendall Co. No. 6, photo ca. 1936; courtesy Historic American Buildings Survey, Library of Congress)

6-30. Freestanding log kitchen of the typical gable-entrance type, East Texas. This kitchen is adjacent to the old Sam Houston homestead in Huntsville. (TLCR, Walker Co. No. 4)

ancestor of the dogtrot house, one of the pens served as a kitchen, separated from the dwelling pen by a roofed dogtrot.

Cellars

Cellars, a common feature of the German continental log house of Pennsylvania and occasionally found through the Upper South and Lower Midwest, are extremely rare in Texas folk houses.[71] The few I have seen are situated beneath the main log room of story-and-a-half single-pen houses, with access by way of an exterior stair on the gable end (Fig. 6-34).[72] In every instance, these cellars were built by settlers who had previously resided in Indiana, Illinois, or Missouri. The principal function of the cellar seems to have been food storage. More commonly, upper southern folk built a dugout cellar separate from the house, a type seen frequently in parts of interior Texas.

Doors and Windows

Doors and windows are not numerous in log houses (Fig. 6-2). Perhaps the principal reason for this paucity of apertures is that each opening weakens the log pen. Even when properly framed in, a door or window remains a weakness. Since most houses had already been weakened by the cutting of a fireplace gap, builders kept doors and windows to a minimum. Another reason for the small number of windows, in some parts of Texas at least, was the danger of Indian attack. Shooting holes appear in many Texas log houses. Usually these are simply gaps in the chinking, "two or three holes in each side and end between the chinking, called port holes, used for the purpose of shooting outside in case of an attack from without."[73] Other shooting holes are formed by cutting away parts of two adjacent logs (Fig. 6-31).

In the single-pen house, one door often suffices, situated in the front wall. Most typically, this door is centrally positioned, but often it is displaced toward one side or the other. Centrally positioned doors reflect British influence, while off-center entrances are derived from the Pennsylvania Germans. British tradition also dictated that a rear door be aligned with the front entrance. One log house in north-central Texas, located in Comanche-plagued Parker County, had no door at all. Entrance was made on hands and knees by way of a tunnel under the front sill log. Unwelcomed Indian intruders were thus in an extremely vulnerable posture as they entered the house. At night, a large rock was placed over the entrance tunnel.[74] A Travis County log schoolhouse of the 1830's also lacked a door, "a couple of the lower logs being left uncut in the doorway, over which the little tots had to be lifted," to prevent "the ingress of the pigs."[75]

When a shed room was added, if not earlier, a rear door was cut to facilitate movement within the house. Similarly, gable-end additions, whether of the basic, dogtrot, or central-chimney type, caused new doors to be cut. If a house was built initially as a dogtrot, the front doors were often omitted, with the two pens opening instead to the passageway.[76]

Only one original window is usually found in the log pen. Most commonly, this is a very small opening situated adjacent to the chimney. Since the fireplace gap is already cut, this small window does not further weaken the pen. Quite a few log houses have no windows at all, at least original ones.[77]

Several types of door construction occur in Texas. The more primitive are simply puncheons. William Banta, recalling the log houses of early northeast Texas, described doors "made of split and hewed puncheons pinned together with an auger, and hung to the log wall with wooden hinges."[78] A Delta County pioneer remembered the hinges as being rawhide.[79] A step above the puncheon door, but very similar, is the board-and-batten type, consisting of milled vertical boards or planks and horizontal battens.[80] Finer log houses have paneled doors.

The small windows of early log cabins and houses were covered with rawhide and a puncheon or board shutter (Fig. 6-32). "The windows were protected with a kind of clarified raw-hide that admitted light into the rooms much better than any one would imagine," recalled Andrew Davis.[81] A visitor to a Brazoria log house in 1831 mentioned "a few windows closing with wooden shutters and destitute of glass."[82] In time, the boards and planks were replaced by larger, glassed windows. Often, additional windows were cut after glass became available. The placement of these varies, but at least one full-sized window is usually cut in the front wall, facing the porch. Front-wall windows are a British tradition that seemingly could not be suppressed indefinitely.

Conclusion

As we have seen, log pens can be left singly or put together in a variety of ways to

6-31. Shooting hole cut into the log walls of a Norwegian house in Bosque County. (TLCR, Bosque Co. No. 3; courtesy Mrs. Rebecca D. Radde)

6-32. Board window shutter, Deep East Texas. The shutter probably antedates the glass. (TLCR, Sabine Co. No. 1; courtesy Texas Historical Commission)

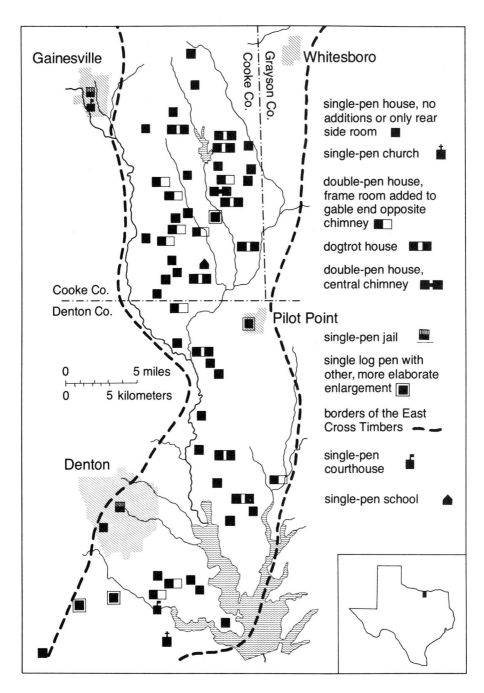

Gainesville

Whitesboro

Grayson Co.
Cooke Co.

single-pen house, no
additions or only rear
side room ■

single-pen church

double-pen house,
frame room added to
gable end opposite
chimney ■□

dogtrot house ■▯■

double-pen house,
central chimney ■▬

Cooke Co.

Denton Co.

Pilot Point

single-pen jail

single log pen with
other, more elaborate
enlargement ▣

0   5 miles

0   5 kilometers

borders of the East
Cross Timbers ━ ━

single-pen
courthouse

Denton

single-pen school ▲

6-33. Log houses, East Cross Timbers.

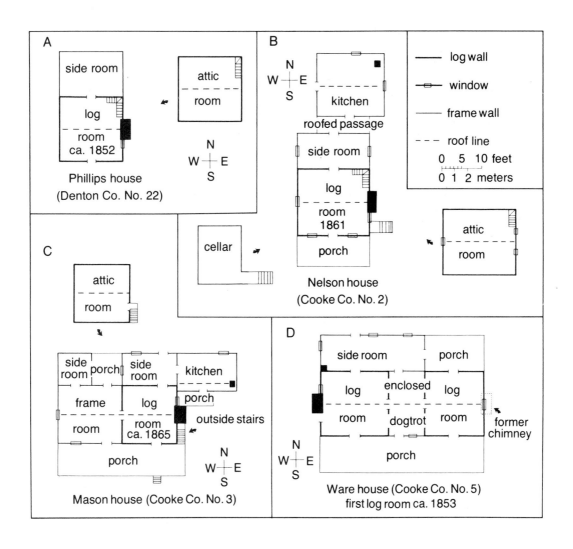

6-34. Log folk houses of the East Cross Timbers. The diversity of floorplans evident in this sketch and in Figure 6-33 is typical of Texas. Single-pen and basic double-pen types are prevalent in this upper southern area in North Texas.

form many different floorplans. Half-pen shed rooms and quarter-pen rooms on the porch add still more flexibility, as does the porch itself. The loft, half-story, or full upper story further augments the options available to the builder. The resultant combinations produce the various log folk houses of Texas (Fig. 6-33). Studied closely, floorplans tell us much about the people who occupied them, revealing their wealth and prestige (or lack of it), the size and growth of the family, the dangers they faced, their regional cultural heritage, and their perception of local climate and weather (Fig. 6-34). It is perhaps the floorplan more than any other feature of folk architecture that describes the life and times of our Texan forefathers. In cultural heritage, as we have seen, Texas log floorplans are predominantly British, representing the blending of a German technology with English and Irish plans.

The log culture complex was by no means confined to houses, for a great variety of other log structures enjoyed a place in the landscape. Perhaps most prominent among them were public buildings, such as inns, churches, courthouses, and jails. Chapter 7 is devoted to these log public buildings.

SEVEN

Log Public Buildings

Visitors to almost any frontier town or hamlet in the eastern half of Texas rarely saw public structures other than those of log. If they sought accommodations for the night, they found lodging at a log inn or hotel; if they had business to transact or purchases to make, they did so in log stores and offices; if they had legal duties or difficulties, they went to the log courthouse or were escorted to the log jail; if they had need of spiritual comfort, they sought it in a log chapel; if they preferred instead the company of "demon rum," they imbibed it at a log tavern. Often it was difficult to distinguish public buildings from ordinary houses, as the floorplans and outward appearance were similar or identical in many cases. It is no accident that the vernacular of that time included such terms as school*house,* church *house,* road*house,* court*house,* and jail*house.* An 1837 visitor to Harrisburgh (now part of Houston) saw "four or five log houses, two of which are used for stores, and another as a place of public accommodation."[1]

Log Courthouses

In most Texas county seat towns, the courthouse is one of the grandest structures to be seen. Many are splendid examples of Victorian architecture, others reflect the glories of the glass-and-steel age. It is hard to realize, when admiring these fine courthouses ensconced in their pleasant public squares, that the same site was originally occupied by a log courthouse. Yet in many counties of the eastern half of Texas, court was initially held in precisely such humble buildings (Fig. 7-1).[2]

The typical Texas log courthouse was a single-pen hewn structure, generally somewhat larger than a dwelling. The dimensions of the pen ranged from Smith County's 20' × 26' courthouse and Fannin County's 18' × 24' structure, both of which reflected the tradition of rectangular pens, to square or nearly square pens, such as Denton County's 20' × 20', Van Zandt's 18' × 18', Ellis' 16' × 18', and Williamson's 16' × 16'.[3] Most were single-story buildings, but some were story-and-a-half. The majority were built to specifications by professional carpenters, at the request of the county commissioners. Often the specifications were rather detailed. The commissioners of a northeast Texas county were promised by the builder, William Richey, that "the building of the Court House in the Town of Greenville in the county of Hunt, [is] to be twenty by twenty-two and the logs to face ten inches in the middle, six inches thick, framed, rough covered [i.e., roofed] with three feet boards, boards to show one foot, two doors, . . . two windows, one in the back end, the other in the side, . . . and a Sturdy Puncheon floare, good doore, shutters, all to be done in workman like manner, and is to be completed by the first day of April next, this the 16th day of

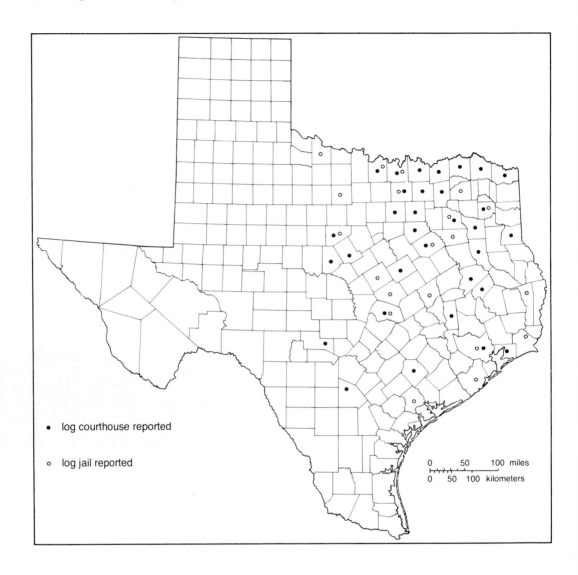

7-1. Log courthouses and jails in Texas. (Published county histories and field observations)

Jany. 1847 . . ."[4] Specifications for the 1838 Fannin County courthouse described "a post oak or cedar log body, 18 × 24 feet, one and one-half stories high, the lower floor of rough plank, the upper floor to be dressed, and a wooden chimney, two doors and four windows . . . with shutters, one flight of stairs, the upper apartment to be divided into two rooms of equal size and one alley; to have a shed room at the opposite end from the chimney . . ."[5]

Certain other counties demanded somewhat grander edifices, usually one-story dogtrots. Harris County had such a courthouse, as did Comanche and Atascosa.[6] The one in Comanche County survives to the present, apparently the only log courthouse in the state remaining in existence. A replica of dubious merit was built of the Atascosa dogtrot courthouse and stands today alongside one of the intersecting highways in Jourdanton.

The county treasury was not much depleted by the construction of the initial log courthouse. Cooke County obtained a small, dirt-floored, chimneyless cabin capitol for $29, while the citizens of Ellis displayed a bit more civic pride in their $59 model. Panola County purchased what must have been a palace for $200.[7]

In every instance where log courthouses were built, the commissioners obviously viewed the structure as temporary. These humble public buildings were generally not afforded the place of honor in the center of the town square, in order not to be in the way when construction began on a more substantial courthouse. Most often, the log building faced the square from one of the sides. The functional life-span of log courthouses varied from two or three years to as much as eight or ten. The existence of the first Cooke County courthouse was ingloriously shortened about 1855, when a fly-crazed steer charged inside seeking respite from his insect tormentors. In the process of an equally hasty egress, the panicked beast ran against one corner of the log building and brought the $29 structure tumbling down.[8]

The log courthouses of Texas belonged to a tradition rooted in the Middle Atlantic culture. All through the log construction areas of the eastern United States, such public buildings had been common. Virginia offers examples from the 1700's, and Ohio, Kentucky, Missouri, and other states continued the tradition, passing it eventually to Texas.[9]

Log Jails

On the frontier, a jail was an even more pressing need than a courthouse. Most communities of any size or ambition had one, and in the early years many were of log construction.[10] For obvious reasons, these public buildings had to be stronger than the average log pen, and the typical solution was to construct double walls, a pen within a pen. Typically, the two log walls were spaced apart, so that some other material could be filled in between. The 1837 Brazoria County jail had "double walls, made of timber 8 inches thick, hewn square and dovetailed at the ends, and sufficiently apart to admit a log of 10 inches in diameter to stand upright between the two walls, and the walls to be filled in this manner."[11] The Denton jail, destroyed by fire about 1866, had triple hewn walls.[12] Notched logs composed the inner and outer walls, and the middle layer consisted of vertically placed beams. The jail had no door, and prisoners were lowered into it from an attic room, an arrangement duplicated at the Belton log jail.[13] If the prisoners contemplated digging out of the Denton jail, they had to cope with the double layer of hewn logs that formed the floor. To spend a July day incarcerated at Denton must have been a memorable experience. At the Athens jail, the foot or so of space between the two log walls was filled with rocks.[14] To keep prisoners from sawing their way out, builders of the Young County jail at Graham drove square nails into the log wall every few inches, a technique also found in the original Hopkins County jail.[15] The builders of Houston's jail made it sturdier by using huge logs, still a foot thick after hewing. Apparently such precautions had the intended results, because the log jail at Athens was in use for thirty years and numerous others lasted ten years or more.[16]

The living space inside one of these log cells was usually limited. The Fannin County jail was only 4′ × 8′, Belton's measured 12′ × 12′, and Athens' pokey 6′ × 10′.[17] Others, such as those at Houston and Brazoria, were larger, perhaps in anticipation of a sizable lawless population.

One particularly fine Texas log jail survives today, situated in Raby Park at Gatesville (Fig. 7-2). The original Coryell County jail, this structure was built in 1858 by John H. Crisman, a professional carpenter of Indiana birth who had also resided in Illinois and Arkansas.[18] The double walls are skillfully half-dovetailed. Regrettably, this unique and priceless structure is being allowed to deteriorate. The inner pen of the double-walled, half-dovetailed Gainesville log jail still exists, though in poor condition. It was moved out of town some years ago and is used as a farm outbuilding. Perhaps because of its superior locking characteristic, the half-dovetail notch seems to have been in almost universal use on Texas log jails. This notch was further strengthened by pins, as at Houston, where the corners were "dovetailed, dowelled, and pinned."[19]

Log jails, like courthouses, were part of the log folk architecture of the eastern states. Examples have been noted in North Carolina and eighteenth-century Louisiana, among others.[20]

Log Churches and Schools

"Scattered over this portion of the State," wrote an Englishman touring northeast Texas in the 1840's, "are seen primitive chapels, built of logs, generally placed in a secluded locality."[21] His observations would have been true for all Anglo frontier settlements in Texas, for the log culture complex extended to the southern Protestant chapel, or church house.[22]

Two distinct types of log chapel were found in frontier Texas. The first was a square single-pen structure with side-facing gables, a centered front door, and a chimney. In short, it was identical in floorplan to many single-pen houses, a similarity reinforced by the absence of a steeple or any other religious symbolism that might have identified it as a church. Prototypes of the side-gable chapel can be found in the mountains of Kentucky and some other poorer parts of the South.[23] The only surviving log church in Texas known to me is of this type (Fig. 7-3). It is situated in a rural cemetery atop a low hill in south-central Denton County and was the original Chinn's Chapel Methodist Church.[24] This humble log chapel may well be the oldest existent Protestant church edifice in Texas. Built by settlers from East Tennessee shortly after 1850 of massive, half-dovetailed post oak logs, the chapel measures twenty feet square, the largest log pen in the county (Fig. 7-4). It has a dirt floor, front and rear doors, and two small windows. Once the chapel boasted a fine sandstone chimney, but it was pulled down many years ago. Chinn's Chapel also served its rural community as a schoolhouse, and newly arrived settlers sometimes set up housekeeping in the building while their homes were being built. For many years now, Chinn's Chapel has been used only as a shed for tools needed in cemetery maintenance. Protected by a sheath of milled siding, its logs remain sound, but the

7-2. Half-dovetail double walls of the original Gatesville jail. Built in 1858 by J. H. Crisman, a professional carpenter from Indiana and Arkansas, the jail is apparently the only one of its kind to survive in Texas. (TLCR, Coryell Co. No. 1, photo 1973)

7-3. Chinn's Chapel Methodist log church in its peaceful cemetery setting in Denton County. This structure is probably the oldest Protestant church structure in Texas, dating from about 1850. (TLCR, Denton Co. No. 13, photo 1973 by Larry Barr)

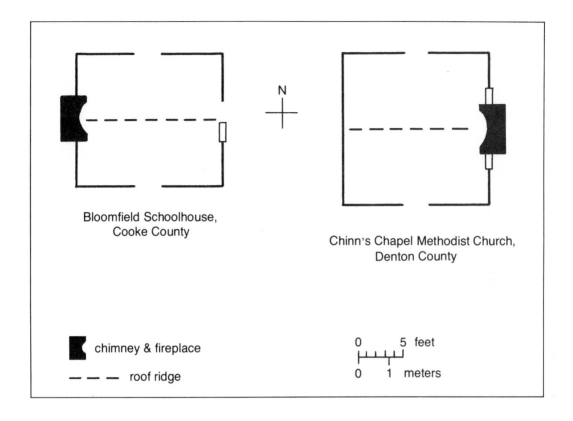

Bloomfield Schoolhouse,
Cooke County

Chinn's Chapel Methodist Church,
Denton County

N

◆ chimney & fireplace

— — — roof ridge

0   5 feet

0   1 meters

7-4. A school and a church built of logs, North Texas.

7-5. Front view of the Chinn's Chapel log church. The logs are well preserved beneath the siding. (TLCR, Denton Co. No. 13, photo 1973 by Larry Barr)

church group that owns the old chapel refuses to consider its restoration (Fig. 7-5). Thus, a folk structure of architectural importance, of significance to the history of Texas Methodism, seems doomed to end its years as a tool shed.

The other type of log chapel once common in Texas was rectangular rather than square and had front- and rear-facing gables, with the entrance in the front gable end. A pulpit or lectern was placed in the rear end of the chapel, and the parishioners sat on wooden pews facing away from the door. A small window or two on each side provided ventilation. This type also lacked a steeple and was not easily identified as a church. The floorplan and general layout can be traced to the Chesapeake Tidewater English settlements and from there to the Dissenter-Protestant districts of the United Kingdom, especially Methodist Wales.[25] The front-gable, steepleless chapel, in frame construction, occurs frequently across the entire South and is very common in Texas. I know of no surviving front-gable log chapels in the state.[26] A log "replica" of this type, purported to be a faithful copy of the seventeenth-century Spanish Tejas Mission near Alto, can only be regarded as an architectural practical joke.[27]

The overall visual impression produced by these chapels and their frame successors is one of simplicity and austerity. This simplicity is deliberate. It is not an index of rural poverty or frontier frugality, but instead a conscious expression of the stern fundamentalism of southern Protestantism. No beauty, grandeur, or religious symbolism distracts the senses. These chapels express, in the simplest possible visual terms, the British Dissenter-Protestant view of the church structure as merely a place of assembly, not an abode of God or the scene of ritual miracle. The structure is not sanctified or sacred and is often used for nonreligious purposes, such as education and secular

meetings.[28] The log church can be a grand and impressive structure, as is seen in numerous surviving examples in Scandinavia and eastern Europe; the humility of the southern chapel is obviously intentional.[29] We should seek its prototypes in the stone chapels of highland Britain rather than the log churches of European Eastern Orthodoxy or Lutheranism.

The log chapel often, or even usually, served as the local schoolhouse.[30] Even when church and school occupied separate buildings, the log schoolhouse was virtually identical in floorplan and design to the chapel. The same two basic chapel types account for the great majority of log schools.

A good example of the side-gable, chimney-and-fireplace schoolhouse, and one which survives to the present day, is an old log structure near Bloomfield in Cooke County (Fig. 7-4). This original Bloomfield school is a single pen measuring 20' × 17 3/4', constructed of half-dovetailed post oak timbers.[31] Unfortunately, the old log school is in an advanced state of decay and cannot be preserved. The front-gable type is well exemplified by a surviving log school built in the hills of Palo Pinto County in 1858, an 18' × 15' single pen with one door, centered in the front gable end, and a single window, in the rear gable directly opposite the door.[32] Other floorplans also existed for log schools. In one Delta County community, the early school occupied one pen of a dogtrot log house, with the other room serving as a residence for the teacher.[33]

Many of these pioneer log schools were extremely primitive structures. Mary Nunley, remembering her Palo Pinto County school of the 1850's, wrote that "the floor was the ground . . . , a plank along one side of the room for a desk, and a big crack in the wall gave us light." Benches were made of "logs split open and holes bored in the round side of the logs and legs put in."[34] Floorless, windowless schools were apparently not uncommon, perhaps an indication of the low value Anglo pioneers in Texas placed on education.[35]

Hotels, Taverns, Stores, and Offices

Approaching the Bowie County village of Boston on a day early in the 1840's, Frederick Marryat "descried between the trees a long building, made of the rough logs of the black pine, and as we advanced, we perceived that the space between the logs (about six inches) had not been filled up, probably to obtain a more free circulation of air. This building, a naked negro informed us, was Ambassadors' Hall, the great and only hotel of Texian Boston."[36] To be sure, most log hostelries were somewhat grander than Ambassadors' Hall and belonged to the hewn, chinked generation of buildings, but the typical hotel of frontier Anglo Texas was indeed of logs.[37] The earliest of these may have been Whiteside's Hotel at San Felipe, a story-and-a-half hewn dogtrot. Whiteside's was already a going concern when Noah Smithwick visited San Felipe in 1827.[38] The most common floorplan for log hotels seems to have been the dogtrot.[39]

A painted sign inviting overnight guests was about the only visible difference between hotels and ordinary log dwellings. In fact, there was no clear distinction in many cases. Particularly in rural areas, overnight accommodations could be had for a price in many farm homes. Even some so-called stagecoach inns were in reality simply "friendly farmhouses" whose gregarious owners enjoyed frequent visitors. Not all farmers welcomed guests. A German traveler seeking bed and board at a farm near Gonzales in 1849 was surprised when the owner "shut the door in my face," forcing the visitor to drag his saddle into the dogtrot and sleep there.[40]

If the distinction between log hotels and private dwellings was blurred, the same was true between hotels and stores. A traveler in northeast Texas in the 1830's described "a large house, divided into two apartments, one of which was occupied as a cooking, eating, and sleeping room, the other . . . contained for sale tomahawks, bowie knives, powder and lead, some Indian trinkets, and a quantity of whiskey."[41] In other cases, such establishments occupied separate structures. Two fine Navarro County log commercial structures, a store and a trading post, have been restored at Jester Park in Corsicana. They are among the few surviving structures of this type in Texas.[42] Grog shops, such as the "double hewed log house which answers as a tavern" at Lynchburg, have apparently vanished altogether from the Texas landscape.[43]

Offices of various types were also built of logs. Perhaps the most famous, and best preserved, is Sam Houston's law office at Huntsville.[44] Unfortunately, such specimens of folk architecture have traditionally been preserved only when some prominent personage is associated with them. Better crafted, finer specimens are often lost because George Washington never slept or worked in them. One Texas exception to this neglect is the restored Blue Gap Post Office, a small single-pen log structure in Runnels County on the far western periphery of the log culture complex zone.[45]

Forts and Blockhouses

The log stronghold has become part of our stereotyped image of the American frontier, apparently with ample justification. The early settlements in New Sweden and even New England contained log blockhouses, forts, and "garrison hous-

7-6. The Peters "Blockhouse" in northwestern Mason County. Built in 1869, the Blockhouse is one of the few of its type to survive in Texas. The distinguishing trait is the projecting, cantilevered upper story. (TLCR, Mason Co. No. 3; "Blockhouse," in *Mason County Historical Book*, p. 310)

es."[46] Two major types seem to have been typical in much of the eastern United States: the freestanding blockhouse and the walled fort.

In Texas, there was no sharp distinction between blockhouses and well-fortified houses. The earliest "fort" in the state, and the one which gave its name to Fort Bend County, was erected about 1822 on the site of the present town of Richmond.[47] It was simply a dogtrot house with a cannon positioned in the open passageway. Most true blockhouses in Texas were distinguished by a cantilevered overhang of the second story. One of the earliest cantilevered blockhouses in the state was Fort Inglish, built at the site of Bonham in 1837. It had a square pen measuring sixteen feet on each side as its first story, with a twenty-four–foot–square second half-story.[48] Fort Inglish apparently became a model for many fortified log houses in northeast Texas, for an observer in the 1840's recalled that "in building houses . . . , the first six logs were fourteen feet in length, the next four rounds sixteen feet long."[49] Cantilevered blockhouses continued to be built in Texas at least as late as the 1860's. A fine surviving example, and one of the very few remaining in existence, was built in 1863 near the San Saba River in northwestern Mason County and is still widely referred to by local residents as the "blockhouse," a usage perhaps encouraged by the sizable German population of the county.[50] The

German word for log house is *Blockhaus*. The Mason County blockhouse is a notable structure, and steps should be taken to preserve it (Fig. 7-6).

Enclosed log forts in Texas date from at least 1834, when Fort Parker in Limestone County was built. Such strongholds often included simply a blockhouse or several cabins surrounded by a picket wall. Others had blockhouses at each corner. In 1840 Fort Houston near present Palestine was described as "150 by 80 feet, containing two rows of log houses, enclosed with pickets."[51] Such structures remained common even into the early statehood period, and Noah Smithwick remembered that Fort Croghan at Burnet in 1848 "consisted of the usual log cabins, enclosed by a stout stockade."[52] No enclosed forts survive in Texas, though a replica of Fort Parker was built.

Soon thereafter, the arrival of federal troops to protect the Texas frontier ushered in a different type of log fort. No longer were hostile Indians capable of mounting attacks against the military posts, and as a consequence the protective wall disappeared from fort architecture. The new forts were simply cantonments, consisting of a loose assemblage of buildings adjacent to a parade ground. Relatively few of these federal posts contained log structures. Fort Merrill in Live Oak County, Fort Lincoln in Medina County, and Fort Griffin in Shackelford County reportedly had some log houses.[53] A procedure followed by some commanders upon establishing a fort was to confiscate some local cabins and transport them to the site of the post as temporary quarters.[54]

Conclusion

Cabins, houses, and the various kinds of public buildings together accounted for much of the craftsmanship associated with the log culture complex, but overall they constituted a minority of the log structures erected in Texas. The remaining majority consisted of various kinds of farm outbuildings. It is to this remaining majority that we turn our attention in Chapter 8.

EIGHT
Rural Log Outbuildings

The typical pioneer farmstead of the eastern half of Texas consisted of five or ten separate buildings. Besides the house and kitchen, many farmers had a small barn or corncrib, a smokehouse, a cotton shed, stables, a chicken coop, a springhouse, and various other special-purpose structures. William Bollaert sketched such log farmsteads in the 1840's, noting in his Texas journal the presence of the log "cook-house, stables, graneries," and other farm outbuildings.[1] The visual effect of such farmsteads was striking. The parallel lines of the logs, almost a striped effect, lent a basic unity to the assemblage of buildings, linking house, barn, kitchen, sheds, and cribs in a harmonious whole. Against the backdrop of remnant forest, these log farmsteads seemed to belong to the land, to blend with the wooded landscape. Such harmony and blending provide much of the appeal of folk architecture, offering a visual joy and satisfaction now denied to the American eye in most of our landscapes.

The purposes of scholarly investigation demand that we now dissassemble this orderly whole in order to look at its constituent parts. Perhaps the most appropriate point of departure is the barn. The ancient meaning of *barn*, "barley house," provides a clear indication that the traditional barn was a granary. Farm animals were housed in stables, built separate from the dwelling. Hay was stored out-of-doors in stacks. Not until the time of the so-called Agricultural Revolution of the late eighteenth and early nineteenth centuries were the functions of storage and stabling combined under one roof. It is for this reason that no clear distinction exists between log barns and corncribs in Texas and much of the American South. Many log barns retain the ancient purpose and are simply for storage of grain and the implements used in grain cultivation. Others contain stables under the same roof and, as a result, also have space for hay storage. I find unprofitable an attempt to define log barns according to function and to differentiate barns from corncribs. In frontier times, when the impact of the Agricultural Revolution remained negligible in Texas, separate granary barns and stables were the rule. Twenty or thirty years later, after the roughness of the frontier had worn off, progressive currents in farming modified pioneer ways and produced some unitary log barns. Not infrequently, original granary barns were enlarged to become multifunctional.

The Single-Crib Barn

The simplest of all Texas log barns is the *single-crib* type. In the vernacular terminology of log construction, "crib" means the same as "pen"—a unit of four log walls notched at the corners—except that "crib" refers only to outbuildings, particularly barns, while "pen" denotes a house or some other log unit for human occupance. The single-crib barn, then, consists of one unit of four walls (Fig. 8-1).

The roof of the single-crib barn has gables at front and rear, with a single roof ridge at right angles to the front. Almost without exception, the entrance is in the front gable, often centered in the wall but sometimes offset to one side. This door varies in size from one barn to another, but most commonly it is very small, nothing more than a crawlway into the grain bins (Figs. 8-2 and 8-3). As such, the single-crib barn represents yet another survival of the ancient mesolithic European gable-entrance log structure.[2]

Texas single-crib barns vary in dimensions, but most are small. As the log barn diffused south and southwest from Pennsylvania into warmer climate zones, the average barn size decreased.[3] Do not search in Texas for the magnificent, sizable log barns of Appalachia or Pennsylvania; they are not to be found. The smallest single-crib barns in Texas are simply corncribs and are so designated by the people who own them (Fig. 8-2). Corncrib dimensions are usually in the 10′ × 12′ to 12′ × 14′ range, with the shorter sides on the gable walls. Larger cribs are usually square, ranging from about 12′ × 12′ up to 18′ × 18′ and are normally called barns. Their function, however, is often identical to that of the corncrib. Many or perhaps even most single-crib barns and corncribs, regardless of dimensions, have enclosed shed rooms on one or both eave sides.[4] These rooms are used as stables and to store farm equipment. In other cases, the sheds are unenclosed by walls, simply shed roofs under which items may be stored. Enclosed or not, the two sheds lend the single-crib barn a distinctive "witch's hat" roof profile, familiar to anyone who has traveled rural Texas (Figs. 8-4 and 8-5). Some single-crib barns also have a shed room or shed roof on the nonentrance gable side, so that

sheds flank three of the four walls. The larger single-crib barns contain an attic hayloft above the granary, particularly when one of the shed rooms is a stable.[5]

The single-crib barn, from the humblest small granary to the largest crib flanked by two enclosed sheds, is the most common farm outbuilding in Texas. Such structures are seen throughout the zone of log construction in the state. They occur frequently in East Texas, perpetuating the modest barn-building tradition of the subtropical Lower South. There is a direct continuity from the Texas single-crib barn back to the log granary of central Europe, from the early twentieth century to prehistoric times.[6]

Most Texas single-crib barns and in fact most log outbuildings, regardless of size or function, are carelessly built of unhewn timbers or split half-logs, saddle notched and unchinked.[7] There are some exceptions, well-crafted barns that reflect the same care and skill that went into the better log houses, but these are rare. The outbuildings, perhaps more than other structure types, reveal the extent to which log craftsmanship had declined in the long journey of diffusion from southeastern Pennsylvania.

Stables occupying a separate log crib were mentioned by numerous observers during the early pioneer period.[8] "We built strong log stables," recalled Noah Smithwick, "with stout doors, which we fastened on the inside, going out at the top of the building," a precaution against Indian thievery.[9] Only horses were stabled; the other farm livestock foraged out-of-doors year round. I have never seen a log stable in Texas, so I must conclude that few if any still exist. Some were converted to other uses, as in Fannin County, where a log stable became a schoolhouse, after being "thoroughly cleaned."[10] Most commonly, stables occupy frame shed rooms attached to log barns.

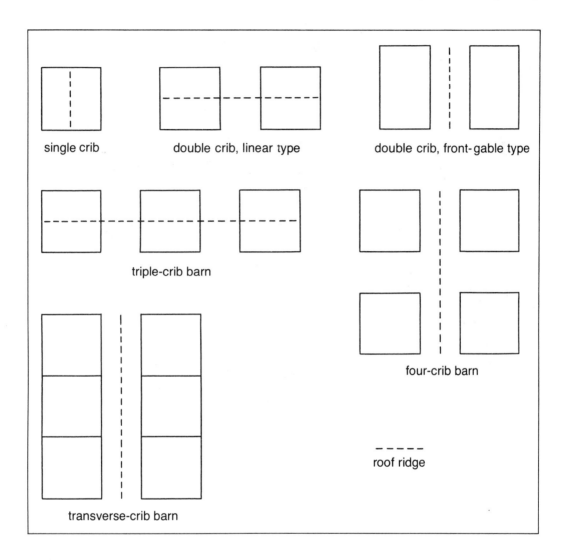

single crib

double crib, linear type

double crib, front-gable type

triple-crib barn

four-crib barn

roof ridge

transverse-crib barn

8-1. Some types of log barns found in Texas.

8-2. A saddle-notched, single-crib log corncrib, the smallest and simplest "barn" found in Texas. This North Texas structure measures 11 1/2' gable width by 13 1/2' on the eaves and is 9 1/2' tall to the eaves. Note the typical small door. (TLCR, Denton Co. No. 19, photo 1973)

8-3. Crib door on a Comal County cedar log barn. (TLCR, Comal Co. No. 4; courtesy Theodore Albrecht)

8-4. Single-crib log barn with two shed rooms and covered with vertical siding, North Texas. Note the "witch's hat" roof profile. This is one of the most typical Texas barns. (TLCR, Cooke Co. No. 18, photo 1972)

The Double-Crib Barn

Also very common in Texas, particularly in the interior, upper southern counties, is the double-crib barn. A linear type of this barn, with a floorplan essentially identical to the dogtrot house, is most frequently seen (Fig. 8-1). The two cribs are separated by an open, roofed runway, equivalent to the passageway or hall of the dogtrot house, and the cribs and runway are covered by a single roof with side-facing gables (Fig. 8-6).[11] Entrances to the cribs generally face the runway, but occasionally one sees double-crib barns with front-facing doors. The farm wagon is parked in the runway, with convenient access to the attic haylofts, or the passage can be used as a threshing floor.[12] These barns are seen in different sizes, varying both in square footage of the cribs and in the height of the structure. Some consist of two small, rectangular cribs, each measuring about 8' × 14', usually with the shorter sides on the gables and occasionally with a cantilevered roof overhanging on one eave side (Fig. 8-7). Much more commonly, the two cribs are square or roughly square, measuring anywhere from about 10' × 10' to 18' × 18', most often about 14' × 14'. The large majority are one story in height, reaching eight or ten feet at the eaves, and only the plate logs connect the two cribs (Fig. 8-8). Some attain greater height, perhaps fifteen feet or even more at the eaves, providing very substantial loft space (Fig. 8-9).

The typical linear double-crib barn was transferred virtually unaltered from the Alpine German lands to America.[13] I have

8-5. Unusually well-built "V"-notched single-crib barn. (TLCR, Cooke Co. No. 48, photo 1973)

seen double-crib barns nearly identical to those of Texas in the Austrian Alps around Badgastein, where they are used for hay storage. Presumably Germans from the Alpine area, possibly Canton Bern in Switzerland, brought this double-crib barn to Pennsylvania in the 1700's, and it spread through the Upper South and into parts of the Gulf Coastal Plain (Figs. 8-10 and 8-11). Its acceptance by settlers of English ancestry was facilitated and encouraged by the similarity to the basic English tripartite barn, which has essentially the same floorplan but with the runway enclosed.[14] The double crib is very common in Appalachia and even beyond the Ohio River in southern Indiana.[15] It is less common in the Lower South but is usually present there as a minority type. In Appalachia, the double crib often takes more elaborate forms,

such as a massive cantilevered loft super-structure, but simpler barns like those of Texas can also be seen in the mountain South.[16] Curiously, the double-crib barn enjoys greatest acceptance in areas different from those of its floorplan twin, the dogtrot house. One is tempted to link the two in origin, so similar are they in concept and design, yet the rather contrasted spatial distributions warn against such a linkage.

The linear double-crib barn, like the single crib, commonly has shed rooms or shed roofs on one or both sides. In East Texas, one occasionally sees shed rooms formed by projections of the log walls of the cribs, but generally the rooms are of frame construction.[17]

Another, much rarer type of double-crib barn has a front-facing gable and consists of two elongated cribs flanking the

8-6. Small double-crib pine log barn, Deep East Texas. (TLCR, Sabine Co. No. 2A; courtesy Texas Historical Commission)

runway (Fig. 8-1). I have seen only one such barn in Texas, located in the hills of Wood County, near Winnsboro.

Triple-Crib Barns

The triple-crib barn apparently has no prototype in Europe or the eastern United States, yet a few examples can be seen in Texas (Figs. 8-1 and 8-10). These are found exclusively among the Hill Country Germans and seemingly represent elaborations of the double-crib barn.[18] The more spectacular of these has two open runways, forming an extremely elongated structure (Fig. 8-12). Another type is simply a double-crib barn with the logs cantilevered to enclose the runway as a threshing floor, leaving a door at the middle of each side (Fig. 8-13). The resultant tripartite floorplan is quite like the basic English frame barn.

Four-Crib and Transverse-Crib Barns

The largest log barn found in Texas is the four crib, sometimes modified to become a transverse crib. A four-crib barn is square, with a log crib at each corner and two intersecting runways at the center (Fig. 8-1). A huge roof covers the entire structure, and gables face the front and rear (Fig. 8-14).[19]

The four-crib type, also called a "four-square" barn, is an Americanism. It seems to have evolved as an enlargement of the double crib in East Tennessee.[20] From there it spread through much of the Upper South, usually as a minority type. A barn of such considerable size is suited to cold climates, where farmers must store large amounts of winter feed and fodder for their livestock. Perhaps for this reason, the four-crib barn is uncommon in the subtropical climate of Texas. Only three examples have been detected

8-7. Double-crib barn with oblong cribs and a cantilevered forebay roof, a rare type in Texas. This structure once stood in Birdville, now part of Fort Worth. (TLCR, Tarrant Co. No. 3, photo 1925; from the Joseph E. Taulman collection, University of Texas Archives, Austin)

through field research, all in the upper southern interior of Texas (Fig. 8-10).[21] One of these is adjacent to Winedale Inn, an old stagecoach stop in Fayette County.[22] The construction of a large barn there was perhaps prompted by the need to feed and shelter the stagecoach horses. Winedale's well-crafted foursquare barn, beautifully preserved and restored, is one of the finest surviving log outbuildings in the state.

The transition from four crib to transverse crib was an easy one. To form a transverse-crib barn, one of the two intersecting runways is closed off with walls, resulting in two additional grain bins or storage bays (Fig. 8-1).[23] Normally, the runway closed is the one opening to the eave sides, allowing the main entrance to remain on a gable end, but occasionally the gable runway is closed instead (Fig. 8-14). The transverse-crib barn is fairly common in frame construction in Texas, but log prototypes are extremely rare. A smaller type of transverse-crib log barn, consisting of two abutting cribs on either side of a single runway, occurs widely in Appalachia, but none have been found in Texas, though frame examples abound.[24]

8-8. Poorly crafted double-crib barn, typical of its North Texas setting. Built of unhewn, saddle-notched oak logs, this barn reflects the deterioration of construction techniques that occurred in Texas. The barn was razed in 1970. (TLCR, Denton Co. No. 9, photo 1969)

8-9. An unusually tall double-crib barn, including spacious lofts, one shed room, and a shed roof. It was built in several stages and is fairly well crafted. The barn has been in continuous use for a century or more on a farm in the East Cross Timbers of North Texas. (TLCR, Cooke Co. No. 7)

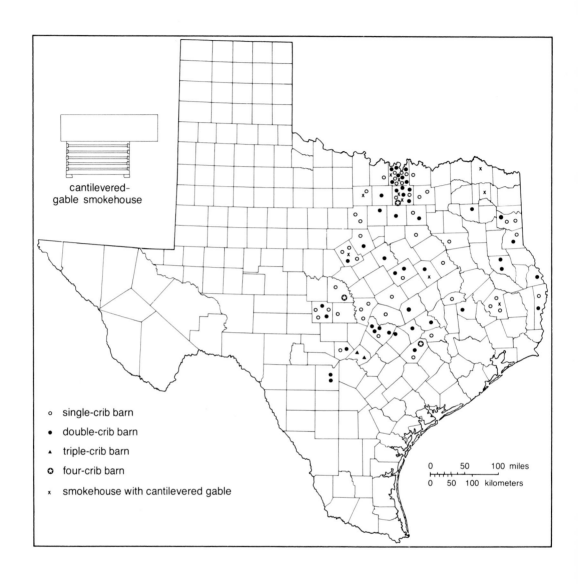

cantilevered-
gable smokehouse

∘   single-crib barn

•   double-crib barn

▲   triple-crib barn

✪   four-crib barn

×   smokehouse with cantilevered gable

8-10. Distribution of selected types of log outbuildings observed in Texas. (TLCR and field observations)

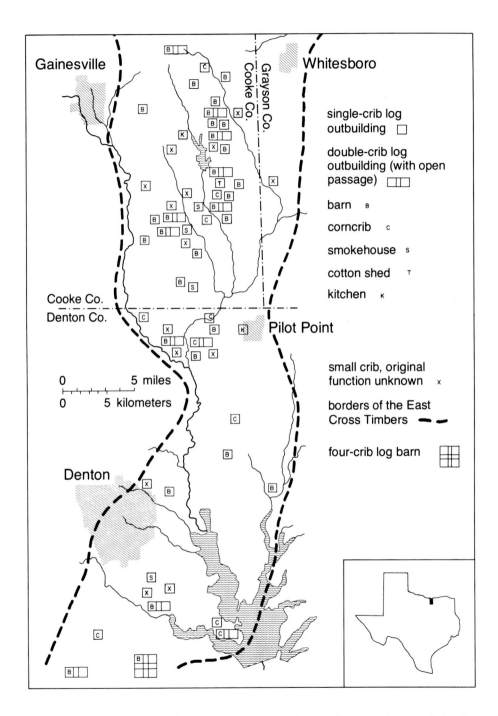

8-11. Log outbuildings of the East Cross Timbers. The prevalence of single- and double-crib barns in Texas is evident from this small area.

8-12. A triple-crib barn with two runways, in the German Hill Country of Texas. This is a very rare type. (TLCR, Comal Co. No. 4; courtesy Theodore Albrecht)

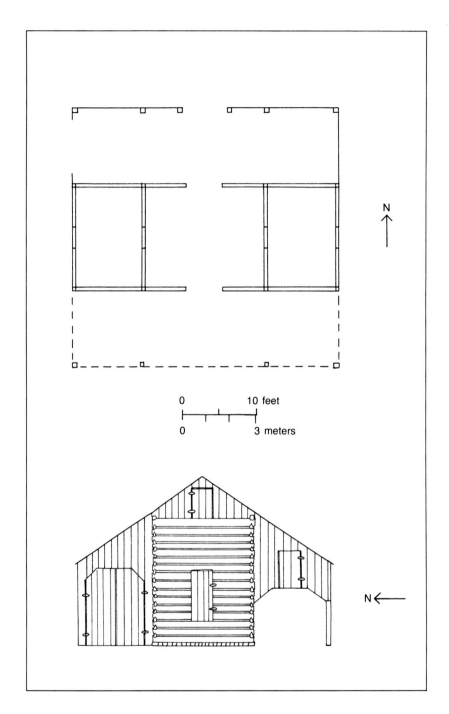

8-13. Cantilevered triple-crib log barn, Comal County. (TLCR, Comal Co. No. 6)

8-14. Four-crib log barn in the hills of San Saba County, Texas. One runway has been closed off with a picket wall to form a transverse-crib barn. (TLCR, San Saba Co. No. 3, photo 1975)

The Log Smokehouse

Next to barns, the most common log outbuilding on Texas farms is the smokehouse. On many farmsteads, the smokehouse is simply a demoted single-pen cabin and therefore not distinguishable in an architectural sense from early dwellings. Others, those of concern to us here, were built as smokehouses, a function clearly revealed by their form.

The typical Texas log smokehouse is a small, slightly rectangular crib, measuring 6' × 8' at the smallest up to about 10' × 12' or 12' × 14'.[25] The height from ground level to the eaves is usually about six to seven feet (Fig. 8-15). Most striking visually is a cantilevered gable overhang of three to five feet on one end (Fig. 8-16).

Resting atop the two cantilevered logs is a pole from which the newly slaughtered hogs are hung for butchering. The entrance to these small meathouses is normally in the cantilevered gable end, but occasionally it is at the opposite gable.[26]

Smokehouses identical to these, distinguished by the cantilevered gable, are found all through the Upper South. North Carolina, Ohio, southern Appalachia, and the Ozarks all offer abundant examples.[27] They are widely distributed in Texas, though greater numbers are seen in the upper southern counties of the interior. The ancestry of these cantilevered smokehouses is traced back to the Pennsylvania Germans, who introduced them from central Europe.[28]

Texas log smokehouses are unique

8-15. Cantilever-gabled log smokehouse, built about 1865 in Central Texas by John E. Chaffin. (TLCR, Limestone Co. No. 2, photo 1907; from the Joseph E. Taulman collection, University of Texas Archives, Austin)

among outbuildings in the relatively high level of craftsmanship they normally display. Smokehouses are often built of hewn logs, fastened together with half-dovetail or "V" notching, instead of the saddle-notched round logs found on most barns and cribs (Table 4-5).

By no means were all smokehouses used to smoke meat. The sugar-curing method was common in the postpioneer period. Even when sugar curing was used, the structure was still referred to in the vernacular as a "smokehouse," though the term "meathouse" could also be heard.

Other Log Outbuildings

Many Texas farmsteads included a variety of other log buildings. Sizable plantations in the antebellum period usually had a log smithy, manned by a slave artisan. Even small-scale farmers often owned a log cotton shed, and some had log spring- or wellhouses. Tool sheds, general-purpose storage cribs, and wash houses were also of logs. Not enough of these have been catalogued in Texas to permit many generalizations about their construction, other than the observation that these smaller outbuildings are usually carelessly built of unhewn, saddle-notched logs and have gable-end entrances.

8-16. Cantilever-gabled smokehouse in North Texas, carefully built of half-dovetailed postoak logs. In contrast to most outbuildings, many smokehouses were built with the same degree of care as houses. The smokehouse measures 10′ × 12′, with the shorter sides on the gables, and it is 6′9″ tall to the eaves. (TLCR, Cooke Co. No. 35, photo 1973)

As we have seen, log outbuildings, like dwellings, exhibit distinct types and regional distributions. In the following, concluding chapter, an attempt will be made to piece these types and patterns into a regional classification of Texas log buildings.

NINE

Texas Log Culture Regions

Cultural geographers, by training and inclination, attempt to group research findings into a regional framework, to postulate a system of culture areas as a device to bring together their data in an orderly spatial classification.[1] To the careful reader of the preceding chapters, many or all of the culture regions of Texas log architecture described in this chapter will already be apparent. They reflect different physical environments and contrasted population origins. I discern five major log culture areas in Texas (Fig. 9-1).

East Texas:
The Lower Southern Region

East Texas is a western appendage of the Deep South.[2] Its environment and people are very similar to those of the coastal plain of Alabama, Mississippi, and Georgia. Not surprisingly, East Texans were derived in the main from these coastal mother states. Duplicates of the East Texan pine forests, humid subtropical climate, and red soils can be found all across the Deep South, and its institutions and culture strengthen these environmental ties. The traditional devotion to the Democratic party, to southern Baptist and Methodist faiths, to King Cotton and the defeated Confederacy—all reflect affiliation to the Deep South. The pleasant local dialect, with its slurred r's and abundant dipthongs, its "peckerwoods" and

"redbugs," speaks to us of the lower southern heartland, as do placenames like Crossroads, bayou, and slough.

As we might expect, its log architecture is also that of the Deep South. Here is the Texas stronghold of the dogtrot house and slave cabin, the square, saddle, and semilunate notches, the cat and brick chimneys. The pine tree provides the most common wood for log structures here, and half-log construction is common. Cantilevered porch and shed-room supports, hooded chimneys, and back porches as well as front characterize the East Texas log house. Foundations of tall brick or wooden pilings are the rule, and chinks are often covered by rived boards instead of being filled. Occasional two-story plantation houses and Louisiana-style roofs add to the deep southern image. Pens are larger here than elsewhere in Texas, and the room on the porch is more often encountered. The first area to receive the log culture complex, about 1815, East Texas was also the last to retain active log construction, in the 1930's.

Central and North Texas:
The Upper Southern Region

West of the lower southern realm in East Texas is the settlement zone of the highland southerner, the Tennessean, Missourian, Arkansan, and Kentuckian.[3] At its

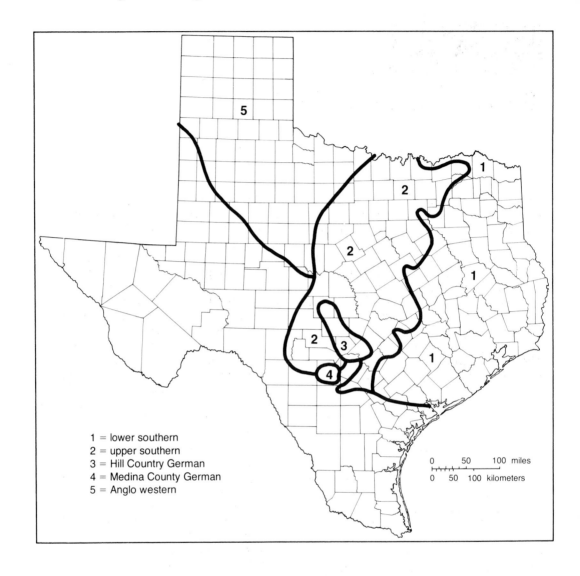

1 = lower southern
2 = upper southern
3 = Hill Country German
4 = Medina County German
5 = Anglo western

9-1. Log construction culture areas in Texas.

core is a hilly zone mildly reminiscent of Appalachia or Ozarkia, replete with hollows, coves, and gaps. The culture, economy, and architecture are those of the Upper South, modified in response to a distinctive environment. Here the single pen and basic double pen prevail over the dogtrot, and the central-chimney house appears as a minority type (Figs. 6-33 and 6-34). Half-dovetailing and "V" notching are overwhelmingly dominant in most counties, and oak is the most common building material. Chinks are filled and plastered, chimneys are of stone, foundations are low, and cantilever-gabled smokehouses occur widely. An occasional four-crib barn or a cellar adds to the upper southern character of the log landscape. Pens and cribs are smaller in dimensions than those of East Texas, and porches are often lacking. The time depth of log construction was shallower here than in East Texas, lasting fifty years or less in many counties.

The Hill Country German Region

Imbedded in the upper southern domain is an alien intrusion zone created by mid-nineteenth-century German immigrants.[4] Stretching from New Braunfels and the northern outskirts of San Antonio up through the Hill Country as far as Mason, this region remained rather isolated even as late as the 1930's. Heavily Teutonized, it has been described as one of the most thoroughly German areas of the United States. German speech, German customs, German frugality still prevail here.

The European immigrants who came to these hills in the 1840's and 1850's were not drawn from the log construction areas of Germany. Instead, they learned how to build log structures from Anglo-Americans after coming to Texas. But, once learned, the techniques were modified by the Germans, and distinctively Teutonic

features were added, to the extent that the Hill Country German log buildings can easily be distinguished from those of the Anglos. "V" notching is dominant in the hilly German counties, and saddle notching is common. Dovetailing is rare, a marked contrast to the log notching in the surrounding upper southern areas. Chinks are unusually wide, particularly in the Fredericksburg area, and filled with hewn, mortared stones. Additions to the original log structure, particularly shed rooms, are typically of stone or half-timbered construction (Fig. 6-10). Chimneys are less common than in Anglo areas, and those that do exist are normally not positioned centrally in a gable wall. Instead, corner chimneys or stovepipe flues are the rule, and many are attached to shed rooms. Fireplaces are rare. Story-and-a-half plans are almost universal. The only triple-crib barns observed in Texas were in Comal County, in the German Hill Country.

Medina County German Region

So distinctive is the log architecture of Medina County, below the Balcones Escarpment just west of San Antonio, that a separate culture region is warranted.[5] Apparently this distinctiveness is the product of the unusual settlement history and ethnic make-up of the county. The log buildings seen in Medina County were built by the Castro colonists, who came beginning in 1844. They were predominantly German-speaking Alsatians, with a smattering of German-Swiss, Germans, and French.

Medina County construction is chinkless, with each log resting snug against the ones above and below it. Double notching and false corner timbering both occur here. In these major respects, the Medina County structures are unlike others anywhere in Texas. Both chinkless walls and double notching are found in Switzerland, suggesting that the Swiss were likely the introducers of this distinctive technology. Most of the Alsatians were derived from villages in the Upper Rhine plain, where half-timbering rather than log construction is found. Conceivably, the chinkless, double-notched method, as well as false corner timbering, could have been introduced from adjacent Mexico, where all occur.

West Texas: The Anglo Western Region

The scattering of log buildings in West Texas, beyond the zone of dominance of log construction, also includes rather distinctive structures.[6] Perhaps the greatest departure from the styles of the East is seen in the log semidugout, built on a hillside and entered through a gable door. Also confined to this area is the gently pitched Anglo western roof, in which the ridgepole rests directly on the highest logs in the gable-end walls. Log construction was never prevalent in West Texas, sharing importance with other building materials and techniques, such as adobe, sod, stone, and pickets. All these were quickly superseded by frame buildings with the coming of the railroads, and the time depth of log construction in West Texas was not more than ten or fifteen years. The best collection of West Texas log buildings is at the Panhandle-Plains

Historical Museum in Canyon, and a well-preserved log semidugout can be seen at the Ranch Headquarters Museum in Lubbock. Log structures in the Davis Mountains of Trans-Pecos Texas have not been sufficiently documented to allow any conclusions concerning style.

Conclusion

The last generation of authentic log house dwellers, much reduced by affluence and social stigma, is now aged. By the end of this century few, if any, occupied log houses and functional log outbuildings will remain, and a tangible tie to the frontier era in Texas will have been severed. For those who have the interest and the time to search patiently, the highly varied log culture complex of Texas is still accessible, still to be seen. In the next twenty years, a concerted effort should be made to seek out worthy examples of the different types and styles and to restore them for the future. More care should be taken in the process of restoration to ensure authenticity, avoiding the lamentable mistakes that characterize the large majority of existing restorations. Unless we undertake, very soon, an effective, intelligent program of restoration, a priceless and beautiful legacy of folk architecture will have been squandered and a building technique thousands of years old will vanish from the Texas countryside.

Appendix 1
A List of Texas Restoration Projects Open to the Public That Include Log Structures

County	Place	Structure
Bell	Temple, grounds of Scott & White Hospital	log house and corncrib, joined as dwelling
Bell	Salado	log house and corncrib, now used as store
Bell	Salado, Stagecoach Inn	log house, now used as store
Bell	Belton, 604 N. Pearl St.	Denman log house, from nearby rural area
Blanco	Johnson City, on Hwy. 290 W., W. Main St.	log house, now used as store
Blanco	Johnson City, Johnson Old Ranch, National Park Service	Johnson family log house*
Burnet	just W. of Burnet, grounds of Fort Croghan	two log houses from rural Burnet County
Caldwell	Luling, Blanche Square	log house from nearby rural area
Comal	New Braunfels, Church Hill Dr.	triple-crib log barn
Comanche	Comanche, Burks Museum, N.W. outskirts on Hwy. 36	original log courthouse; barn, smokehouse
Coryell	Gatesville, Raby Park	original log jailhouse
Dallas	Dallas, Old City Park	two log homes, from Dallas and Tarrant counties
Dallas	Dallas, adjacent to old courthouse	John Neely Bryan log cabin
Denton	Little Elm, park	log home from nearby rural area
Ellis	Waxahachie, Getzendaner Park	log house

* = Structure in Original Location

County	Place	Structure
Erath	Dublin, City Hall grounds	one pen of a dogtrot log house from local area
Fayette	Round Top, Henkel Square	log houses and kitchens from Fayette and Colorado counties
Fayette	Winedale, U. of Texas Winedale Inn Properties	log kitchen,* four-crib barn,* and smokehouse*
Fayette	Schulenburg, Wolters Park	Jacob Wolters log house from Austin County
Freestone	Fairfield, adjacent to old jail, 302 E. Main	two log houses from rural Freestone County
Gillespie	near Stonewall, LBJ State Park	several German-built log houses, including some on original site*
Gonzales	Gonzales, 1300 block of St. Louis St.	Eggleston log house
Grimes	Anderson, on Hwy. 90	Steinhagen log house
Hays	Wimberly, Pioneer Town	several log houses from Hays and Comal counties
Hays	San Marcos, Aquarena Park	two antebellum log houses
Hood	Granbury, E. edge of town on Hwy. 377	log house, original ferry keeper's residence*
Houston	near Weches, Mission Tejas State Park	Rice family log house, formerly at Crockett
Kimble	Junction, intersection of Pecan and N. 3rd St.	log cabin from rural Kimble County
Lubbock	Lubbock, Texas Tech Campus, Ranch Headquarters Museum	log cabins and houses from Mason, Dickens, and Gonzales counties
Montague	Forestburg, on Hwy. 455	log house from nearby rural area
Montague	Montague, courthouse square	log house from nearby rural area
Montague	Bowie, city park	log house from nearby rural area
Navarro	Corsicana, Jester Park	numerous log structures, including houses, cabins, stores, shops, from rural Navarro County
Parker	Weatherford, Holland's Lake Park	two single-pen log houses from rural Parker County joined together as fake dogtrot

County	Place	Structure
Polk	Alabama-Coushatta Indian Reservation	traditional log house
Randall	Canyon, Panhandle-Plains Historical Museum	log house, cabins, smokehouse from Randall, Armstrong, Hemphill, and Oldham counties
San Jacinto	Hill Herb Garden, S.W. part of county on Hwy. 1725	log cabin, used as office
San Saba	San Saba, Mill Pond Park	log house from nearby rural area
Tarrant	Arlington, Johnson Cemetery Park	two early log houses from local area
Tarrant	Grapevine, Liberty Park	early log house from local area
Tarrant	Fort Worth, Trinity Park, near intersection of University Dr. and Parkway Dr.	log house with rectangular floorplan
Tarrant	Fort Worth, Forest Park, Log Cabin Village	a number of log homes from Tarrant, Parker, Hood, and Milam counties
Travis	Austin, Zilker Park	Swenson Swedish log cabin
Tyler	Woodville, Heritage Garden Village	log house from rural Tyler County
Upshur	Gladewater, 303 S. Center St.	log jail
Walker	Huntsville, Sam Houston Park	log house,* kitchen, and law office once used by Sam Houston
Williamson	Round Rock, Harrell Memorial Park	log house
Williamson	Georgetown, residential area	log house
Wise	on rural road 8 mi. S.E. of Decatur	earliest house in county, the Woody log house*

Appendix 2
A List of Replicas or Reconstructions
of Log Buildings in Texas

County	Place	Structure
Anderson	1 mi. W. of Elkhart	replica of early church
Atascosa	Jourdanton, 703 Oak St.	replica of first courthouse
Fannin	Bonham	replica of early blockhouse
Houston	near Weches, Mission Tejas State Park	"replica" of seventeenth-century Spanish mission, of dubious merit, since the original church was likely of picket rather than log construction
Limestone	just N. of Groesbeck, off Hwy. 14, Fort Parker State Park	replica of log Fort Parker
Van Zandt	Wills Point	replica of early dogtrot house

Notes

1. A Regional Folk Architecture

1. For examples of the ethnic imprint on Texas architecture, see Ernest A. Connally, "The Ecclesiastical and Military Architecture of the Spanish Province of Texas," Ph.D. dissertation; Edith M. Hanna, "The Indigenous Architecture of Fredericksburg, Texas," M.S. thesis; Terry G. Jordan, "German Houses in Texas," *Landscape* 14, no. 1 (Autumn 1964): 24–26; Dinah Lee Lamb, "Selected Historic Domestic Architecture of San Antonio, Texas, Influenced by the Spanish-Mexican Culture," M.A. thesis; Ada L. K. Newton, "The Anglo-Irish House of the Rio Grande," *Pioneer America* 5, no. 1 (January 1973): 33–38; and Elliot A. P. Evans, "The East Texas House," *Journal of the Society of Architectural Historians* 11, no. 4 (December 1952): 1–7.
2. Folk architecture has long received the attention of cultural geographers. See, for example, Fred B. Kniffen, "Louisiana House Types," *Annals, Association of American Geographers* 26 (1936): 179–193; Fred B. Kniffen, "Folk Housing: Key to Diffusion," *Annals, Association of American Geographers* 55 (1965): 549–577; Robert Finley and E. M. Scott, "A Great Lakes-to-Gulf Profile of Dispersed Dwelling Types," *Geographical Review* 30 (1940): 412–419; Richard Pillsbury and Andrew Kardos, *A Field Guide to the Folk Architecture of the Northeastern United States*; and Peirce F. Lewis, "Common Houses, Cultural Spoor," *Landscape* 19, no. 2 (January 1975): 1–21.
3. Wilbur Zelinsky, "The Log House in Georgia," *Geographical Review* 43 (1953): 173.
4. Noah Smithwick, *The Evolution of a State*, p. 55; *A Visit to Texas*, p. 30.
5. Mary James Eubank, "A Journal of Our Trip to Texas, Oct. 6, 1853," *Texana* 10 (1972): 39.
6. William Bollaert, *William Bollaert's Texas*, facing p. 233.
7. Eugene C. Barker, ed., *The Austin Papers*, 1:1359.
8. J. Marvin Hunter, *The Trail Drivers of Texas*, p. 673.
9. This house is "Cooke Co. No. 3," the Texas Log Cabin Register (hereafter cited as TLCR).
10. Martha E. Hotchkiss Whitten, *Author's Edition of Texas Garlands*, pp. 231–234.
11. U.S. Department of Agriculture, *Farm Housing Survey*, pp. 5–6.
12. See Terry G. Jordan, "Reflections on Log Cabins and Architectural Zoos," *Texas Uniques, Antiques & Art* 3, no. 7 (July 1974): 7.
13. For the reader who is unfamiliar with the settlement of Texas by the various ethnic groups who built log structures, I recommend the following books and articles. For general sources, see Terry G. Jordan, "Population Origin Groups in Rural Texas," *Annals, Association of American Geographers* 60 (1970): 404–405 plus colored map; Terry G. Jordan, "Population Origins in Texas, 1850," *Geographical Review* 59 (1969): 83–103; Homer L. Kerr, "Migration into Texas, 1860–1880," *Southwestern Historical Quarterly* 70 (1966): 184–216; and Donald W. Meinig, *Imperial Texas*.

    For sources on Anglo- and Afro-Americans, see Barnes F. Lathrop, *Migration into East Texas, 1835–1860*; Terry G. Jordan, "The Imprint of the Upper and Lower South on Mid-Nineteenth-Century Texas," *Annals, Association of American Geographers* 57 (1967): 667–

690; Frank L. Owsley, "The Pattern of Migration and Settlement on the Southern Frontier," *Journal of Southern History* 11 (1945): 147–176; and W. O. Lynch, "The Westward Flow of Southern Colonists before 1861," *Journal of Southern History* 9 (1943): 303–327.

For the various European groups, see Axel Arneson, "Norwegian Settlements in Texas," *Southwestern Historical Quarterly* 45 (1941–42): 125–135; Carl M. Rosenquist, "The Swedes of Texas," *Yearbook, American Swedish Historical Museum*, 1945, pp. 16–30; Anne Blasig, *The Wends of Texas*; Henry R. Maresh and Estelle Hudson, *Czech Pioneers of the Southwest*; William H. Oberste, *Texas Irish Empresarios and Their Colonies*; Terry G. Jordan, *German Seed in Texas Soil*; and Rudolph L. Biesele, *The History of the German Settlements in Texas, 1831–1861*.

For sources on Texas Indian tribes that used log construction, see Harriet Smither, "The Alabama Indians of Texas," *Southwestern Historical Quarterly* 36 (1932): 83–108; Ernest W. Winkler, "The Cherokee Indians in Texas," *Texas State Historical Association Quarterly* 7 (1903): 95–165; and John H. Bounds, "The Alabama-Coushatta Indians of Texas," *Journal of Geography* 70 (1971): 175–182.

14. Young and Comanche counties files, TLCR.

15. W. W. White, "Dog-Run Houses," in *The Handbook of Texas*, ed. Walter Prescott Webb and H. Bailey Carroll, 1: 510.

16. Hunter, *Trail Drivers*, p. 746.

17. Lawrence R. Sharp, "History of Panola County, Texas, to 1860," M.A. thesis, p. 187; Rupert Richardson, *The Frontier of Northwest Texas, 1846 to 1876*, p. 128; Frances Terry Ingmire, ed. and comp., *Archives and Pioneers of Hunt County, Texas*, 1: 18; Brutus C. Chrisman, *Early Days in Callahan County*, p. 83; and Joseph C. McConnell, *The West Texas Frontier*, p. 124.

18. Edward Smith, *Account of a Journey through North-Eastern Texas*, p. 101.

19. Sharp, "History of Panola County," p. 187.

20. "Colorado Co. No. 2," TLCR.

2. The Origin & Diffusion of Log Folk Architecture

1. Fred B. Kniffen and Henry H. Glassie, "Building in Wood in the Eastern United States: A Time-Place Perspective," *Geographical Review* 56 (1966): 58.

2. For additional information on European log construction, see Hermann Phelps, *Holzbaukunst*; Hermann Schilli, *Das Schwarzwaldhaus*; Richard Weiss, *Häuser und Landschaften der Schweiz*; Gerda Boëthius, *Studier i den nordiska Timmerbyggnadskonsten från vikingatiden till 1800-talet*; Sigurd Erixon, "The North-European Technique of Corner-Timbering," *Folk-Liv* 1 (1937): 13–60; and David Buxton, "Wooden Churches of Eastern Europe," *Architectural Review* 157, no. 935 (1975): 41–54.

3. See Harold R. Shurtleff, *The Log Cabin Myth*.

4. Swedish-Finnish log structures in the Delaware Valley are the subject of several articles by C. A. Weslager: "Log Structures in New Sweden during the Seventeenth Century," *Delaware History* 5 (September 1952): 77–95; "Log Houses in Pennsylvania during the Seventeenth Century," *Pennsylvania History* 22 (1955): 256–266; and *The Excavation of a Colonial Log Cabin near Wilmington, Delaware, Bulletin, Archeological Society of Delaware* 16, no. 1 (April 1954).

5. Some scholars feel that the Swedish-Finnish influence was significant (see C. A. Weslager, *The Log Cabin in America from Pioneer Days to the Present*, pp. 197–201).

6. Warren E. Roberts, "Folk Architecture in Context: The Folk Museum," *Proceedings of the Pioneer America Society* 1 (1972): 41; Warren E. Roberts, *Some Comments on Log Construction in Scandinavia and the United States,* Preprint Series 1, no. 3 (September 1973): 1–5; Henry Glassie, "The Types of the Southern Mountain Cabin," in *The Study of American Folklore,* ed. Jan. H. Brunvand, p. 345.

7. Weslager, "Log Houses in Pennsylvania," p. 264.

8. C. A. Weslager, "Log Houses in Maryland during the 17th Century," *Quarterly Bulletin, Archaeological Society of Virginia* 9, no. 2 (1954): 2–8.

9. George C. Gregory, "Log Houses at Jamestown, 1607," *Virginia Magazine of History & Biography* 44, no. 4 (October 1936): 287–295. For the contrary, prevailing view, see Shurtleff, *The Log Cabin Myth.*

10. J. Frederick Kelly, "A Seventeenth-Century Connecticut Log House," *Old-Time New England* 31, no. 2 (October 1940): 28–40.

11. Pierre Deffontaines, *L'Homme et la Forêt,* pp. 120–121.

12. Richard W. Hale, Jr., "The French Side of the 'Log Cabin Myth,'" *Proceedings of the Massachusetts Historical Society* 3d ser., 72 (October 1957–December 1960): 121.

13. Carol Wells, "Earliest Log Cabins of Natchitoches," *North Louisiana Historical Association Journal,* Spring 1975, pp. 117–118.

14. Weslager, *Log Cabin in America,* p. 211; Henry Glassie, "The Old Barns of Appalachia," *Mountain Life and Work* 40 [41], no. 2 (Summer 1965): 30.

15. Glassie, "The Types of the Southern Mountain Cabin," p. 345.

16. John J. Winberry, "The Log House in Mexico," *Annals, Association of American Geographers* 64 (1974): 54–69; Charles F. Gritzner, "Spanish Log Construction in New Mexico," Ph.D. dissertation; Charles F. Gritzner, "Log Housing in New Mexico," *Pioneer America* 3, no. 2 (July 1971): 54–62.

17. Winberry, "The Log House in Mexico," pp. 54–55, 59, 61.

18. Michael Karni and Robert Levin, "Finnish Log Buildings in Minnesota," *North West Architect,* May–June 1972, pp. 92–99; Richard W. E. Perrin, "Log Sauna and the Finnish Farmstead: Transplanted Architectural Idioms in Northern Wisconsin," *Wisconsin Magazine of History* 44 (1961): 284–286; Richard W. E. Perrin, "German Timber Farmhouses in Wisconsin: Terminal Examples of a Thousand-Year Building Tradition," *Wisconsin Magazine of History* 44, no. 3 (Spring 1961): 199–202; Lawrence R. Brandt and Ned E. Braatz, "Log Buildings in Portage County, Wisconsin: Some Cultural Implications," *Pioneer America* 4, no. 1 (January 1972): 29–39.

19. Wells, "Earliest Log Cabins of Natchitoches," pp. 117–118.

20. Thelma Hall, "Swisher County," in *Handbook of Texas,* ed. Webb and Carroll, 2: 700.

21. See "Oldham Co. No. 1," TLCR.

22. Mary L. Williams, Park Technician, Fort Davis National Historic Site, letter to T. G. J. dated March 24, 1973.

23. Roberta F. Biles, "The Frame House Era in Northwest Texas," *West Texas Historical Association Year Book* 46 (1970): 167–183.

3. Raising a Log Wall

1. H. H. Halsell, *Cowboys and Cattleland,* p. 16.

2. Terry G. Jordan, "Log Construction in the East Cross Timbers of Texas," *Proceedings of the Pioneer America Society* 2 (1973): 118.

3. John Barrow, *Facts Relating to North-Eastern Texas, Condensed from Notes Made during a Tour*, p. 48.

4. Roberts, "Folk Architecture in Context," p. 38.

5. Fred R. Cotten, "Log Cabins of the Parker County Region," *West Texas Historical Association Year Book* 29 (1953): 101.

6. Henry Glassie, *Pattern in the Material Folk Culture of the Eastern United States*, p. 215; Henry Glassie, "The Appalachian Log Cabin," *Mountain Life and Work* 39, no. 4 (Winter 1963): 9.

7. Zelinsky, "Log House in Georgia," p. 180.

8. Weslager, "Log Houses in Pennsylvania during the Seventeenth Century," p. 263; Roberts, *Some Comments on Log Construction*, p. 1.

9. John B. Billingsley, "A Trip to Texas," *Texana* 7 (1969): 203–204.

10. Smithwick, *Evolution of a State*, p. 55.

11. Roberts, "Folk Architecture in Context," p. 38.

12. W. B. Bates, letter to T. G. J. from Houston, Texas, October 10, 1973.

13. Glassie, "Types of the Southern Mountain Cabin," p. 343.

14. J. M. Franks, *Seventy Years in Texas*, p. 17.

15. Ibid.; Halsell, *Cowboys and Cattleland*, p. 16.

16. Warren E. Roberts, "The Waggoner Log House Near Paragon, Indiana," in *Forms upon the Frontier*, ed. Austin Fife et al., p. 29; Glassie, *Pattern in the Material Folk Culture*, p. 113.

17. Halsell, *Cowboys and Cattleland*, p. 16.

18. Glassie, "Types of the Southern Mountain Cabin," p. 343.

19. W. R. Strong, "Reminiscences," *Gainesville Register*, June 16, 1914.

20. Glassie, *Pattern in the Material Folk Culture*, p. 215; Goodloe R. Stuck, "Log Houses in Northwest Louisiana," *Louisiana Studies* 10 (1971): 228–229.

21. Glassie, "Types of the Southern Mountain Cabin," p. 343.

22. Ellen Polk, as quoted in Ronnie C. Tyler and Lawrence R. Murphy, eds., *The Slave Narratives of Texas*, p. 45.

23. Roberts, *Some Comments on Log Construction*, pp. 1–2.

24. Eugene M. Wilson, "The Single Pen Log House in the South," *Pioneer America* 2, no. 1 (January 1970): 21; Roberts, "Waggoner Log House," p. 29; Glassie, "Types of the Southern Mountain Cabin," p. 343.

25. Wilson, "Single Pen Log House," p. 24.

26. Glassie, "Types of the Southern Mountain Cabin," p. 343.

27. Ibid.

28. Ibid., p. 341; Roberts, "Waggoner Log House," p. 29; John M. Vlach, "The 'Canada Homestead': A Saddlebag Log House in Monroe County, Indiana," *Pioneer America* 4, no. 2 (July 1972): 13.

29. Vlach, "The 'Canada Homestead,'" p. 13.

30. Ibid., pp. 11–12.

31. Eliot Wigginton, ed., *The Foxfire Book*, p. 86.

32. Vlach, "The 'Canada Homestead,'" p. 13.

33. Stanley Willis, "Log Houses in Southwest Virginia: Tools Used in Their Construction," *Virginia Cavalcade* 21, no. 4 (Spring 1972): 42; Donald A. Hutslar, "The Log Architecture of Ohio," *Ohio History* 80 (1971): 219.

34. Frederick Marryat, *Narrative of the Travels and Adventures of Monsieur Violet*, 3: 21.

35. Glassie, "Types of the Southern Mountain Cabin," p. 345; Jaromin Demek and Miroslav Strida, *Geography of Czechoslovakia*, following p. 192.

36. Roberts, *Some Comments on Log Construction*, p. 2.

37. See "Newton Co. No. 4," TLCR.
38. Glassie, *Pattern in the Material Folk Culture*, p. 215.
39. Francis E. Abernethy, ed., *Tales from the Big Thicket*, p. 60.
40. Gilbert Hathaway, *Travels in the Two Hemispheres*, 1: 287; Cotten, "Log Cabins of the Parker County Region," p. 102.
41. Halsell, *Cowboys and Cattleland*, p. 17.
42. William Banta and J. W. Caldwell, Jr., *Twenty-Seven Years on the Texas Frontier*, p. 4.
43. Cotten, "Log Cabins of the Parker County Region," p. 102.
44. Douglas K. Meyer, "Diffusion of Upland South Folk Housing to the Shawnee Hills of Southern Illinois," *Pioneer America* 7, no. 2 (July 1975): 60; Nancy McDonough, *Garden Sass*, p. 44; Roberts, *Some Comments on Log Construction*, p. 2; Glassie, "Appalachian Log Cabin," p. 9.
45. Cotten, "Log Cabins of the Parker County Region," p. 102; Franks, *Seventy Years in Texas*, p. 18; James Randolph Ward, "The Log Cabin in Texas History," M.A. thesis, p. 25.
46. Maryan McCamey, "The Lost Art of Chinking: Refound!" *Mother Earth News*, no. 36 (November 1975), p. 58; "Denton Co. No. 16," TLCR.
47. Cotten, "Log Cabins of the Parker County Region," p. 102; McDonough, *Garden Sass*, p. 44.
48. Ward, "Log Cabin in Texas History," p. 25.
49. Tyler and Murphy, *Slave Narratives of Texas*, p. 45.
50. Glassie, "Appalachian Log Cabin," p. 9; Zelinsky, "Log House in Georgia," p. 174.
51. George B. Erath, "Memoirs of Major George Bernard Erath," *Southwestern Historical Quarterly* 26 (1923): 223; Smithwick, *Evolution of a State*, p. 57.
52. Marryat, *Narrative of the Travels*, 3:6.
53. Vlach, "The 'Canada Homestead,'" p. 12.
54. *Visit to Texas*, p. 68; Webb and Carroll, eds., *Handbook of Texas*, 1:162.
55. See the files for Jack and DeWitt counties, TLCR.

4. Corner Notching

1. A good general source on corner notching is Fred B. Kniffen, "On Corner Timbering," *Pioneer America* 1, no. 1 (January 1969): 1–8; see also Terry G. Jordan, "Log Corner-Timbering in Texas," *Pioneer America* 8, no. 1 (January 1976): 8–18.
2. Glassie, "Types of the Southern Mountain Cabin," p. 350; Hutslar, "Log Architecture of Ohio," p. 237; Buxton, "Wooden Churches of Eastern Europe," p. 43; Kniffen and Glassie, "Building in Wood," pp. 54, 56, 63; and Glassie, "Appalachian Log Cabin," p. 11.
3. Kniffen and Glassie, "Building in Wood," p. 56.
4. Weslager, *Log Cabin in America*, pp. 152–153; Demek and Strida, *Geography of Czechoslovakia*, following p. 192.
5. Peter O. Wacker and Roger T. Trindell, "The Log House in New Jersey: Origins and Diffusion," *Keystone Folklore Quarterly* 13 (1968): 253, 258; Weslager, *Log Cabin in America*, pp. 169, 188; Glassie, "Appalachian Log Cabin," p. 10; Glassie, "Types of the Southern Mountain Cabin," p. 351.
6. Hutslar, "Log Architecture of Ohio," p. 247; Roberts, *Some Comments on Log Construction*, p. 2.
7. Richard W. E. Perrin, "Log Houses in Wisconsin," *Antiques* 89, no. 6 (June 1966): 867–871; Brandt and Braatz, "Log Buildings in Portage County," pp. 29–39.
8. Kniffen and Glassie, "Building in Wood," p. 61.
9. Glassie, "Types of the Southern Mountain Cabin," p. 350.

10. Kniffen and Glassie, "Building in Wood," pp. 56, 63; Glassie, "Appalachian Log Cabin," p. 10; Hutslar, "Log Architecture of Ohio," p. 247; Roberts, *Some Comments on Log Construction*, p. 2; Willis, "Log Houses in Southwest Virginia," p. 40; Vlach, "The 'Canada Homestead,'" p. 12; McDonough, *Garden Sass*, p. 44.

11. Wilson, "Single Pen Log House in the South," pp. 24–25; Hutslar, "Log Architecture of Ohio," p. 247.

12. Halsell, *Cowboys and Cattleland*, p. 16.

13. Roberts, "Folk Architecture in Context," p. 38.

14. Glassie, "Types of the Southern Mountain Cabin," p. 345.

15. Wigginton, ed., *Foxfire Book*, p. 75.

16. Ibid., pp. 65–69.

17. Roberts, "Folk Architecture in Context," p. 38.

18. Kniffen and Glassie, "Building in Wood," p. 54.

19. Ibid., p. 59.

20. Weslager, *Log Cabin in America*, p. 168; Hutslar, "Log Architecture of Ohio," p. 247.

21. Zelinsky, "Log House in Georgia," p. 174.

22. Roberts, "Folk Architecture in Context," p. 38.

23. Kniffen and Glassie, "Building in Wood," p. 59; Brandt and Braatz, "Log Buildings in Portage County," p. 38.

24. Glassie, "Appalachian Log Cabin," p. 10; Kniffen and Glassie, "Building in Wood," pp. 54, 59.

25. Weslager, *Log Cabin in America*, p. 167.

26. Roberts, *Some Comments on Log Construction*, p. 2; Vlach, "The 'Canada Homestead,'" p. 12.

27. Glassie, "Appalachian Log Cabin," p. 10.

28. Jaroslav Pacovský, *Český Ráj* [Bohemian paradise], plates 25, 104, 147, 153.

29. Glassie, "Appalachian Log Cabin," p. 11.

30. Jennifer E. Attebury, "Log Construction in the Sawtooth Valley of Idaho," *Pioneer America* 8, no. 1 (January 1976): 39; Philip W. Sultz, "Architectural Values of Early Frontier Log Structure," in *Forms upon the Frontier*, ed. Fife et al., pp. 35, 37; Hutslar, "Log Architecture of Ohio," p. 247; Brandt and Braatz, "Log Buildings in Portage County," p. 34; Wilson, "Single Pen Log House in the South," p. 245.

31. Glassie, "Appalachian Log Cabin," p. 11; Kniffen and Glassie, "Building in Wood," p. 56.

32. Glassie, "Appalachian Log Cabin," p. 11.

33. Meyer, "Diffusion of Upland South Folk Housing," p. 60; Hutslar, "Log Architecture of Ohio," p. 247; Glassie, "Types of the Southern Mountain Cabin," pp. 340, 363.

34. Roger N. Conger, *Historic Log Cabins of McLennan County, Texas*, declared square notching to be dominant even into Central Texas.

35. Kniffen and Glassie, "Building in Wood," p. 57.

36. Winberry, "Log House in Mexico," p. 56.

37. Kniffen and Glassie, "Building in Wood," p. 57.

38. Winberry, "Log House in Mexico," p. 56.

39. Weslager, *Log Cabin in America*, pp. 152–153; Kniffen and Glassie, "Building in Wood," p. 57; Buxton, "Wooden Churches of Eastern Europe," p. 43.

40. Gritzner, "Log Housing in New Mexico," p. 60.

41. Perrin, "Log Sauna and the Finnish Farmstead," pp. 284–286; Kniffen and Glassie, "Building in Wood," p. 57.

42. Winberry, "Log House in Mexico," p. 55; Gritzner, "Log Housing in New Mexico," p. 58.

43. See, for example, "Newton County No. 4," TLCR.

44. Kniffen and Glassie, "Building in Wood," p. 64.
45. Hutslar, "Log Architecture of Ohio," p. 237; Buxton, "Wooden Churches of Eastern Europe," p. 43.
46. Kniffen and Glassie, "Building in Wood," pp. 54, 56, 63.
47. Brandt and Braatz, "Log Buildings in Portage County," p. 30.
48. Roberts, "Folk Architecture in Context," p. 38.
49. See "Washington County No. 4," TLCR.
50. *Preservation Plan and Program for Rice Family Log Home, Houston County, Texas*, p. 25.

5. Construction of Floors, Roofs, & Chimneys

1. Billingsley, "A Trip to Texas," pp. 203–204.
2. McDonough, *Garden Sass*, pp. 37–38; for references to dirt floors in Texas, see Smithwick, *Evolution of a State*, p. 56, and E. F. Bates, *History and Reminiscences of Denton County*, p. 300.
3. Banta and Caldwell, *Twenty-Seven Years on the Texas Frontier*, p. 5.
4. McDonough, *Garden Sass*, pp. 37–38.
5. Banta and Caldwell, *Twenty-Seven Years on the Texas Frontier*, p. 5.
6. Ward, "Log Cabin in Texas History," p. 29.
7. Erath, "Memoirs of Major George Bernard Erath," p. 223.
8. Cooke County No. 47 and Comanche County No. 3 files, TLCR.
9. Glassie, "Types of the Southern Mountain Cabin," p. 347.
10. Wilson, "Single Pen Log House in the South," p. 22; Hutslar, "Log Architecture of Ohio," p. 172; Frances B. Johnston and Thomas T. Waterman, *The Early Architecture of North Carolina*, p. 4.
11. Strong, "Reminiscences."
12. Roberts, *Some Comments on Log Construction*, p. 3.
13. Franks, *Seventy Years in Texas*, p. 18.
14. Cotten, "Log Cabins of the Parker County Region," p. 100; Vlach, "The 'Canada Homestead,'" p. 14; Glassie, "Types of the Southern Mountain Cabin," p. 347.
15. Gritzner, "Log Housing in New Mexico," p. 60; Attebury, "Log Construction in the Sawtooth Valley," pp. 39–40.
16. Willis, "Log Houses in Southwest Virginia," p. 42; Henry Glassie, "A Central Chimney Continental Log House," *Pennsylvania Folklife* 18, no. 2 (Winter 1968–69): 35; Roberts, "Waggoner Log House," p. 29; Roberts, *Some Comments on Log Construction*, p. 3; Wilson, "Single Pen Log House in the South," p. 22; Glassie, "Types of the Southern Mountain Cabin," p. 347.
17. Evans, "East Texas House," p. 4. See also Washington County No. 1 file, TLCR.
18. San Jacinto County No. 5 file, TLCR.
19. Zelinsky, "Log House in Georgia," pp. 178, 180; Stuck, "Log Houses in Northwest Louisiana," p. 235; Glassie, *Pattern in the Material Folk Culture*, p. 215.
20. Smithwick, *Evolution of a State*, p. 55; Cotten, "Log Cabins of the Parker County Region," p. 102.
21. Strong, "Reminiscences."
22. Rex W. Strickland, "History of Fannin County, 1836–1843," *Southwestern Historical Quarterly* 33 (1929–30): 281; Abernethy, *Tales from the Big Thicket*, p. 60; John H. Jenkins, *Recollections of Early Texas*, p. 7; Franks, *Seventy Years in Texas*, p. 18.
23. Halsell, *Cowboys and Cattleland*, p. 16.

24. This roof structure is illustrated in Hutslar, "Log Architecture of Ohio," p. 172. See also Wilson, "Single Pen Log House in the South," pp. 21, 22; Billingsley, "A Trip to Texas," pp. 203–204.
25. Strong, "Reminiscences."
26. Banta and Caldwell, *Twenty-Seven Years on the Texas Frontier*, p. 4.
27. Strickland, "History of Fannin County," p. 281.
28. Weslager, *Log Cabin in America*, p. 238; Roberts, *Some Comments on Log Construction*, p. 3.
29. Willis, "Log Houses in Southwest Virginia," p. 42.
30. McDonough, *Garden Sass*, p. 42.
31. Ibid.
32. Willis, "Log Houses in Southwest Virginia," p. 44.
33. Hutslar, "Log Architecture of Ohio," p. 254.
34. Llano County No. 2 file, TLCR.
35. Attebury, "Log Construction in the Sawtooth Valley," p. 40.
36. Glassie, "Types of the Southern Mountain Cabin," p. 343.
37. Eugene M. Wilson, "Some Similarities between American and European Folk Houses," *Pioneer America* 3, no. 2 (July 1971): 10; Roberts, "Folk Architecture in Context," p. 40; Glassie, "Types of the Southern Mountain Cabin," p. 362; Roberts, *Some Comments on Log Construction*, p. 4.
38. Wacker and Trindell, "The Log House in New Jersey," pp. 258, 265; Roberts, "Folk Architecture in Context," p. 41; Roberts, *Some Comments on Log Construction*, p. 4.
39. Robert C. Bucher, "The Continental Log House," *Pennsylvania Folklife* 12, no. 4 (Summer 1962): 14–19; Wacker and Trindell, "Log House in New Jersey," p. 265.
40. Glassie, "Types of the Southern Mountain Cabin," p. 343.
41. Andrew Davis, "Folk Life in Early Texas: The Autobiography of Andrew Davis," *Southwestern Historical Quarterly* 43 (1939–40): 167.
42. McDonough, *Garden Sass*, p. 53.
43. Bates, *History and Reminiscences of Denton County*, p. 300; Billingsley, "A Trip to Texas," pp. 203–204; Smithwick, *Evolution of a State*, p. 126; Johnston and Waterman, *Early Architecture of North Carolina*, p. 4.
44. Hathaway, *Travels in the Two Hemispheres*, 1:287; Strickland, "History of Fannin County," p. 281.
45. Banta and Caldwell, *Twenty-Seven Years on the Texas Frontier*, p. 5.
46. Strong, "Reminiscences."
47. William R. Thomas, *Life among the Hills and Mountains of Kentucky*, p. 5.
48. For sources on the cat chimney in Texas, see Cecil V. Overstreet, "Chimney Dobbin' in the Big Thicket," in *Some Still Do*, pp. 77–87; A. R. Fillingim, "Chimney Daubing," in *Buzzard Eggs and Other Big Thicket Recollections*, ed. Robert Pierce and W. G. Regier, pp. 15–16. See also Abernethy, *Tales from the Big Thicket*, p. 61; McDonough, *Garden Sass*, pp. 50–51.
49. Glassie, *Pattern in the Material Folk Culture*, p. 113; Weslager, *Log Cabin in America*, p. 231.
50. Hutslar, "Log Architecture of Ohio," p. 198; Weslager, *Log Cabin in America*, p. 198.
51. Wells, "Earliest Log Cabins of Natchitoches," p. 119.
52. Stuck, "Log Houses in Northwest Louisiana," pp. 229, 230; Zelinsky, "Log House in Georgia," p. 180; Glassie, *Pattern in the Material Folk Culture*, p. 113; McDonough, *Garden Sass*, p. 48.
53. Traylor Russell, ed., *History of Titus County, Texas*, p. 148; Abernethy, *Tales from the Big Thicket*, p. 61.

54. See, for example, Tyler Co. No. 2, located at Heritage Garden Village at Woodville.
55. Erath, "Memoirs of Major George Bernard Erath," pp. 223–224.
56. Russell, *History of Titus County*, p. 148.
57. Evans, "East Texas House," p. 3; Overstreet, "Chimney Dobbin' in the Big Thicket," p. 80.
58. Hunter, *Trail Drivers of Texas*, pp. 792–793.
59. D. Port Smythe, "D. Port Smythe's Journey across Early Texas," *Texas Geographic Magazine* 6 (Fall 1942): 4; Erath, "Memoirs of Major George Bernard Erath," p. 223; Bollaert, *William Bollaert's Texas*, p. 184.
60. Hathaway, *Travels in the Two Hemispheres*, 1:287.
61. Banta and Caldwell, *Twenty-Seven Years on the Texas Frontier*, p. 5; Bates, *History and Reminiscences of Denton County*, p. 302.
62. Glassie, "Types of the Southern Mountain Cabin," pp. 343, 346–347; McDonough, *Garden Sass*, pp. 50–51.
63. McDonough, *Garden Sass*, p. 48.
64. Edna Scofield, "The Evolution and Development of Tennessee Houses," *Journal of the Tennessee Academy of Science* 11 (1936): 239; Glassie, "Central Chimney Continental Log House," p. 36; Johnston and Waterman, *Early Architecture of North Carolina*, p. 13; Glassie, "Types of the Southern Mountain Cabin," pp. 343, 346.
65. Evans, "East Texas House," p. 3.
66. Roberts, "Folk Architecture in Context," pp. 39–41.
67. *Visit to Texas*, p. 31.
68. William E. Sawyer, ed., "A Young Man Comes to Texas in 1852," *Texana* 7 (1969): 33.

6. Log Dwelling Types & Floorplans

1. *Texas in 1837*, p. 74. See also Glassie, "Appalachian Log Cabin," pp. 8–9.
2. Billingsley, "A Trip to Texas," pp. 203–204.
3. Marryat, *Narrative of the Travels*, 3:1.
4. William A. McClintock, "Journal of a Trip through Texas and Northern Mexico in 1846–1847," *Southwestern Historical Quarterly* 34 (1930–31): 24; Smithwick, *Evolution of a State*, p. 14.
5. Mary A. Nunley, "The Interesting Story of a Pioneer Mother," *Frontier Times* 4, no. 11 (August 1927): 17.
6. Strong, "Reminiscences."
7. Tyler and Murphy, *Slave Narratives of Texas*, pp. 34, 45.
8. *Texas in 1837*, p. 74; Erath, "Memoirs of Major George Bernard Erath," p. 223.
9. Wilson, "Single Pen Log House in the South," pp. 21–28; Johnston and Waterman, *Early Architecture of North Carolina*, pp. 5, 8; Meyer, "Diffusion of Upland South Folk Housing," p. 60; Hutslar, "Log Architecture of Ohio," p. 242; Glassie, "Types of the Southern Mountain Cabin," pp. 349–355; Warren E. Roberts, "Field Work in DuBois County, Indiana," *Echoes of History* 6, no. 1 (January 1976): 12–14.
10. Bucher, "Continental Log House," pp. 14–19; Glassie, "Central Chimney Continental Log House," pp. 32–39.
11. Glassie, "Types of the Southern Mountain Cabin," pp. 353–355.
12. Wells, "Earliest Log Cabins of Natchitoches," p. 120.
13. Glassie, "Types of the Southern Mountain Cabin," pp. 349–353.
14. Ibid., p. 362; Glassie, "Appalachian Log Cabin," pp. 7–8.
15. Wilson, "Some Similarities between American and European Folk Houses," p. 9.

16. Ibid., p. 10.
17. Glassie, "Types of the Southern Mountain Cabin," pp. 353–355.
18. Gritzner, "Log Housing in New Mexico," p. 61.
19. Pillsbury and Kardos, *A Field Guide to the Folk Architecture*, p. 78; Eugene M. Wilson, "Form Changes in Folk Houses," in *Man and Cultural Heritage*, ed. Bob F. Perkins, p. 71.
20. Glassie, "Types of the Southern Mountain Cabin," p. 349.
21. Norbert F. Riedl et al., *A Survey of Traditional Architecture and Related Material Folk Culture Patterns in the Normandy Reservoir, Coffee County, Tennessee*, pp. 81–86; Roberts, "Waggoner House," pp. 28–29; Zelinsky, "Log House in Georgia," p. 175; Scofield, "Evolution and Development of Tennessee Houses," pp. 236–237; Glassie, *Pattern in the Material Folk Culture*, pp. 78–79, 82–83.
22. Fred and Hettie Worley, "The Mogford Homestead: Texas Historical Architecture," *Texas Architect* 20, no. 4 (April 1970): 18–21.
23. Johnston and Waterman, *Early Architecture of North Carolina*, p. 20; Wilson, "Form Changes in Folk Houses," p. 67.
24. In Texas vernacular a "saddlebag" is a one-and-a-half-story open-passage (dogtrot) house.
25. Glassie, "Appalachian Log Cabin," p. 12; Wilson, "Form Changes in Folk Houses," p. 71; Johnston and Waterman, *Early Architecture of North Carolina*, p. 7.
26. Vlach, "The 'Canada Homestead,'" pp. 8–13; Richard H. Hulan, "Middle Tennessee and the Dogtrot House," *Pioneer America* 7, no. 2 (July 1975): 42; David Sutherland, "Folk Housing in the Woodburn Quadrangle," *Pioneer America* 4, no. 2 (July 1972): 22; Meyer, "Diffusion of Upland South Folk Housing," p. 60; Kniffen, "Folk Housing," p. 561; Johnston and Waterman, *Early Architecture of North Carolina*,. pp. 16, 20; Hutslar, "Log Architecture of Ohio," p. 243; Glassie, "Appalachian Log Cabin," p. 12.
27. Pillsbury and Kardos, *Field Guide to Folk Architecture*, p. 51.
28. For an example, see J. L. and L. J. Stambaugh, *A History of Collin County, Texas*, pp. 215–216.
29. Smithwick, *Evolution of a State*, p. 232.
30. Wacker and Trindell, "Log House in New Jersey," p. 259; Martin Wright, "The Antecedents of the Double-Pen House Type," *Annals, Association of American Geographers* 48 (1958): 109–117; Evans, "East Texas House," p. 2; McDonough, *Garden Sass*, p. 34; Kniffen, "Folk Housing," p. 561.
31. *Visit to Texas*, p. 31.
32. Data derived from TLCR.
33. Glassie, *Pattern in the Material Folk Culture*, p. 101; Zelinsky, "Log House in Georgia," p. 175.
34. Loren N. Horton, "Early Architecture in Dubuque," *Palimpsest* 55, no. 5 (September–October 1974): 133; Sutherland, "Woodburn Quadrangle," p. 22; Meyer, "Diffusion of Upland South Folk Housing," pp. 59–60; Hutslar, "Log Architecture of Ohio," pp. 203, 242–243; Weslager, *Log Cabin in America*, p. 303.
35. Evans, "East Texas House," p. 1–7.
36. Hathaway, *Travels in the Two Hemispheres*, 1:287; *Visit to Texas*, p. 40.
37. Smithwick, *Evolution of a State*, pp. 56–57; Alex W. Terrell, "The City of Austin from 1839 to 1865," *Texas State Historical Association Quarterly* 14 (1910): 117.
38. Files for Cooke and Polk counties, TLCR.
39. Smithwick, *Evolution of a State*, p. 232; John Barrow, *Facts Relating to North-Eastern Texas*, p. 48.
40. Cecil E. Burney, "Home of Heroes: The Story of the Holland House," *East Texas Historical*

Journal 9, no. 2 (1971): 109–128; Franks, *Seventy Years in Texas*, p. 17; Davis, "Folk Life in Early Texas," p. 167; files for Sabine Co. No. 1 and Walker Co. No. 5, TLCR.

41. Barrow, *Facts Relating to North-Eastern Texas*, p. 48.
42. Wilson, "Form Changes in Folk Houses," pp. 68–70.
43. For examples of first-generation dogtrot houses, see Cooke Co. No. 5 and Cooke Co. No. 15, TLCR; for examples of second-generation dogtrot houses, see Gonzales Co. No. 1 and Mason Co. No. 1, TLCR.
44. Wright, "Antecedents of the Double-Pen House," p. 113; Wilson, "Some Similarities between American and European Folk Houses," p. 11; Weslager, *Log Cabin in America*, pp. 73, 153.
45. Evans, "East Texas House," p. 2; Wacker and Trindell, "Log House in New Jersey," p. 259.
46. Glassie, "Appalachian Log Cabin," p. 12.
47. Ibid., p. 12; Wright, "Antecedents of the Double-Pen House," p. 111.
48. Wilson, "Some Similarities between American and European Folk Houses," pp. 8, 10.
49. Ibid., pp. 8–12; Glassie, *Pattern in the Material Folk Culture*, p. 96.
50. Hulan, "Middle Tennessee and the Dogtrot House," pp. 37, 42–44; Johnston and Waterman, *Early Architecture of North Carolina*, p. 7.
51. Glassie, *Pattern in the Material Folk Culture*, pp. 88–89; Hulan, "Middle Tennessee and the Dogtrot House," p. 37.
52. Cotten, "Log Cabins of the Parker County Region," pp. 99, 101; Glassie, "Appalachian Log Cabin," p. 11.
53. For an example of an ell separated by a passageway, see Palo Pinto Co. No. 4, TLCR.
54. *Preservation Plan and Program for Rice Family Log Home*, pp. 1–43; Houston Co. No. 1 and Red River Co. No. 2 files, TLCR.
55. Amos A. Parker, *Trip to the West and Texas*, p. 126.
56. Drury B. Alexander and Todd Webb, *Texas Homes of the Nineteenth Century*, pp. 22, 235; Hays Co. No. 1 file, TLCR.
57. Henry Glassie, *Folk Housing in Middle Virginia*, pp. 142–143.
58. Tyler and Murphy, *Slave Narratives of Texas*, p. 36.
59. Bell Co. No. 8 file, TLCR.
60. McDonough, *Garden Sass*, p. 42.
61. Glassie, "Appalachian Log Cabin," p. 9.
62. Warren E. Roberts, *Some Comments on Log Construction*, p. 4; Glassie, "Types of the Southern Mountain Cabin," p. 362; Wacker and Trindell, "Log House in New Jersey," p. 265.
63. Glassie, "Appalachian Log Cabin," p. 9; Glassie, "Central Chimney Continental Log House," pp. 35, 38.
64. For an example of a full two-story basic double-pen house, see Grimes Co. No. 8 file, TLCR.
65. Kniffen, "Folk Housing," pp. 553–555.
66. Milam Co. No. 1 file, TLCR.
67. Wilson, "Single Pen Log House in the South," p. 26.
68. For an example of a log shed room, see Palo Pinto Co. No. 8 file, TLCR; for an example of a stone shed room, see Mason Co. No. 1 file, TLCR. German stone shed rooms also occur in Pennsylvania; see Henry C. Mercer, "The Origin of Log Houses in the United States," *Old-Time New England* 18, no. 1 (July 1927): 16, 18.
69. Glassie, "Types of the Southern Mountain Cabin," pp. 348–349.
70. Ibid., p. 349; Wilson, "Single Pen Log House in the South," p. 26.
71. Bucher, "Continental Log House," pp. 14–19; Vlach, "The 'Canada Homestead,'" p. 13.
72. See, for example, Cooke Co. No. 2 file, TLCR.

73. Banta and Caldwell, *Twenty-Seven Years on the Texas Frontier*, p. 4.
74. Cotten, "Log Cabins of the Parker County Region," p. 98.
75. Smithwick, *Evolution of a State*, p. 231.
76. *Visit to Texas*, p. 31.
77. For a windowless example, see Tarrant Co. No. 2 file, TLCR.
78. Banta and Caldwell, *Twenty-Seven Years on the Texas Frontier*, p. 4.
79. Ikie Gray Patteson, *Loose Leaves*, p. 39.
80. Roberts, *Some Comments on Log Construction*, p. 4; Evans, "East Texas House," p. 4.
81. Davis, "Folk Life in Early Texas," p. 167; Evans, "East Texas House," p. 4; Patteson, *Loose Leaves*, p. 39; McDonough, *Garden Sass*, p. 41; Ward, "Log Cabin in Texas History," p. 29.
82. *Visit to Texas*, p. 31.

7. Log Public Buildings

1. *Texas in 1837*, p. 24.
2. Adolphus Sterne, *Hurrah for Texas!* p. 227; Marryat, *Narrative of the Travels*, 3:6; Willard B. Robinson and Todd Webb, *Texas Public Buildings of the Nineteenth Century*, pp. 21, 30; Jordan, "Log Construction in the East Cross Timbers," p. 118; Weldon Hart, "Old Cora and the Comanche Courthouse," *Texas Star*, May 7, 1972, p. 4; Hattie J. Roach, *The Hills of Cherokee*, pp. 40–41; Graham Landrum and Allan Smith, *Grayson County*, p. 20; Sawyer, "A Young Man Comes to Texas," p. 25.
3. "Fannin County's First Court House," *Frontier Times* 1, no. 11 (August 1924): 15; *A Memorial and Biographical History of Ellis County, Texas*, p. 78; W. S. Mills, *History of Van Zandt County*, p. 17; McConnell, *West Texas Frontier*, pp. 118, 124.
4. Ingmire, *Archives and Pioneers of Hunt County*, 1:18.
5. Strickland, "History of Fannin County," p. 281.
6. Robinson and Webb, *Texas Public Buildings*, p. 21; Hart, "Old Cora and the Comanche Courthouse," p. 4.
7. McConnell, *West Texas Frontier*, p. 124; *Memorial and Biographical History of Ellis County*, p. 78.
8. McConnell, *West Texas Frontier*, p. 124; Strong, "Reminiscences."
9. Paul Goeldner, "1846 Specifications for Building a Log Courthouse in Maryville, Missouri," *Bulletin, Association for Preservation Technology* 5, no. 1 (1973): 75; William H. Gaines, Jr., "Courthouses of Bedford and Charlotte Counties," *Virginia Cavalcade* 21, no. 1 (Summer 1971): 9; Hutslar, "Log Architecture of Ohio," p. 212.
10. M. K. Kellogg, *M. K. Kellogg's Texas Journal, 1872*, p. 82; Robinson and Webb, *Texas Public Buildings*, p. 21; Tyler and Murphy, *Slave Narratives of Texas*, p. 29.
11. Robinson and Webb, *Texas Public Buildings*, p. 21.
12. "First Pokey Had Trap-Door Entry," *Denton Record-Chronicle*, February 3, 1957, sec. 3, p. 5.
13. Robinson and Webb, *Texas Public Buildings*, p. 21.
14. J. J. Faulk, *History of Henderson County, Texas*, p. 37.
15. Carrie J. Crouch, *Young County History and Biography*, p. 139; Gladys St. Clair, *A History of Hopkins County, Texas*, p. 16.
16. Faulk, *History of Henderson County*, p. 37; Robinson and Webb, *Texas Public Buildings*, p. 21.
17. Ibid.; Strickland, "History of Fannin County," p. 67.
18. Free population schedules, U.S. Census, Coryell Co., Texas, 1860; Webb and Carroll, *Handbook of Texas*, 1:344.

19. Robinson and Webb, *Texas Public Buildings*, p. 21.
20. Johnston and Waterman, *Early Architecture of North Carolina*, p. 5; Wells, "Earliest Log Cabins of Natchitoches," p. 118.
21. Barrow, *Facts Relating to North-Eastern Texas*, p. 62.
22. Erath, "Memoirs of Major George Bernard Erath," p. 224; Patteson, *Loose Leaves*, p. 61.
23. Thomas, *Life among the Hills and Mountains of Kentucky*, p. 123; for examples of early log churches in New Sweden, see Weslager, *Log Cabin in America*, p. 257.
24. Jordan, "Reflections on Log Cabins and Architectural Zoos," p. 7; Jordan, "Log Construction in the East Cross Timbers," p. 118; Bates, *History and Reminiscences of Denton County*, pp. 74–75, 404–405.
25. Terry G. Jordan, "The Traditional Southern Rural Chapel in Texas," *Ecumene* 8 (1976): 6–17.
26. For a surviving example in Alabama, see Wilson, "Single Pen Log House in the South," p. 23.
27. Rex Z. Howard and F. M. McCarty, *Texas Guidebook*, pp. 60–61.
28. Jordan, "Traditional Southern Rural Chapel," pp. 12–13.
29. Buxton, "Wooden Churches of Eastern Europe," p. 43.
30. Patteson, *History of Delta County*, p. 61; Erath, "Memoirs of Major George Bernard Erath," p. 224.
31. Cooke Co. No. 64 file, TLCR.
32. Palo Pinto Co. No. 18 file, TLCR.
33. Patteson, *History of Delta County*, p. 39.
34. Nunley, "Interesting Story of a Pioneer Mother," p. 19.
35. Smithwick, *Evolution of à State*, p. 231; Patteson, *History of Delta County*, p. 39.
36. Marryat, *Narrative of the Travels*, 3:5.
37. Kathryn T. Carter, *Stagecoach Inns of Texas*, pp. 34–36, 60–62, 84, 91–93; Bates, *History and Reminiscences of Denton County*, p. 319.
38. Smithwick, *Evolution of a State*, p. 57.
39. *Visit to Texas*, p. 31.
40. W. Steinert, "W. Steinert's View of Texas in 1849," *Southwestern Historical Quarterly* 80 (1976–77): 73.
41. Edward Stiff, *The Texan Emigrant*, p. 114.
42. Navarro Co. No. 3 and No. 6 files, TLCR.
43. *Texas in 1837*, p. 20.
44. Walker Co. No. 3 file, TLCR.
45. Runnels Co. No. 1 file, TLCR.
46. Mercer, "Origin of Log Houses in the United States," pp. 7–8; Weslager, *Log Cabin in America*, pp. 257, 265.
47. J. De Cordova, *Texas*, p. 287.
48. Strickland, "History of Fannin County," p. 270.
49. Banta and Caldwell, *Twenty-Seven Years on the Texas Frontier*, p. 4.
50. "Blockhouse," *Mason County Historical Book*, p. 310.
51. Stiff, *Texan Emigrant*, p. 108.
52. Smithwick, *Evolution of a State*, p. 296.
53. Webb and Carroll, *Handbook of Texas*, 1:626, 628, 629.
54. Roy E. Graham, "Federal Fort Architecture in Texas during the Nineteenth Century," *Southwestern Historical Quarterly* 74 (1970–71): 182–183.

8. Rural Log Outbuildings

1. Bollaert, *William Bollaert's Texas*, p. 117.
2. Glassie, "Old Barns of Appalachia," p. 21.
3. Pillsbury and Kardos, *Field Guide to the Folk Architecture*, p. 58; Kniffen, "Folk Housing," p. 563.
4. Jordan, "Log Construction in the East Cross Timbers," p. 118; Kniffen, "Folk Housing," p. 564. See also Polk Co. No. 8 and No. 9, Panola Co. No. 2 files, TLCR.
5. Pillsbury and Kardos, *Field Guide to the Folk Architecture*, p. 58. See also Panola Co. No. 2 and Polk Co. No. 9 files, TLCR.
6. Glassie, "Old Barns of Appalachia," p. 22; Pillsbury and Kardos, *Field Guide to Folk Architecture*, p. 58; Eric Sloane, *An Age of Barns*, pp. 24, 77; Meyer, "Diffusion of Upland South Folk Housing," p. 61.
7. Even as far east as Appalachia, some barns are carelessly built; see Glassie, "Old Barns of Appalachia," pp. 21–22.
8. Bollaert, *William Bollaert's Texas*, p. 117.
9. Smithwick, *Evolution of a State*, p. 240.
10. Strickland, "History of Fannin County," p. 63.
11. For sources on the linear double-crib barn, see Henry Glassie, "The Double Crib Barn in South-Central Pennsylvania," *Pioneer America* 1, no. 1 (January 1969): 9–16; 1, no. 2 (July 1969): 40–45; 2, no. 1 (January 1970): 47–52; 2, no. 2 (July 1970): 23–34; Pillsbury and Kardos, *Field Guide to Folk Architecture*, pp. 58, 71–72; Glassie, "Old Barns of Appalachia," pp. 28–29; Sloane, *An Age of Barns*, pp. 24, 27; Jordan, "Log Construction in the East Cross Timbers," p. 118; Eric Arthur and Dudley Witney, *The Barn*, pp. 65, 70–71.
12. Kniffen, "Folk Housing," p. 563.
13. Glassie, *Pattern in the Material Folk Culture*, p. 89; Glassie, "Old Barns of Appalachia," p. 28.
14. Glassie, "Old Barns of Appalachia," p. 30.
15. Roberts, "Field Work in DuBois County, Indiana," p. 13; Hutslar, "Log Architecture of Ohio," pp. 220, 224; Joe K. Kindig and Frank J. Schmidt, *Architecture in York County*, pp. 17–18; McDonough, *Garden Sass*, p. 90; Pillsbury and Kardos, *Field Guide to Folk Architecture*, p. 58; Glassie, "Old Barns of Appalachia," pp. 28–29; Glassie, *Pattern in the Material Folk Culture*, p. 89.
16. Pillsbury and Kardos, *Field Guide to Folk Architecture*, pp. 71–72; Glassie, "Old Barns of Appalachia," pp. 28–29.
17. See Newton Co. No. 9 file, TLCR.
18. See Comal Co. No. 4 and No. 6 files, TLCR.
19. Glassie, "Old Barns of Appalachia," pp. 28–29; Sloane, *An Age of Barns*, p. 26.
20. Kniffen, "Folk Housing," pp. 564–566.
21. See San Saba Co. No. 3 and Denton Co. No. 40 files, TLCR.
22. "Stagecoach Inn, Winedale," *Texas Architect* 16, no. 6 (June 1966): 13; Fayette Co. No. 10 file, TLCR.
23. Glassie, "Old Barns of Appalachia," p. 29; Kniffen, "Folk Housing," p. 565.
24. Glassie, "Old Barns of Appalachia," p. 29.
25. See the following files in TLCR; Comanche Co. No. 2, Cooke Co. Nos. 35 and 41, Denton Co. Nos. 31 and 36, Limestone Co. No. 2, Polk Co. No. 11B, Red River Co. No. 2B, and Titus Co. No. 4A.
26. Comanche Co. No. 2 file, TLCR.

27. Johnston and Waterman, *Early Architecture of North Carolina*, p. 10; Hutslar, "Log Architecture of Ohio," p. 225; McDonough, *Garden Sass*, pp. 67–68; Glassie, "Old Barns of Appalachia," p. 22.
28. Henry Glassie, "The Smaller Outbuildings of the Southern Mountains," *Mountain Life and Work* 40, no. 1 (Spring 1964): 23.

9. Texas Log Culture Regions

1. See, for example, Meinig, *Imperial Texas*, pp. 91–109.
2. On the log architecture of East Texas, see Evans, "East Texas House," pp. 1–7; Charlotte Phelan, "Log Cabins in Grimes County," *Houston Post*, December 1, 1963; Burney, "Home of Heroes," pp. 109–128; and Rebecca F. Fitch, "The Use of Native Materials in the Ante Bellum Buildings of Harrison County, Texas," M.A. thesis.
3. On the log architecture of Central and North Texas, see Conger, *Historic Log Cabins of McLennan County*; Cotten, "Log Cabins of the Parker County Region," pp. 99–102; Jordan, "Log Construction in the East Cross Timbers," pp. 107–124; and Terry G. Jordan, "The Texan Appalachia," *Annals, Association of American Geographers* 60 (1970): 409–427.
4. On the log architecture of the German Hill Country, see Worley, "The Mogford Homestead," pp. 18–21; J. Roy White and Joe B. Frantz, *Limestone and Log*; Hubert G. H. Wilhelm, "German Settlement and Folk Building Practices in the Hill Country of Texas," *Pioneer America* 3, no. 2 (July 1971): 15–24; Hubert G. H. Wilhelm, "Organized German Settlement and Its Effects on the Frontier of South-Central Texas," Ph.D. dissertation; and Hanna, "Indigenous Architecture of Fredericksburg, Texas."
5. On the log architecture of Medina County, see Kilian Fehr, "Castroville and Medina County: Texas Historical Architecture," *Texas Architect* 19, no. 3 (March 1969): 18–23.
6. On the log architecture of West Texas, see Duncan G. Muckelroy, "Ranching History of the American West: Revitalized through the Preservation of Its Architecture," *Pioneer America* 6, no. 2 (July 1974): 34–42.

Glossary of
Log Construction Terms
Encountered in Texas

adze (or adz): a cutting tool with an arching blade at right angles to the handle, used in the shaping of logs.

Anglo western roof: a low-pitched roof supported by a ridgepole resting directly atop the highest logs in the gable walls.

basic double-pen house: formed by placing a second pen on the gable end opposite from the chimney gable of the first pen; sometimes called a "Cumberland house."

basic ell house: a triple-pen house formed by adding a pen directly behind one of the pens of a basic double-pen house.

basic "T" house: a triple-pen house formed by adding a pen centrally at the rear of a basic double-pen house.

bay: a compartment of about sixteen feet square that formed the typical living area in one end of the Medieval English house, hence a room about sixteen feet on a side.

block four-pen house: formed of four pens, one at each corner of a square floorplan, separated from one another by two intersecting halls or passages.

blockhouse: a fortified single-pen dwelling or garrison house, characterized by a cantilevered second story that projects to overhang the first story on two or all four sides.

box(ed) corner: the corner of a log pen with the projecting logs sawed off flush with the walls to form a neat, square corner.

boxed-in stairs: a stairway enclosed with board walls to separate it from the room.

butting pole: a pole that rests atop cantilevered logs from the gable walls and lies parallel to and out beyond the plates; helps hold roofing in place.

butt log: same as a butting pole.

cabin: a small crudely built log dwelling, consisting of logs left in the round, a dirt floor, and a stick-and-dirt chimney.

capping: shingles, shakes, or roof boards that project a foot or so beyond the ridgecrest of a roof, usually in the direction of the prevailing winds.

cat(ted) chimney: a mud-and-stick chimney constructed of a framework of poles and sticks covered with "cats," which are matlike, pliable strips made of clay mixed with moss, horsehair, grass, or straw.

central-chimney house: a double-pen house formed by placing two log pens together at their gable ends with a chimney and fireplace between them.

central-hall ell house: a triple-pen house formed by adding a pen directly behind one of the pens of a central-hall house.

central-hall house: a double-pen house formed by placing two pens gable to gable, separated by an enclosed hallway and covered by a single roof.

central-hall "T" house: a triple-pen house formed by adding a pen directly behind the hall of a central-hall house.

chimney gap. See *fireplace gap*.

chink: the open space left between the logs in a wall.

chinking: the substance used to fill the open spaces between logs.

continental log house: a Pennsylvania German house having one pen; subdivided by light partitions into three or four rooms; further characterized by a central chimney, off-center front door, story-and-a-half construction, and a cellar.

cook house: a kitchen built separate from the dwelling.

corner man: the carpenter who fashions the corner notching on the logs, particularly the final fitting which is performed while atop the wall.

crib: a log outbuilding; the name given to one log unit of an outbuilding, consisting of four log walls notched together at the corners.

Cumberland house: a basic double-pen house with two front doors, one in each pen; especially common in the Cumberland Plateau of Middle Tennessee.

diamond notch: a type of log corner notching characterized by a diamond-shaped tongue; does not occur in Texas.

dogrun house. See *dogtrot house*.

dogtrot ell house: a dogtrot house to which a third pen is added directly behind one of the two front pens, forming a triple-pen house with an L-shaped floorplan; the third pen has its own roof ridge at right angles to that of the main part of the house.

dogtrot house: a double-pen house formed by placing two pens gable to gable, separated by an open passageway and covered by a single roof.

dogtrot "I" house: a dogtrot house two full stories in height.

dogtrot "T" house: a dogtrot house to which a third pen is added directly behind the open passageway, forming a triple-pen house with a T-shaped floorplan; the third pen has its own roof ridge at right angles to that of the main part of the house.

double-crib barn: a barn consisting of two cribs arranged gable to gable and separated by an open runway.

double notch: a type of log corner notching fashioned by cutting a square-shaped depression near the end of the log, both top and bottom.

double-pen house: any log house consisting of two pens, such as the central-hall, central-chimney, and dogtrot types.

double saddle notch: a saddle notch involving notching of both the top and bottom of the log.

dovetail notch. See *full-dovetail notch* and *half-dovetail notch*.

dugout. See *semidugout*.

eave(s): the projecting lower edge of a roof, overhanging the nongabled walls.

ell: an addition to a house which forms an L-shaped floorplan.

false corner timbering: when the tiers of logs on adjacent walls are even (the same distance above the ground) instead of alternated, with no chinks, typically achieved by use of the half notch, cut so that the tongue of each log is exactly half the height of the log, in the manner of a lap joint.

fireplace gap: the opening cut in a log pen to permit construction of a fireplace.

foot adze: a long-handled adze, used in a manner similar to a hoe.

four-crib barn: formed of four cribs, one at each corner of a square floorplan, separated from one another by two intersecting runways.

foursquare. See *block four-pen house* and *four-crib barn*.

froe: an L-shaped cleaving tool with a handle at right angles to and at one end of the blade, used in the preparation of boards, puncheons, shakes, and shingles.

full-dovetail notch: a type of log corner notching, formed by cutting slopes (splays) in the end of the log, both top and bottom, in such a manner that a wider portion remains to the inside of the wall, in the manner of a common cabinetmaker's joint.

gable: the vertical, triangle-shaped end of a roof, reaching from the ridge of the roof down to the level of the eaves.

half-dovetail notch: a type of corner notching in which the top side of the end of the log is sloped down toward the outside of the joint, leaving the wider remaining portion to the inside of the wall.

half-log construction: when logs are split in half lengthwise prior to use, so that each timber in the wall is half-round.

half notch: a simplified version of the square notch, in which only one cube-shaped piece of wood is removed from the bottom of the end of the log.

hand adze: a short-handled adze.

hewn: a log that has been flattened off on the side, usually on all four sides to produce a square beam; see also *planked*.

hooded chimney: as used in folk vernacular, a gable-end chimney surrounded by a cantilevered projection of the roof.

house: when used to describe a log dwelling, implies a carefully constructed, hewn, floored structure with a brick or stone chimney, as contrasted to the hastily built, poorly crafted cabin.

"I" house: a full two-story double-pen house, with side-facing gables; a basic double-pen, dogtrot, central-hall, or central-chimney house with a full second story; thus two pens (or two pens and a hall) wide and one pen deep.

joists: beams reaching between the sill logs upon which the floorboards rest; joists for the attic or second story rest upon logs higher than the sill.

knee: a short slat of wood serving as a spacer between weight poles on a roof.

lap joint: the joining of two pieces of wood by cutting a cubic block of wood from the underside of the end of one piece; sometimes a block of equal size and shape was cut from the second piece of wood to provide a flush fit; lap joints can be used to join beams end to end, forming a long beam, or to join members at right angles to one another.

lathing: boards one or two inches thick and about four inches wide that are attached to the rafters and onto which the roofing material is placed.

linear basic triple-pen house: formed by placing three pens in a row, with no intervening halls.

linear dogtrot four-pen house: formed by adding a pen to each gable end of a dogtrot house.

linear dogtrot triple-pen house: formed by adding a pen to one gable end of a dogtrot house.

loft: a floored, unpartitioned space in an attic used for sleeping or storage; often occupies only part of the attic space, in which case the loft is completely open to the room below on one side; the loft usually has vertical walls only at each gable, the others being sloped roof; found generally in cabins and barns rather than houses; usually reached by a ladder.

Louisiana roof: consists of two unbroken slopes of about 40° extending over the entire house, with no break in profile for the porch and shed room; side-facing gables.

mitre-dovetail notch: the same as a half-dovetail notch.

overhanging dovetail: a dovetail-notched corner with the ends of the logs left projecting slightly beyond the corner.

pen: a log dwelling unit consisting of four walls notched together at the corners; generally forms one room but can be subdivided by partitions into two or more rooms.

pen chimney: one type of stick-and-dirt chimney; the firebox is built of short logs notched together and notched into the wall logs where the fireplace gap is cut.

pier: foundation pillar two feet or more in length which raises the structure considerably above ground level; made of wood or brick.

planked: a log hewn only on two sides, facing the inside and outside of the wall.

plate: the top log on a nongabled wall, just below the eaves, upon which the rafters rest.

pole rafter: a rafter left in the round, unhewn.

pole shack: another term to describe a small, crudely built low dwelling, consisting of logs left in the round, a dirt floor, and a mud-and-stick chimney; basically synonomous with "log cabin."

puncheon: a split log or log plank of about two to four feet in length used as floorboard in log houses, often resting loosely on the joists, occasionally pegged, more rarely resting directly on a bed of sand or dirt; containing one carefully smoothed face; doors and shutters can also be made of puncheons.

purlin: a roof support reaching from one gable to the other, parallel to the roof ridge, supporting the rafters or the roof boards.

quarter notch: same as the square notch.

rafter: a roof support reaching from the plate log on the eaves to the roof ridge.

rib pole: another name for a purlin.

ridgepole: a roof support running the length of the roof ridge from one gable peak to the other.

room on the porch: a small room, usually about eight feet square, situated at one end of a front porch, covered by the porch roof.

rough hewn: a slightly hewn log, with some of the natural rotundity of the log still exposed; generally hewn *after* the log wall has been erected.

runway: the open passageway in double-, triple-, and four-crib barns.

saddle notch: a type of log corner notching fashioned by hollowing out a saddle-shaped depression near the end of the log, on the top and/or the bottom of the log.

saddlebag house: a term variously used to mean (a) a central-chimney double-pen house or (b) a story-and-a-half dogtrot house.

score: to make numerous broadaxe cuts an inch or two deep in the rounded sides of a log preparatory to hewing; accomplished by striking the log at about a 45° angle at regular, closely spaced intervals; most hewn log walls retain the deeper parts of the score marks.

semidugout: a gable-entrance log dwelling built on a hillside and partially excavated into the slope; the log wall forms only a superstructure above the excavation.

semilunate notch: a type of log corner notching applied in half-round construction; the natural half-round shape is retained in the notch.

shake: an untapered roof board measuring about 12" to 15" wide, 2' to 3' long, and 1/2" to 1 1/2" thick.

shed room: an oblong room half the size of a pen, attached to the rear side of a pen and covered by a single-slope shed roof projecting from the rear eaves; less commonly positioned on a gable wall.

shingle: a roof board somewhat smaller than a shake and distinguished by tapered thickness.

side room: the same as a shed room.

siding: milled lumber nailed over the exterior of a log wall, concealing the logs.

sill: the lowest log on the front and back walls of a pen, resting directly on the foundation of the house.

single-crib barn: a barn consisting of only one log crib, sometimes flanked by shed rooms; has a front-facing gable.

single notch: a type of log corner notching similar to the double notch but differing in that only the top or bottom of each log is notched.

single-pen house: a log dwelling consisting of only one pen.

single saddle notch: a saddle notch with hollowed-out saddle depressions on only one side of the log, either the top or the bottom.

skid: an inclined plane consisting of two or more poles reaching from the ground to the top of a
 log wall under construction; used as a device to facilitate raising logs to the top of the
 wall.

sleepers: another term for joists, beams that support the floorboards.

splay: a slope or slant cut to form dovetail, "V," or diamond notches.

square notch: a type of log corner notching fashioned by removing small cube-shaped blocks of
 wood from both the top and bottom of the end of the log.

"T" house: a triple-pen house with a T-shaped floorplan.

transverse-crib barn: a barn consisting of two or three cribs on each side of a central runway; a
 gable normally faces the front.

triple-crib barn: a barn consisting of three log cribs arranged in a row, with or without intervening runways.

triple-pen house: consisting of three full-sized pens, with several different floorplans possible.

"turkey feather" roof: a shake roof weathered so that the shakes stick out at odd angles.

"V" notch: a type of log corner notching fashioned by making an inverted V shape in the top and
 bottom of the end of the log.

weight pole: lies atop the boards of a roof to hold them in place; parallel to ridgepole and at right
 angles to the rafters.

Bibliography

Unpublished Materials

Bates, W. B. Letter to Terry G. Jordan from Houston, Texas, dated October 10, 1973.

Connally, Ernest A. "The Ecclesiastical and Military Architecture of the Spanish Province of Texas." Ph.D. dissertation, Harvard University, Cambridge, Mass., 1955.

Fitch, Rebecca F. "The Use of Native Materials in the Ante Bellum Buildings of Harrison County, Texas." M.A. thesis, North Texas State University, Denton, 1952.

Gordon, Michael H. "The Upland Southern–Lowland Southern Culture Areas: A Field Study of Building Characteristics in Southern Virginia." M.A. thesis, Rutgers University, New Brunswick, N.J., 1968.

Gritzner, Charles F. "Spanish Log Construction in New Mexico." Ph.D. dissertation, Louisiana State University, Baton Rouge, 1969.

Hanna, Edith M. "The Indigenous Architecture of Fredericksburg, Texas." M.S. thesis, North Texas State University, Denton, 1942.

Hollingsworth, S. W., Jr. "Profiles of Big Thicket Architecture." Graduate research paper, North Texas State University, Denton, 1974. Geography 501 collection, Special Materials, Main Library.

Jordan, Terry G., comp. Texas Log Cabin Register. Collection of documents, sketches, and photographs. North Texas State University, Denton. Historical collection, Historical Building.

Lamb, Dinah Lee. "Selected Historic Domestic Architecture of San Antonio, Texas, Influenced by the Spanish-Mexican Culture." M.A. thesis, East Texas State University, Commerce, 1969.

Sharp, Lawrence R. "History of Panola County, Texas, to 1860." M.A. thesis, University of Texas, Austin, 1940.

Texas Historical Commission. Files of applications for state historical markers. Carrington-Covert House, headquarters of the Texas Historical Commission, Austin.

United States Census. Free population schedules, Texas, 1860. Texas State Archives, Austin.

Ward, James Randolph. "The Log Cabin in Texas History." M.A. thesis, Texas Christian University, Fort Worth, 1963.

Wilhelm, Hubert G. H. "Organized German Settlement and Its Effects on the Frontier of South-Central Texas." Ph.D. dissertation, Louisiana State University, Baton Rouge, 1968.

Williams, Mary L., Park Technician, Fort Davis National Historic Site. Letter to Terry G. Jordan from Fort Davis, Texas, dated March 24, 1973.

Wilson, Eugene M. "Folk Houses of Northern Alabama." Ph.D. dissertation, Louisiana State University, Baton Rouge, 1969.

Winberry, John J. "The Log House in Mexico: Distribution, Origin and Diffusion." Ph.D. dissertation, Louisiana State University, Baton Rouge, 1971.

Wright, Martin. "The Log Cabin in the South." M.A. thesis, Louisiana State University, Baton Rouge, 1950.
———. "Log Culture in Hill Louisiana." Ph.D. dissertation, Louisiana State University, Baton Rouge, 1956.

Published Materials

SOURCES DEALING SPECIFICALLY WITH LOG CONSTRUCTION

Aldrich, Chilson D. *The Real Log Cabin.* New York: Macmillan Co., 1928.
Attebury, Jennifer Eastman. "Log Construction in the Sawtooth Valley of Idaho." *Pioneer America* 8, no. 1 (January 1976): 36–46.
Boëthius, Gerda. *Studier i den nordiska Timmerbyggnadskonsten från vikingatiden till 1800-talet . . .* Stockholm: Fritzes Hovbokhandel i Distribution, 1927.
Brandt, Lawrence R., and Ned E. Braatz. "Log Buildings in Portage County, Wisconsin: Some Cultural Implications." *Pioneer America* 4, no. 1 (January 1972): 29–39.
Bucher, Robert C. "The Continental Log House." *Pennsylvania Folklife* 12, no. 4 (Summer 1962): 14–19.
Burney, Cecil E. "Home of Heroes: The Story of the Holland House." *East Texas Historical Journal* 9, no. 2 (October 1971): 109–128.
Conger, Roger N. *Historic Log Cabins of McLennan County, Texas.* Waco: Heritage Society of Waco, 1954.
Connor, Seymour V. "Log Cabins in Texas." *Southwestern Historical Quarterly* 53 (1949–50): 105–116.
Cotten, Fred R. "Log Cabins of the Parker County Region." *West Texas Historical Association Year Book* 29 (1953): 99–102.
Davidson, William H. *Pine Log and Greek Revival: Houses and People of Three Counties in Georgia and Alabama.* Chattahoochee Valley Historical Society Publication, no. 6. Alexander City, Ala.: Outlook, 1965.
Erixon, Sigurd. "Är den Nordamerikanska Timringstekniken Överförd från Sverige?" *Folk-Liv* 19 (1955–56): 56–68.
———. "The North-European Technique of Corner-Timbering." *Folk-Liv* 1 (1937): 13–60.
"Fannin County's First Court House." *Frontier Times* 1, no. 11 (August 1924): 15.
Glassie, Henry. "The Appalachian Log Cabin." *Mountain Life and Work* 39, no. 4 (Winter 1963): 5–14.
———. "A Central Chimney Continental Log House." *Pennsylvania Folklife* 18, no. 2 (Winter 1968–69): 32–39.
———. "The Double Crib Barn in South-Central Pennsylvania." *Pioneer America* 1, no. 1 (January 1969): 9–16; 1, no. 2 (July 1969): 40–45; 2, no. 1 (January 1970): 47–52; 2, no 2 (July 1970): 23–34.
———. "The Old Barns of Appalachia." *Mountain Life and Work* 40 [41], no. 2 (Summer 1965): 21–30 (see also cover illustration).
———. "The Smaller Outbuildings of the Southern Mountains." *Mountain Life and Work* 40, no. 1 (Spring 1964): 21–25.
———. "The Types of the Southern Mountain Cabin." In *The Study of American Folklore: An Introduction,* ed. Jan H. Brunvand, pp. 338–370. New York: W. W. Norton Co., 1968.

Goeldner, Paul. "1846 Specifications for Building a Log Courthouse in Maryville, Missouri." *Bulletin, Association for Preservation Technology* 5, no. 1 (1973): 75.

Gregory, George C. "Log Houses at Jamestown, 1607." *Virginia Magazine of History & Biography* 44, no. 4 (October 1936): 287–295.

Gritzner, Charles F. "Log Housing in New Mexico." *Pioneer America* 3, no. 2 (July 1971): 54–62.

Hale, Richard W., Jr. "The French Side of the 'Log Cabin Myth.'" *Proceedings of the Massachusetts Historical Society* 3d ser. 72 (October 1957–December 1960): 118–125.

"Historic Jackson Cabin." *Frontier Times* 4, no. 4 (January 1927): 30–31.

Hulan, Richard H. "Middle Tennessee and the Dogtrot House." *Pioneer America* 7, no. 2 (July 1975): 37–46.

Hunt, W. Ben. *Building a Log Cabin*. Milwaukee: Bruce Publishing Co., 1947.

Hutslar, Donald A. "The Log Architecture of Ohio." *Ohio History* 80 (1971): 172–271.

———. *Log Cabin Restoration: Guidelines for the Historical Society*. American Association for State and Local History, Technical Leaflet, no. 74. Reprinted in *History News* 29, no. 5 (May 1974).

Jordan, Terry G. "Log Construction in the East Cross Timbers of Texas." *Proceedings of the Pioneer America Society* 2 (1973): 107–124.

———. "Log Corner-Timbering in Texas." *Pioneer America* 8, no. 1 (January 1976): 8–18.

———. "Some Comments on Log Construction in Texas." In *The Architecture of the Texas Frontier: A Series of Papers Delivered at the 1972 Winedale Workshop*, pp. 59–76. N.p.: Texas State Historical Survey Committee, [1973].

Karni, Michael, and Robert Levin. "Finnish Log Buildings in Minnesota." *North West Architect*, May–June 1972, pp. 92–99.

Kelly, J. Frederick. "A Seventeenth-Century Connecticut Log House." *Old-Time New England* 31, no. 2 (October 1940): 28–40.

Kniffen, Fred B. "On Corner Timbering." *Pioneer America* 1, no. 1 (January 1969): 1–8.

Lewis, Thomas M. N., ed. "Cherokee Log Cabins." *Tennessee Archaeologist* 7, no. 2 (1951): 60–61.

McCamey, Maryan. "The Lost Art of Chinking: Refound!" *Mother Earth News*, no. 36 (November 1975), pp. 58–59.

Marshall, Howard W. "The 'Thousand Acres' Log House, Monroe County, Indiana." *Pioneer America* 3, no. 1 (January 1971): 48–56.

Mercer, Henry C. "The Origin of Log Houses in the United States." *Old-Time New England* 18, no. 1 (July 1927): 2–20; 18, no. 2 (October 1927): 51–63.

———. "The Origin of Log Houses in the United States." *Papers, Bucks County Historical Society* 5 (1926): 568–583.

Morey, Philip R., and Jerry L. Rogers. "El Capote Cabin: Biological History of Wood Used in an Early Texas Ranch House." *Texas Journal of Science* 25 (March 1974): 3–13.

Perrin, Richard W. E. "An Architectural Remnant of Old Muskego: John Bergen's Log House." *Wisconsin Magazine of History* 44, no. 1 (Autumn 1960): 12–14.

———. "Log Houses in Wisconsin." *Antiques* 89, no. 6 (June 1966): 867–871.

———. "Log Sauna and the Finnish Farmstead: Transplanted Architectural Idioms in Northern Wisconsin." *Wisconsin Magazine of History* 44 (1961): 284–286.

Phelps, Hermann. *Holzbaukunst: Der Blockbau*. Karlsruhe: Dr. Albert Bruder, 1942.

Preservation Plan and Program for Rice Family Log Home, Houston County, Texas. Austin: Texas Parks & Wildlife Department, Historic Sites & Restoration Branch, 1974.

Price, Beulah M. D'Olive. "The Dog-Trot Log Cabin: A Development in American Folk Architecture." *Mississippi Folklore Register* 4, no. 3 (1970): 84–89.

Roberts, Warren E. *Some Comments on Log Construction in Scandinavia and the United States*. Folklore Students Association, Indiana University, *Preprint Series*, 1, no. 3 (September 1973).

———. "The Waggoner Log House near Paragon, Indiana." In *Forms upon the Frontier: Folklife and Folk Arts in the United States*, ed. Austin and Alta Fife and Henry H. Glassie, pp. 28–30. Logan: Utah State University Press, 1969.

———. "The Whitaker-Waggoner Log House from Morgan County, Indiana." In *American Folklife*, ed. Don Yoder, pp. 185–207. Austin: University of Texas Press, 1976.

Roe, Frank G. "The Old Log House in Western Canada." *Alberta Historical Review* 6 (1958): 1–9.

Rustrum, Calvin. *The Wilderness Cabin*. New York: Macmillan Co., 1961.

Schilli, Hermann. *Das Schwarzwaldhaus*. Stuttgart: W. Kohlhammer, 1953.

Shurtleff, Harold R. *The Log Cabin Myth: A Study of the Early Dwellings of the English Colonists in North America*, ed. Samuel Eliot Morison. Cambridge, Mass.: Harvard University Press, 1939.

Stuck, Goodloe R. "Log Houses in Northwest Louisiana." *Louisiana Studies* 10 (1971): 225–237.

Sultz, Philip W. "Architectural Values of Early Frontier Log Structure." In *Forms upon the Frontier: Folklife and Folk Arts in the United States*, ed. Austin and Alta Fife and Henry H. Glassie, pp. 31–40. Logan: Utah State University Press, 1969.

United States Department of Agriculture, Forest Service. *Building with Logs*. Miscellaneous Publication, no. 579. Washington, D.C.: Government Printing Office, 1957.

Vlach, John M. "The 'Canada Homestead': A Saddlebag Log House in Monroe County, Indiana." *Pioneer America* 4, no. 2 (July 1972): 8–17.

Wacker, Peter O., and Roger T. Trindell. "The Log House in New Jersey: Origins and Diffusion." *Keystone Folklore Quarterly* 13 (1968): 248–268.

Wells, Carol. "Earliest Log Cabins of Natchitoches." *North Louisiana Historical Association Journal*, Spring 1975, pp. 117–122.

Weslager, C. A. *The Excavation of a Colonial Log Cabin near Wilmington, Delaware. Bulletin, Archeological Society of Delaware* 16, no. 1 (April 1954).

———. *The Log Cabin in America from Pioneer Days to the Present*. New Brunswick, N.J.: Rutgers University Press, 1969.

———. "Log Houses in Maryland during the 17th Century." *Quarterly Bulletin, Archaeological Society of Virginia* 9, no. 2 (1954): 2–8.

———. "Log Houses in Pennsylvania during the Seventeenth Century." *Pennsylvania History* 22 (July 1955): 256–266.

———. "Log Structures in New Sweden during the Seventeenth Century." *Delaware History* 5 (September 1952): 77–95.

Willis, Stanley. "Log Houses in Southwest Virginia: Tools Used in Their Construction." *Virginia Cavalcade* 21, no. 4 (Spring 1972): 36–47.

Wilson, Eugene M. "The Single Pen Log House in the South." *Pioneer America* 2, no. 1 (January 1970): 21–28.

Winberry, John J. "The Log House in Mexico." *Annals, Association of American Geographers* 64 (1974): 54–69.

Worley, Fred, and Hettie Worley. "The Mogford Homestead: Texas Historical Architecture." *Texas Architect* 20, no. 4 (April 1970): 18–21.

Wright, Martin. "The Antecedents of the Double-Pen House Type." *Annals, Association of American Geographers* 48 (1958): 109–117.

Zelinsky, Wilbur. "The Log House in Georgia." *Geographical Review* 43 (1953): 173–193.

GENERAL SOURCES

Abernethy, Francis E., ed. *Tales from the Big Thicket*. Austin: University of Texas Press, 1966.

Alexander, Drury B., and Todd Webb. *Texas Homes of the Nineteenth Century*. Austin: University of Texas Press, 1966.

Arneson, Axel. "Norwegian Settlements in Texas." *Southwestern Historical Quarterly* 45 (1941–42): 125–135.

Arthur, Eric, and Dudley Witney. *The Barn: A Vanishing Landmark in North America*. Toronto: McClelland & Stewart, 1972.

Banta, William, and J. W. Caldwell, Jr. *Twenty-Seven Years on the Texas Frontier*. Council Hill, Okla: L. G. Park, 1933 [originally published 1893].

Barker, Eugene C., ed. *The Austin Papers*. 3 vols. Vol. 1, *Annual Report of the American Historical Association*, 1919; Vol. 2, ibid., 1922. Washington, D.C.: Government Printing Office, 1924, 1928. Vol. 3, Austin: University of Texas, [ca. 1926].

Barrow, John. *Facts Relating to North-Eastern Texas, Condensed from Notes Made during a Tour . . .* London: Simpkin, Marshall & Co., 1849.

Bates, E. F. *History and Reminiscences of Denton County*. Denton: McNitzky Printing Co., 1918.

Biesele, Rudolph L. *The History of the German Settlements in Texas 1831–1861*. Austin: Von Boeckmann-Jones, 1930.

Biles, Roberta F. "The Frame House Era in Northwest Texas." *West Texas Historical Association Year Book* 46 (1970): 167–183.

Billingsley, John B. "A Trip to Texas." Ed. Robert L. and Pauline Jones. *Texana* 7 (1969): 201–219.

Blasig, Anne. *The Wends of Texas*. San Antonio: Naylor Co., 1954.

"Blockhouse." In *Mason County Historical Book*, pp. 310–311. Mason, Tex.: Mason County Historical Commission and Mason County Historical Society, 1976.

Bollaert, William. *William Bollaert's Texas*. Ed. W. Eugene Hollon and Ruth Lapham Butler. Norman: University of Oklahoma Press, 1956.

Bounds, John H. "The Alabama-Coushatta Indians of Texas." *Journal of Geography* 70 (1971): 175–182.

Bracken, Dorothy K., and Maurine W. Redway. *Early Texas Homes*. Dallas: S.M.U. Press, 1956.

Buxton, David. "Wooden Churches of Eastern Europe." *Architectural Review* 157, no. 935 (January 1975): 41–54.

Bywaters, Jerry. "More about Southwestern Architecture." *Southwest Review* 18, no. 3 (April 1933): 234–264.

Campbell, Harry H. *The Early History of Motley County*. San Antonio: Naylor Co., 1958.

Carter, Kathryn T. *Stagecoach Inns of Texas*. Waco: Texian Press, [ca. 1972].

Chrisman, Brutus C. *Early Days in Callahan County*. 2d ed. Abilene, Tex.: Abilene Printing & Stationery Co., 1972.

Clark, Anne; Carolyn Allen; and Jim Alvis. *Historic Homes of San Augustine*. Austin: Encino Press and San Augustine Historical Society, 1972.

Clopper, J. C. "J. C. Clopper's Journal and Book of Memoranda for 1828." *Texas State Historical Association Quarterly* 13 (1909–10): 44–80.

Connally, Ernest A. "Architecture at the End of the South: Central Texas." *Journal of the Society of Architectural Historians* 11, no. 4 (December 1952): 8–12.

———. "Texas Architecture." *Historic Preservation* 16, no. 6 (November–December 1964): 220–228.

Cox, C. C. "Reminiscences of C. C. Cox." *Texas State Historical Association Quarterly* 6 (1902–03): 113–138, 204–235.

Crouch, Carrie J. *Young County History and Biography*. Dallas: Dealey and Lowe, 1937.

Davis, Andrew. "Folk Life in Early Texas: The Autobiography of Andrew Davis." Ed. R. L. Jones. *Southwestern Historical Quarterly* 43 (1939–40): 158–175, 323–341.

De Cordova, J. *Texas: Her Resources and Her Public Men . . .* Philadelphia: E. Crozet, 1858.

Deffontaines, Pierre. *L'Homme et la Forêt*. Paris: Gallimard, 1933.

Demek, Jaromin, and Miroslav Strida. *Geography of Czechoslovakia*. Prague: Academia, 1971.

Dewees, William B. *Letters from an Early Settler of Texas*. Comp. Cara Cardelle [pseud.] Louisville: Morton & Griswold, 1852; Louisville: Hull & Brother, 1854.

DeWitt, Roscoe. "After Indigenous Architecture, What?" *Southwest Review* 16, no. 3 (April 1931): 314–324.

Eastman, Seth. *A Seth Eastman Sketchbook, 1848–1849*. Austin: University of Texas Press, 1961.

Erath, George B. "Memoirs of Major George Bernard Erath." Ed. Lucy A. Erath. *Southwestern Historical Quarterly* 26 (1923): 207–233, 255–280.

Eubank, Mary James. "A Journal of Our Trip to Texas, Oct. 6, 1853." Ed. W. C. Nunn. *Texana* 10 (1972): 30–44.

Evans, E. Estyn. "The Ulster Farmhouse." *Ulster Folklife* 1 (1955): 27–31.

Evans, Elliot A. P. "The East Texas House." *Journal of the Society of Architectural Historians* 11, no. 4 (December 1952): 1–7.

———. "The Old Homes of Rusk County." *Humble Way* 6, no. 2 (July–August 1950): 83–91, 102.

Faulk, J. J. *History of Henderson County, Texas*. Athens, Tex.: Athens Printing Co., 1929.

Fehr, Kilian. "Castroville and Medina County: Texas Historical Architecture." *Texas Architect* 19, no. 3 (March 1969): 18–23.

Fillingim, A. R. "Chimney Daubing." In *Buzzard Eggs and Other Big Thicket Recollections*, ed. Robert Pierce and W. G. Regier, pp. 15–16. N.p.: Mayhaw Press, 1973.

Finley, Robert, and E. M. Scott. "A Great Lakes-to-Gulf Profile of Dispersed Dwelling Types." *Geographical Review* 30 (1940): 412–419.

Franks, J. M. *Seventy Years in Texas*. Gatesville, Tex., 1924.

Gage, Duane. *Scenes from the Past: A Mid-Cities Album*. N.p.: Duane Gage, printed by X Press, 1975.

Gaines, William H., Jr. "Courthouses of Bedford and Charlotte Counties." *Virginia Cavalcade* 21, no. 1 (Summer 1971): 4–13.

Glassie, Henry. "Eighteenth-Century Cultural Process in Delaware Valley Folk Building." In *Winterthur Portfolio*, 7, pp. 29–57. Charlottesville: University of Virginia Press, 1972.

———. *Folk Housing in Middle Virginia: Structural Analysis of Historic Artifacts*. Knoxville: University of Tennessee Press, 1975.

———. *Pattern in the Material Folk Culture of the Eastern United States*. University of Pennsylvania Monographs in Folklore and Folklife, no. 1. Philadelphia: University of Pennsylvania Press, 1968.

Graham, Roy E. "Federal Fort Architecture in Texas during the Nineteenth Century." *Southwestern Historical Quarterly* 74 (1970–71): 165–188.

Gray, Wm. F. *From Virginia to Texas, 1835, Diary of Col. Wm. F. Gray . . .* Ed. A. C. Gray. Houston: Gray, Dillaye & Co., 1909.

Gschwend, Max. "Bäuerliche Haus- und Hofformen" and "Bäuerlicher Hausbau." In *Atlas der Schweiz . . .*, plates 36, 36a, 37. Wabern-Bern: Verlag der Eidgenössischen Landestopographie, 1965–1966.

———. *Schwyzer Bauernhäuser*. Bern: Paul Haupt, 1957.

Hall, Thelma. "Swisher County." In *The Handbook of Texas*, ed. Walter Prescott Webb and H. Bailey Carroll, 2:700. Austin: Texas State Historical Association, 1952.

Halsell, H. H. *Cowboys and Cattleland*. Nashville, Tenn.: Parthenon Press, n.d.

Harris, Mrs. Dilue. "Reminiscences of Mrs. Dilue Harris." *Texas State Historical Association Quarterly* 4 (1900–01): 85–127, 155–189; 7 (1903–04): 214–222.

Hart, John F., and Eugene Mather. "The Character of Tobacco Barns and Their Role in the Tobacco Economy of the United States." *Annals, Association of American Geographers* 51 (1961): 274–293.

Hathaway, Gilbert. *Travels in the Two Hemispheres . . .* 2 vols. 2d ed. Detroit: Doughty, Straw & Co. and Raymond & Selleck, 1858.

Heimsath, Clovis. *Pioneer Texas Buildings*. Austin: University of Texas Press, 1968.

Holland, Ellen B. *Gay as a Grig: Memories of a North Texas Girlhood*. Austin: University of Texas Press, 1963.

Holland, G. A. *History of Parker County and the Double Log Cabin*. Weatherford, Tex.: Herald Publishing Co., 1937.

Holley, Mary Austin. *Texas*. Lexington, Ky.: J. Clarke & Co., 1836.

Horton, Loren N. "Early Architecture in Dubuque." *Palimpsest* 55, no. 5 (September–October 1974): 130–151.

Howard, Rex Z., and F. M. McCarty. *Texas Guidebook*. 5th ed. Amarillo: F. M. McCarty Co., 1970.

Hunter, J. Marvin. *The Trail Drivers of Texas*. Nashville: Cokesbury Press, 1925.

Ingmire, Frances Terry, ed. & comp. *Archives and Pioneers of Hunt County, Texas*. Vol. 1. N.p., 1975.

Jackson, Ralph S. *Home on the Double Bayou: Memories of an East Texas Ranch*. Austin: University of Texas Press, 1961.

Jeffries, Charles. "Early Texas Architecture." *Bunker's Monthly* 1, no. 6 (June 1928): 905–915.

Jenkins, John H. *Recollections of Early Texas*. Ed. John H. Jenkins III. Austin: University of Texas Press, 1958.

Johnston, Frances B., and Thomas T. Waterman. *The Early Architecture of North Carolina: A Pictorial Survey*. Chapel Hill: University of North Carolina Press, 1941.

Jordan, Terry G. "German Houses in Texas." *Landscape* 14, no. 1 (Autumn 1964): 24–26.

———. *German Seed in Texas Soil: Immigrant Farmers in Nineteenth-Century Texas*. Austin: University of Texas Press, 1966.

———. "The Imprint of the Upper and Lower South on Mid-Nineteenth-Century Texas." *Annals, Association of American Geographers* 57 (1967): 667–690.

———. "Population Origin Groups in Rural Texas." *Annals, Association of American Geographers* 60 (1970): 404–405 plus colored map.

———. "Population Origins in Texas, 1850." *Geographical Review* 59 (1969): 83–103.

———. "Reflections on Log Cabins and Architectural Zoos." *Texas Uniques, Antiques & Art* 3, no. 7 (July 1974): 7.

———. "The Texan Appalachia." *Annals, Association of American Geographers* 60 (1970): 409–427.

———. "The Traditional Southern Rural Chapel in Texas." *Ecumene* 8 (1976): 6–17.

Kellogg, M. K. *M. K. Kellogg's Texas Journal, 1872*. Ed. Llerena Friend. Austin: University of Texas Press, 1967.

Kerr, Homer L. "Migration into Texas, 1860–1880." *Southwestern Historical Quarterly* 70 (1966): 184–216.

Kindig, Joe K., and Frank J. Schmidt. *Architecture in York County*. York, Pa.: Trimmer Printing, for the Historical Society of York County Booklet Series and Colonial York Tourist Bureau, [ca. 1975].

Kniffen, Fred B. *Folk Houses of Louisiana*. Extension Bulletin. Baton Rouge: Louisiana State University, 1942.

———. "Folk Housing: Key to Diffusion." *Annals, Association of American Geographers* 55 (1965): 549–577.

———. "Louisiana House Types." *Annals, Association of American Geographers* 26 (1936): 179–193.

———. "The Physiognomy of Rural Louisiana." *Louisiana History* 4, no. 4 (Fall 1963): 291–299.

———, and Henry H. Glassie. "Building in Wood in the Eastern United States: A Time-Place Perspective." *Geographical Review* 56 (1966): 40–66.

Landrum, Graham, and Allan Smith. *Grayson County: An Illustrated History of Grayson County, Texas*. 2d ed. Fort Worth: Historical Publishers, 1967.

Langman, R. C. *Patterns of Settlement in Southern Ontario*. Toronto: McClelland & Stewart, 1971.

Lathrop, Barnes F. *Migration into East Texas, 1835–1860*. Austin: Texas State Historical Association, 1949.

Lewis, Peirce F. "Common Houses, Cultural Spoor." *Landscape* 19, no. 2 (January 1975): 1–21.

———. "The Geography of Old Houses." *Earth and Mineral Sciences* 39, no. 5 (February 1970): 33–37.

Lynch, W. O. "The Westward Flow of Southern Colonists before 1861." *Journal of Southern History* 9 (1943): 303–327.

McClintock, William A. "Journal of a Trip through Texas and Northern Mexico in 1846–1847." *Southwestern Historical Quarterly* 34 (1930–31): 20–37, 141–158, 231–256.

McConnell, Joseph C. *The West Texas Frontier*. Palo Pinto, Tex.: Texas Legal Bank & Book Co., 1939.

McDonough, Nancy. *Garden Sass: A Catalog of Arkansas Folkways*. New York: Coward, McCann & Geoghegan, 1975.

Maresh, Henry R., and Estelle Hudson. *Czech Pioneers of the Southwest*. Dallas: Southwest Press, 1934.

Marryat, Frederick. *Narrative of the Travels and Adventures of Monsieur Violet . . .* 3 vols. London: Longman, Brown, Green & Longmans, 1843.

Meinig, Donald W. *Imperial Texas: An Interpretive Essay in Cultural Geography*. Austin: University of Texas Press, 1969.

A Memorial and Biographical History of Ellis County, Texas. Chicago: Lewis Publishing Co., 1892.

Meyer, Douglas K. "Diffusion of Upland South Folk Housing to the Shawnee Hills of Southern Illinois." *Pioneer America* 7, no. 2 (July 1975): 56–66.

Mills, W. S. *History of Van Zandt County*. Canton, Tex.: Privately printed, 1950.

Morrell, Z. N. *Flowers and Fruits from the Wilderness; or, Thirty-Six Years in Texas and Two Winters in Honduras*. Boston: Gould and Lincoln, 1873.

Muckelroy, Duncan G. "Ranching History of the American West: Revitalized through the Preservation of Its Architecture." *Pioneer America* 6, no. 2 (July 1974): 34–42.

Mueller, Esther L. "Log Cabins to Sunday Houses." In *Diamond Bessie & the Shepherds*, pp. 51–60. Publications of the Texas Folklore Society, no. 36. Austin: Encino Press, 1972.

Newton, Ada L. K. "The Anglo-Irish House of the Rio Grande." *Pioneer America* 5, no. 1 (January 1973): 33–38.

Newton, Janet Foster. "Log Cabin or Frame." *Antiques* 46 (November 1944): 270–273.

Newton, Milton B., Jr. *Louisiana House Types: A Field Guide*. Melanges, no. 2. Baton Rouge: Museum of Geoscience, Louisiana State University, 1971.

Nunley, Mary A. "The Interesting Story of a Pioneer Mother." *Frontier Times* 4, no. 11 (August 1927): 17–22.

Oberste, William H. *Texas Irish Empresarios and Their Colonies*. Austin: Von Boeckmann-Jones Co., 1953.

Overstreet, Cecil V. "Chimney Dobbin' in the Big Thicket." In *Some Still Do: Essays on Texas Customs*, pp. 77–87. Publications of the Texas Folklore Society, no. 39. Austin: Encino Press, 1975.

Owsley, Frank L. "The Pattern of Migration and Settlement on the Southern Frontier." *Journal of Southern History* 11 (1945): 147–176.

Pacovský, Jaroslav. *Český Ráj* [Bohemian paradise]. Praha: Olympia, 1970.

Paddock, B. B., ed. *A Twentieth Century History and Biographical Record of North and West Texas*. Chicago & New York: Lewis Publishing Co., 1906.

Parker, Amos A. *Trip to the West and Texas . . .* Concord, N.H.: White & Fisher, 1835.

Patteson, Ikie Gray. *Loose Leaves: A History of Delta County, Texas*. Dallas: Mathis Publishing Co., 1935.

Perrin, Richard W. E. "German Timber Farmhouses in Wisconsin: Terminal Examples of a Thousand-Year Building Tradition." *Wisconsin Magazine of History* 44, no. 3 (Spring 1961): 199–202.

Pickrell, Annie Doom. *Pioneer Women in Texas*. Austin: E. L. Steck Co., 1929.

Pillsbury, Richard, and Andrew Kardos. *A Field Guide to the Folk Architecture of the Northeastern United States*. Geography Publications at Dartmouth, ed. Robert E. Huke and John W. Sommer, no. 8. Hanover, N.H.: Dartmouth College, 1970.

Prewett, S. W. F. "The Adventurous Career of Charles Barnard." *Texas Magazine* 3, no. 2 (December 1910): 48–52.

Rempel, John I. *Building with Wood*. Toronto: University of Toronto Press, 1967.

Richardson, Rupert. *The Frontier of Northwest Texas, 1846 to 1876*. Glendale, Calif.: Arthur H. Clark Co., 1963.

Riedl, Norbert F.; Donald B. Ball; and Anthony P. Cavender. *A Survey of Traditional Architecture and Related Material Folk Culture Patterns in the Normandy Reservoir, Coffee County, Tennessee*. Department of Anthropology Report of Investigations, no. 17. Knoxville: University of Tennessee and Tennessee Valley Authority, 1976.

Roach, Hattie J. *The Hills of Cherokee*. N.p., 1952.

Roberts, Warren E. "Field Work in DuBois County, Indiana." *Echoes of History* 6, no. 1 (January 1976): 12–14.

———. "Folk Architecture in Context: The Folk Museum." *Proceedings of the Pioneer America Society* 1 (1972): 34–50.

Robinson, Willard B., and Todd Webb. *Texas Public Buildings of the Nineteenth Century*. Austin: University of Texas Press, 1974.

Rosenquist, Carl M. "The Swedes of Texas." *Yearbook, American Swedish Historical Museum*, 1945, pp. 16–30.

Russell, Traylor, ed. *History of Titus County, Texas*. Waco: W. M. Morrison, 1965.

St. Clair, Gladys. *A History of Hopkins County, Texas*. Waco: Texian Press, 1965.

St. George, R. A. *Protecting Log Cabins, Rustic Work, and Unseasoned Wood from Injurious Insects in the Eastern United States*. United States Department of Agriculture, Farmers' Bulletin, no. 2104. Washington, D.C.: Government Printing Office, 1970.

Sawyer, William E., ed. "A Young Man Comes to Texas in 1852." *Texana* 7 (1969): 17–37.

Schoen, Harold, comp. *Monuments Erected by the State of Texas to Commemorate the Centenary of Texas Independence*. Austin: Commission of Control for Texas Centennial Celebrations, 1938.

Scofield, Edna. "The Evolution and Development of Tennessee Houses." *Journal of the Tennessee Academy of Science* 11 (1936): 229–240.

Sealsfield, Charles. *The Cabin Book; or, Sketches of Life in Texas*. New York: J. Winchester, 1844.

Sloane, Eric. *An Age of Barns*. New York: Funk & Wagnalls, 1967.

Smith, Edward. *Account of a Journey through North-Eastern Texas, Undertaken in 1849 . . .* London: Hamilton, Adams, & Co., 1849.

Smith, Erwin E., and J. Evetts Haley. *Life on the Texas Range*. Austin: University of Texas Press, 1953.

Smither, Harriet. "The Alabama Indians of Texas." *Southwestern Historical Quarterly* 36 (1932): 83–108.

Smithwick, Noah. *The Evolution of a State; or, Recollections of Old Texas Days*. Austin: Gammel Book Co., 1900.

Smythe, D. Port. "D. Port Smythe's Journey across Early Texas." Ed. Donald Day & Samuel W. Geiser. *Texas Geographic Magazine* 6, no. 2 (1942): 1–20.

"Stagecoach Inn, Winedale." *Texas Architect* 16, no. 6 (June 1966): 7–14.

Stambaugh, J. L., and L. J. Stambaugh. *A History of Collin County, Texas*. Austin: Texas State Historical Association, 1958.

Steinert, W. "W. Steinert's View of Texas in 1849." Ed. and trans. Gilbert J. Jordan. *Southwestern Historical Quarterly* 80 (1976–77): 57–78, 177–200.

Sterne, Adolphus. *Hurrah for Texas! The Diary of Adolphus Sterne, 1838–1851*. Ed. Archie P. McDonald. Waco: Texian Press, 1969.

Strickland, Rex W. "History of Fannin County, 1836–1843." *Southwestern Historical Quarterly* 33 (1929–30): 262–298; 34 (1930–31): 38–68.

Stiff, Edward. *The Texan Emigrant, Being a Narrative of the Adventures of the Author in Texas . . .* Cincinnati: George Conclin, 1840.

Strong, W. R. "Reminiscences." *Gainesville* (Tex.) *Register*, June 16, 1914.

Sutherland, David. "Folk Housing in the Woodburn Quadrangle." *Pioneer America* 4, no. 2 (July 1972): 18–24.

Swanton, John R. *The Indians of the Southeastern United States*. Bureau of American Ethnology Bulletin, no. 137. Washington, D.C.: Government Printing Office, 1946.

Terrell, Alex W. "The City of Austin from 1839 to 1865." *Texas State Historical Association Quarterly* 14 (1910): 113–128.

Texas in 1837: An Anonymous, Contemporary Narrative. Ed. Andrew Forest Muir. Austin: University of Texas Press, 1958.

Thomas, William R. *Life among the Hills and Mountains of Kentucky*. Louisville, Ky.: Standard Printing Co., 1930.

Tyler, Ronnie C., and Lawrence R. Murphy, eds. *The Slave Narratives of Texas*. Austin: Encino Press, 1974.

United States Department of Agriculture. *The Farm-Housing Survey*. Miscellaneous Publication, no. 323. Washington, D.C.: Government Printing Office, 1939.

A Visit to Texas: Being the Journal of a Traveller Through Those Parts Most Interesting to American Settlers. With Descriptions of Scenery, Habits, &c. &c. New York: Goodrich & Wiley, 1834; Austin: Steck Co., 1952.

Webb, Walter Prescott, and H. Bailey Carroll, eds. *The Handbook of Texas*. 2 vols. Austin: Texas State Historical Association, 1952.

Weiss, Richard. *Häuser und Landschaften der Schweiz*. Erlenbach, Zürich, and Stuttgart: Eugen Rentsch, 1959.

White, J. Roy, and Joe B. Frantz. *Limestone and Log: A Hill Country Sketchbook*. Austin: Encino Press, 1968.

White, W. W. "Dog-Run Houses." In *The Handbook of Texas*, ed. Walter Prescott Webb and H. Bailey Carroll, 1:510. Austin: Texas State Historical Association, 1952.

Whitten, Martha E. Hotchkiss. *Author's Edition of Texas Garlands*. Austin: Triplett & Hutchings, 1886.

Wigginton, Eliot, ed. *The Foxfire Book*. Garden City, N.J.: Anchor Press, 1972.

Wilhelm, Hubert G. H. "German Settlement and Folk Building Practices in the Hill Country of Texas." *Pioneer America* 3, no. 2 (July 1971): 15–24.

Williams, David R. "An Indigenous Architecture." *Southwest Review* 14, no. 1 (October 1928): 60–74.

Wilson, Eugene M. *Alabama Folk Houses*. Montgomery: Alabama Historical Commission, 1975.

————. "Form Changes in Folk Houses." In *Man and Cultural Heritage: Papers in Honor of Fred B. Kniffen*, ed. H. J. Walker and W. G. Haag, pp. 65–71. Geoscience and Man, ed. Bob F. Perkins, vol. 5. Baton Rouge: School of Geoscience, Louisiana State University, 1974.

————. "Some Similarities between American and European Folk Houses." *Pioneer America* 3, no. 2 (July 1971): 8–13.

Winberry, John J. "The Origin and Dispersal of the Shingle Roof: A Preliminary Consideration." In *Geographic Dimensions of Rural Settlements*, pp. 190–198. National Geographical Society of India, Research Publication Series, no. 16. Varanasi, India, 1976.

Winkler, Ernest W. "The Cherokee Indians in Texas." *Texas State Historical Association Quarterly* 7 (1903): 95–165.

ARTICLES IN TEXAS NEWSPAPERS AND SUNDAY SUPPLEMENT MAGAZINES

"Ancient F W Log Cabin Goes on Sale for $500." *Fort Worth Press*, June 12, 1960.

"An Appeal to Register All Log Cabins Here." *Redland Herald*, supp. to *Daily Sentinel* (Nacogdoches), June 10, 1973, p. 1.

"Aubrey Home Still Reflects Pioneer's Handiwork." *Denton Record-Chronicle*, November 10, 1976, p. 1B.

Buckner, Marsha. "Henry Briden Cabin Restored, Now on Display at Rio Vista." *Times-Review* (Cleburne), August 25, 1974, sec. 2, p. 9.

"Caster Cabin Takes Its Place in History." *Irving Daily News*, July 2, 1975, p. 3.

"Civil War 'Soldier Homes' near Dew." *Teague Chronicle*, October 9, 1969, p. 6.

Clift, John. "Century-Old Log House Found inside House Being Torn Down." *Denison Herald*, February 17, 1974, sec. C, p. 1.

Crume, Paul. "Cabin Still Stands near Original Site." *Dallas Morning News*, May 6, 1973, sec. J, pp. 1, 4.

"Dedication at Texas Tech for Hedwig's Hill Log Cabin." *Mason County News*, October 10, 1974.

Domeier, Doug. "Cabin Gives a Chance to Branch Out." *Dallas Morning News*, November 15, 1976, p. D-1.

————. "Log Cabin, Barn Built around 1850 Still Stand on Dallas County Farm." *Dallas Morning News*, November 15, 1975, p. D-1.

————. "Log Cabins Were Built to Stay." *Dallas Morning News*, February 29, 1976, p. 6H.

Doyle, Paula. "The Vanishing Log Cabin." *Texas Magazine*, supp. to *Houston Chronicle*, September 16, 1973, pp. 6–8.

Ewing, Etta. "Committee Studies Briden Cabin." *Johnson County News*, August 22, 1974.

"First Pokey Had Trap-Door Entry." *Denton Record-Chronicle*, February 3, 1957, sec. 3, p. 5.

Fisher, Binnie. "Historic Cabin Resettled Log by Log." *Fort Worth Star-Telegram*, December 9, 1976, p. 4A.

"Five Log Cabins at Longhorn." *Longhorn Missile*, August 15, 1968, p. 8. [Thiokol Chemical Corp., Marshall]

Fredericksen, Barbara. "Touch of the Past Tucked in the Woods." *Daily Courier* (Conroe), June 16, 1974, sec. 2, pp. 1, 8.

Garber, D. D. "Log House, Built in 1847, Stands on Original Bonnie View Road Site." *Dallas Morning News*, November 4, 1956.

Gunn, Catherine. "Park Log Cabins Reminders of Past." *Fort Worth Star-Telegram*, February 25, 1973, sec. G, p. 7.

Hamilton, Caroline. "Six Cabins from Pioneer Days to be Rebuilt in Forest Park." *Fort Worth Press*, June 22, 1958, p. 4B.

Hart, Weldon. "Old Cora and the Comanche Courthouse." *Texas Star*, May 7, 1972, p. 4.

Hawley, Douglas. "Pioneers' 1847 Log House Damaged by Raiding Vandals." *Dallas Times Herald*, December 1, 1953.

Hess, R. B. "Log Cabin Still Strong though 126 Years Old." *Austin American*, March 1, 1962.

"Historical Structure Survey Includes King Place North of Teague." *Teague Chronicle*, September 12, 1968, p. 1.

Kowert, Elise. "Original Part of Oestreich Home Once Log Cabin." *Fredericksburg Standard*, October 1, 1975, sec. 2, pp. 1, 4.

————. "Pape Log Cabin–Dangers Home Now Restored." *Fredericksburg Standard*, October 27, 1976, sec. 2, pp. 1, 8.

Ledbetter, Barbara. "1880 Log Cabin Still in Use in 1972." *Graham News*, April 16, 1972, sec. 6, p. 2.

————. "Lakey Log Cabin Once Stood on Golf Course Site." *Graham News*, April 16, 1972, sec. 4, p. 5.

————. "McCloud Mud-Chinked Log Cabin Once Stood West of Bryson." *Graham News*, May 13, 1973, p. 6.

"Log Cabins Counted." *Gilmer Mirror*, April 12, 1973, pp. 1, 14.

"Log House Erected in 1852." *Semi-Weekly Farm News* (Dallas), March 22, 1940.

"Longhorn's Last Log Structure Registered, but Still a Puzzle." *Longhorn Missile*, May 15, 1973, p. 4. [Thiokol Chemical Corp., Marshall]

McGinnis, Rosalie. "Cabin at Grand Prairie Due Historical Marker." *Dallas Morning News*, February 23, 1972, sec. A, p. 25.

"Mystery Solved: Cabin Was Crib." *Longhorn Missile*, June 15, 1973, p. 3. [Thiokol Chemical Corp., Marshall]

"The Old Barbee Log Cabin." *Newsletter, Dublin Historical Society* 2, no. 6 (1973): 1–2; supp. to *Dublin Progress*.

Phelan, Charlotte. "Log Cabins in Grimes County." *Houston Post*, December 1, 1963.

Robinson, Ferol. "Log House Defies Elements." *Houston Post*, June 4, 1964, sec. 4, p. 13.

Scarbrough, Clara. "Log Cabins Still Survive in Williamson County." *Williamson County Sun* (Georgetown), June 6, 1974, sec. 1, p. 6.

"Tentative Agreement Reached on Log Cabin Homesite in Arlington." *Fort Worth Star-Telegram*, September 30, 1973, p. 19A.

Index